"What a rich offering this is! The book . . . and theological threads. The weavers bring important and fresh insights from the fields of biblical studies, theology, and liturgy. What ties the contributions together is a shared focus on the essence of spiritual formation: being conformed to Christ under the guidance and power of the Holy Spirit. I highly recommend this valuable resource."

Neil Pembroke, coauthor of *Spiritual Formation in Local Faith Communities: A Whole-of-Person, Prompt Card Approach*

"*Spiritual Formation for the Global Church* is a unique and substantial contribution to spiritual formation. It covers a multidenominational and multicultural approach with a diverse group of authors that better reflects and represents the global church and not just the North American or Western church. It also emphasizes theology as involving spiritual formation at its core and the crucial ministry of the Holy Spirit. This book is essential reading for a more broad-based and biblical perspective on spiritual formation."

Siang-Yang Tan, senior professor of clinical psychology at Fuller Theological Seminary and author of *Shepherding God's People*

"Spiritual formation exists in its own right as an end in itself. But for the teacher in a theology department or seminary, it can offer an otherwise missing or hard-to-find connection between Bible and doctrine and church life and ethics. This volume attempts that in programmatic form, and the contributors get on to the topic of the spiritual life right away. For doctrine and biblical study exist to serve the latter, not vice versa. There is an urgency present even in the introduction, calling the readers to prayer as they read. The ethos is Christ centered, Spirit filled, and mission focused, where mission means hearing God in and through the praying church and cultures of the wide world. In all these contributions there is a striking openness to life transformation in Christ as informed by the biblical witness, offering their own version of a narrative theology with an emphasis on divine power and human emotion as sanctified with the correspondingly correct words and thoughts serving that spiritual life. Take and read!"

Mark W. Elliott, professor of divinity and biblical criticism at the University of Glasgow and professorial fellow at Wycliffe College, Toronto

"Through an accomplished ensemble of international scholars and practitioners, this volume sounds a clarion call to the church and academy, inviting practitioners and academics to foreground spiritual formation in their respective vocations. The tendency to bifurcate academic enterprise and sanctification is addressed via integrated, multidenominational reflections from across the globe. The editors are to be commended for a resource that will certainly influence the tenor of global disciple making and theological instruction for years to come."

Batanayi I. Manyika, academic dean at South African Theological Seminary

"The growing, indeed exploding interest in spiritual formation around the world is deeply encouraging. Readers interested in global interpretations of the dynamics of spiritual formation—Korean, African, Chinese, European, North American, Australian, and others—will find these essays of interest and significant help."

Chris Hall, president of Renovaré

"The Spirit does not form us in isolation. It takes the family of God to help us grow up as children of God. This volume brings together scholars from a variety of perspectives and theological disciplines to illuminate a subject that is urgently needed today. Harnessing the strength of the global church, Brandt and Frederick widen the conversation and deepen our understanding of Christian spiritual formation for the life of the world."

Glenn Packiam, associate senior pastor at New Life Church, Colorado Springs, and author of *Worship and the World to Come*

"This edited volume presents a rich collection of scholarship that provides theological and practical resources for the global church in the field of spiritual formation. The volume assembles a globally diverse team of contributors that not only draws on the cultural resources represented in world Christianity geographically, but also elucidates vital resources across historical contexts. The contexts are also varied, as the writers contextualize formation practices for ecclesial, academic, and broader civic arenas. This book will prove to be a valuable resource to the global body for embracing and reframing Christian traditions of spiritual formation."

Vince L. Bantu, ohene (president) of Meachum School of Haymanot, assistant professor of church history and Black church history at Fuller Theological Seminary

"This cohesive yet diverse collection of outstanding essays is important for several reasons: it concretizes the ideal of reading Scripture with and for the global and historic church, it emphasizes the trinitarian nature of spiritual formation and the inherently formative character of biblical and theological study, it highlights the potential for unique expressions of spiritual theology in diverse contexts, and it identifies avenues of authentic, communal, worshipful, and missional spiritual formation for the global church. In so doing, this thought-provoking volume furthers both the theory and praxis of spiritual formation, in multiple places moving me to prayer, reflection, and gratitude for its contribution."

Catherine Wright, associate professor of New Testament at Bethel University, St. Paul, Minnesota, and author of *Spiritual Practices of Jesus: Learning Simplicity, Humility, and Prayer with Luke's Earliest Readers*

"The evangelical spiritual formation movement has proven surprisingly expansive. Spiritual formation has made significant headway in the local church, the academy, and the practicalities of daily life. With this book, we find evidence that spiritual formation has gone global. Or more accurately, global work on Christian spirituality is reaching North American spiritual formation. Brandt and Frederick have gathered a culturally, ethnically, and denominationally diverse set of authors from a variety of lived contexts addressing Christian formation with cross-cultural sensitivity. Given the importance of learning from underrepresented voices and points of view, this book is timely and welcome. I can think of many colleagues and students for whom these authors and their topics will be a breath of fresh air."

Steve L. Porter, professor of spiritual formation and theology at Biola University

"For every reader there is scholarship to ponder from traditions and cultures that are not their own, which can be both challenging and refreshing. The diversity of voices alone is a desperately needed step forward in the field of Christian formation. As a missiologist, I am delighted to see the integration of Christian formation and cultural engagement. The call to both a communal and a missional approach to Christian life is joyfully unmistakable."

Brian M. Wallace, executive director of the Fuller Center for Spiritual and Missional Formation

SPIRITUAL FORMATION
for the
GLOBAL CHURCH

A MULTI-DENOMINATIONAL, MULTI-ETHNIC APPROACH

RYAN A. BRANDT AND **JOHN FREDERICK**, EDS.

ivp
Academic
An imprint of InterVarsity Press
Downers Grove, Illinois

InterVarsity Press
P.O. Box 1400, Downers Grove, IL 60515-1426
ivpress.com
email@ivpress.com

InterVarsity Press® is the book-publishing division of InterVarsity Christian Fellowship/USA®, a movement
of students and faculty active on campus at hundreds of universities, colleges, and schools of nursing
in the United States of America, and a member movement of the International Fellowship of Evangelical Students.
For information about local and regional activities, visit intervarsity.org.

Scripture quotations, unless otherwise noted, are from the New Revised Standard Version Bible, copyright © 1989
National Council of the Churches of Christ in the United States of America. Used by permission.
All rights reserved worldwide.

The publisher cannot verify the accuracy or functionality of website URLs used in this book beyond the date
of publication.

Cover design and image composite: David Fassett
Interior design: Daniel van Loon
Images: white dirty painted background: © Dmytro_Skorobogatov / iStock / Getty Images
        Palm branch © drpnncpp / iStock / Getty Images Plus

ISBN 978-0-8308-5518-6 (print)
ISBN 978-0-8308-5519-3 (digital)

Printed in the United States of America ♾

InterVarsity Press is committed to ecological stewardship and to the conservation of natural resources
in all our operations. This book was printed using sustainably sourced paper.

Library of Congress Cataloging-in-Publication Data

Names: Brandt, Ryan A., 1985- editor. | Frederick, John, 1981- editor.
Title: Spiritual formation for the global church : a multi-denominational,
    multi-ethnic approach / edited by Ryan A. Brandt and John Frederick.
Description: Downers Grove, IL : InterVarsity Press, [2021] | Includes
    bibliographical references and index.
Identifiers: LCCN 2021024257 (print) | LCCN 2021024258 (ebook) | ISBN
    9780830855186 (print) | ISBN 9780830855193 (digital)
Subjects: LCSH: Spiritual formation—Christianity. |
    Globalization—Religious aspects—Christianity.
Classification: LCC BV4511 .S685 2021 (print) | LCC BV4511 (ebook) | DDC
    248.4—dc23
LC record available at https://lccn.loc.gov/2021024257
LC ebook record available at https://lccn.loc.gov/2021024258

P   25 24 23 22 21 20 19 18 17 16 15 14 13 12 11 10 9 8 7 6 5 4 3 2 1
Y   38 37 36 35 34 33 32 31 30 29 28 27 26 25 24 23 22 21

For the church catholic:

May we be conformed further to the image of Christ across continents,

time, and cultures as one family and fellowship of God—

the communion of the saints.

CONTENTS

ACKNOWLEDGMENTS

PUTTING TOGETHER A VOLUME that aspires to a high degree of global collaboration and theological coherence is a daunting task, but one that has proven to be well worth the effort. The communion of the saints is more than a good idea or an abstract line in a creed; it is the spiritual reality of our supernatural, transdenominational fellowship in the resurrection life of God as the one body of Christ across cultures, continents, and time. What a privilege and adventure it is to be able to explore the faith once delivered to the saints and to learn from one another as a communion of brothers and sisters in the Lord. As the editors, therefore, it is our great joy to express our sincere thanks to the contributors to this volume. The task of editing this book has itself been a spiritually formative process. We have grown in the faith and in our knowledge of God through our contributions and our editorial labors, and for this we are exceedingly grateful.

We likewise are thankful for our excellent experience with IVP Academic, and especially with David McNutt. We've been consistently impressed with the quality of IVP's catalog, and we count ourselves blessed to be able to see this project to fruition with such a capable, excellent, and exciting publishing house.

Ryan wishes to thank John Frederick for all the fun and productive collaboration in putting this project together. Between the emails and video conferencing, the strategizing and deliberation, we became better friends and attained a greater joy in Christ. Ryan is also grateful to Joshua Farris for their endless discussions about theology and its connection to spirituality in the beatific vision. He would also like to extend thanks to all of his colleagues—especially Sammy Alfaro, Christina Larsen, Justin McLendon, and Amanda Jenkins—for their ongoing conversations and collaboration around the college. This project originally arose out of the context of collegial discussions between John's office and mine, a reminder of the importance of passing conversations in the college hallways and seemingly fleeting visions for future projects. In this vein, Ryan would like to thank his dean, Jason Hiles, for supporting his scholarly endeavors and creating an environment at Grand Canyon University (GCU) where writing and research can thrive. Most of all, he is thankful for the continued support and encouragement from his wife, Laura, and their daughter, Evelyn.

John wishes to express deep gratitude to all of his colleagues through the years. In this season of life, he is particularly grateful for Belinda Hoadley, Janet Nibbs, and Deon Naudé at Trinity College Queensland, without whose academic support, endless patience, collegial warmth, and unmatchable administrative and creative skill his experience as a researcher, lecturer, and his second year as an expat in Australia would not have been as fun, rich, or spiritually formative. John wishes to extend thanks to all of his students and colleagues at Trinity College Queensland for allowing him to turn his office into a virtual rubbish bin while he wrote and edited this book. He is also very sorry about the piece of forgotten uneaten cake he left under a stack of crumpled papers for six or seven months near the dry-erase board in his office. It has now been disposed of in a reasonable manner, and therefore, he will not have to attend purgatory for the egregious sin of breaking the protocol of proper office decorum. Lord, hear our prayer. Lastly, John is eternally thankful for the overflow of God's grace through the sacramental power of marriage and the joy of family. He is especially thankful for his wife Tara and their kids Liam and Zoe.

INTRODUCTION

Ryan A. Brandt and John Frederick

IN RECENT DECADES, the world has undoubtedly grown closer and smaller, becoming a global village through the advent and proliferation of communication technology and the internet. Yet, despite these advances, evangelicals often remain fixed and focused on theological conversations and practices that take place within narrow regional, national, denominational, and racial/ethnic boundaries. This is nowhere more evident than in discussions about spirituality, spiritual formation, and sanctification.

This present volume, *Spiritual Formation for the Global Church*, is a global, multidenominational, multiethnic effort in which evangelical biblical scholars, theologians, and practitioners from around the world join together to represent the one body of Christ in pursuit of a cohesive yet diverse constructive theology and praxis of spiritual formation for the global church in the twenty-first century. In what follows, we introduce spiritual formation and its recent revival in evangelical circles and provide an overview of the book for the reader.

WHAT IS SPIRITUAL FORMATION?

There are certainly numerous ways to define and approach spiritual formation. With the global volume in hand, the reader can be sure that the different contributors from distinctive backgrounds and denominational heritages will have unique (though often complementary) definitions of and approaches to spiritual formation.

With that being said, it is helpful to provide at least a minimal definition of spiritual formation for those readers less familiar with the subject. While there are many different understandings of spiritual formation out there, including various religious and philosophical perspectives, this book approaches spiritual formation through a Christian perspective. Our definition of spiritual formation will thus assume our Christian heritage. We define spiritual formation broadly to refer to the process by which personal change takes place in Christ by the power of the Spirit. That is, spiritual formation is a Spirit-empowered and Spirit-led transformation of the person into conformity with Christ, who is the image of God.[1] As Christians, we believe that spiritual formation is trinitarian, meaning that it occurs primarily in the context of being conformed to the image of the Son, by the power of the Spirit, to the glory of God the Father. While each contributor will have a unique approach to spiritual formation, this preliminary definition should suffice to provide coherence to the discussions of spiritual formation in the volume as a whole.

THE RECENT REVIVAL OF SPIRITUAL FORMATION

The last sixty years have seen a maturing revival of spirituality and spiritual formation within evangelicalism in the West.[2] Since the mid-twentieth century, evangelicals have increasingly read some of the spiritual classics of Augustine and Jonathan Edwards, among others, as well as more contemporary works such as those from Dietrich Bonhoeffer, C. S. Lewis, Henri Nouwen, and A. W. Tozer. Furthermore, as Roman Catholicism since Vatican II began to emphasize the importance of spiritual formation for their clergy,[3] evangelicals steadily followed suit, noticing their own "sanctification

---

[1]For a helpful survey of definitions of spiritual formation, see Evan B. Howard, *A Guide to Christian Spiritual Formation: How Scripture, Spirit, Community, and Mission Shape Our Souls* (Grand Rapids, MI: Baker Academic, 2018), 3-20.
[2]For a good survey of the spiritual formation movement, see Nathan A. Finn and Keith S. Whitfield, "The Missional Church and Spiritual Formation," in *Spirituality for the Sent: Casting a New Vision for the Missional Church*, ed. Nathan A. Finn and Keith S. Whitfield (Downers Grove, IL: InterVarsity, 2017), 17-27. See also Chris Armstrong, "The Rise, Frustration, and Revival of Evangelical Spiritual Ressourcement," *Journal of Spiritual Formation and Soul Care*, 2/1 (2009): 113-21.
[3]See Vatican II's *Decree on Priestly Training (Optatam Totius)*, section IV ("The Careful Development of the Spiritual Training"), which articulates the nature and method of formation of the Church's priests, also using the explicit language of "spiritual formation": "Those practices of piety that are commended by the long usage of the Church should be zealously cultivated; but care should be taken lest the spiritual formation consist in them alone or lest it develop only a religious affectation. The students should learn to live according to the Gospel ideal, to be strengthened in faith, hope and charity, so that, in the exercise of these practices, they may

gap"—as Richard Lovelace prophetically termed it[4]—within evangelical spiritual life. Since then there has been a sustained revival of spiritual formation within evangelicalism, most famously through the work of such authors as Richard Foster, Dallas Willard, and Eugene Peterson.[5]

Meanwhile, academic books and articles related directly or indirectly to the field of spiritual formation have been steadily growing since 2010,[6] as well as increased attention to virtue, character formation, and moral formation in general.[7] This coincides with the rise of discussions of the dogmatic and pastoral place of sanctification among evangelicals.[8] The

---

acquire the spirit of prayer, learn to defend and strengthen their vocation, obtain an increase of other virtues and grow in the zeal to gain all men for Christ." Available online at: www.vatican .va/archive/hist_councils/ii_vatican_council/documents/vat-ii_decree_19651028_optatam -totius_en.html.

[4]Richard Lovelace, "The Sanctification Gap," *Theology Today* 29 (January, 1973): 363-69.

[5]See Richard J. Foster, *Celebration of Discipline: A Path to Spiritual Growth* (San Francisco: HarperSanFrancisco, 1998); Richard J. Foster, *Life with God: Reading the Bible for Spiritual Transformation* (New York: HarperOne, 2010); Richard J. Foster, Dallas Willard, Walter Brueggemann, Eugene H. Peterson, eds., *The Life with God Bible, NRSV* (New York: HarperOne, 2009); Dallas Willard, *The Spirit of the Disciplines: Understanding How God Changes Lives* (New York: HarperOne, 1999); Dallas Willard, *Renovation of the Heart: Putting On the Character of Christ* (Colorado Springs: NavPress, 2002); Dallas Willard, *Hearing God: Developing a Conversational Relationship with God* (Downers Grove, IL: IVP Academic, 2012); Eugene Peterson, *A Long Obedience in the Same Direction: Discipleship in an Instant Society* (Downers Grove, IL: IVP Academic, 1980); Eugene Peterson, *The Contemplative Pastor: Returning to the Art of Spiritual Direction* (Grand Rapids, MI: Eerdmans, 1989).

[6]See, for example, Howard, *A Guide to Christian Spiritual Formation*; Thomas Crisp, Steven L. Porter, and Gregg A. Ten Elshof, eds., *Psychology and Spiritual Formation in Dialogue: Moral and Spiritual Change in Christian Perspective* (Downers Grove, IL: IVP Academic, 2019). The *Journal of Spiritual Formation and Soul Care* has particularly been leading the charge, especially in integrating spiritual formation into other fields, such as theology, philosophy, psychology, and education. See, for example, the special issue, "Spiritual Formation in the Academy and the Church: A State of the Union," 7/2 (Fall 2014): 175-323; and the two-part special issue, "Christian Spiritual Formation and Soul Care: Teaching and Practice," 11/2 and 12/1 (November 2018 and May 2019): 121-313 and 1-164.

[7]See Edward Allen Jones III, John Frederick et al., eds., *Ecclesia and Ethics: Moral Formation and the Church* (New York: T & T Clark, 2015); N. T. Wright, *After You Believe: Why Christian Character Matters* (New York: HarperOne, 2012); Nancy E. Snow, ed., *Cultivating Virtue: Perspectives from Philosophy, Theology, and Psychology* (Oxford: Oxford University Press, 2015); Jonathan Pennington, *The Sermon on the Mount and Human Flourishing: A Theological Commentary* (Grand Rapids, MI: Baker Academic, 2017); Grant Macaskill, *Living in Union with Christ: Paul's Gospel and Christian Moral Identity* (Grand Rapids, MI: Baker Academic, 2019).

[8]See Michael Allen, *Sanctification.* New Studies in Dogmatics Book 2 (Grand Rapids, MI: Zondervan, 2017); Sinclair Ferguson, *Devoted to God: Blueprints for Sanctification* (Edinburgh: Banner of Truth, 2016); Kelly M. Kapic, ed., *Sanctification: Explorations in Theology and Practice* (Downers Grove, IL: IVP Academic, 2014); Robert A. Peterson, *Salvation Applied by the Spirit: Union with Christ* (Wheaton, IL: Crossway, 2014); Kent Eliers and Kyle Strobel, eds., *Sanctified by Grace: A Theology of the Christian Life* (New York: Bloomsbury, 2014).

advance of these fields is not coincidental but reflects the emerging real-ization among evangelicals that topics such as these need fresh revisiting and ressourcement in our day. Indeed, Nathan A. Finn and Keith S. Whit-field have rightly noted that due to the success of the spiritual formation movement within evangelicalism, it has further evolved into a broader, interdisciplinary movement:

> As scholars and practitioners have written about spiritual formation and closely related themes, the spiritual formation movement has become inter-disciplinary, transcending the theological and practical disciplines. Much like mission, spiritual formation has become an important aspect of applied the-ology that attracts attention from various types of scholars, ministry practi-tioners, and laypersons.[9]

Therefore, in addition to the development of studies on spirituality, spiritual formation, and sanctification, the closely associated fields of biblical studies and theology show a particularly astounding flurry of activity. The theological study and practice of contemplation, a subject typically included in spiritual formation historically, is one such re-claimed field by evangelicals.[10] Moreover, dogmatic and pastoral treatises on the beatific vision and theosis have seen a revival among evangelicals.[11] As the beatific vision is the final vision in which we see God and are transformed, and theosis is the process of being changed into a partaker of the divine nature, these two dogmatic loci are closely related to spir-itual formation. Ryan Brandt's chapter in the present volume shows the close connection between the beatific vision and spiritual formation. While these subjects have remained predominant in Roman Catholic and

---

[9]Finn and Whitfield, "The Missional Church and Spiritual Formation," 26-27.

[10]See John H. Coe and Kyle C. Strobel, eds., *Embracing Contemplation: Reclaiming a Chris-tian Spiritual Practice* (Downers Grove, IL: IVP Academic, 2019); P. Gregg Blanton, *Contem-plation and Counseling: An Integrative Model for Practitioners* (Downers Grove, IL: IVP Academic, 2019).

[11]See Michael J. Gorman, *Inhabiting the Cruciform God: Kenosis, Justification, and Theosis in Paul's Narrative Soteriology* (Grand Rapids, MI: Eerdmans, 2009); Hans Boersma, *Seeing God: The Beatific Vision in Christian Tradition* (Grand Rapids, MI: Eerdmans, 2018); Michael Allen, *Grounded in Heaven: Recentering Christian Hope and Life on God* (Grand Rapids, MI: Eerdmans, 2018); Joshua R. Farris and Ryan A. Brandt, eds., "Baptist and Reformed Theologies of Vision and Deification," *Perichoresis* 17/2 and 18/1 (Summer 2019 and June 2020): 1-93, 1-115; Joshua R. Farris and Ryan A. Brandt, *The Beatific Vision in Modern Context* (Eugene, OR: Cascade Books, forthcoming 2022).

Eastern Orthodox theology,[12] they have only relatively recently hit center stage among evangelicals.

SPIRITUAL FORMATION FOR THE GLOBAL CHURCH: AN OVERVIEW

While it would be easier and tempting to section off the different branches of theological study as the modern academy does, the spiritual formation movement attempts, among other things, to foster the organic relationship between them for the purposes of personal and ecclesiastical change within our particular contexts. It is truly an interdisciplinary movement. Spiritual formation attempts to see all biblical and theological studies within the context of our formation and transformation in Christ. Christians have too often separated the informational and transformational aspects of the Christian life. This is no doubt true in the Western world from which the editors write. This book is an attempt to engage with evangelical voices from different cultures to help one another chart spiritual courses away from dangerously dichotomous paths that separate the heart from the head in the pursuit of spiritual growth into conformity with Christ. As you read, we invite you to examine yourself through the various cultural and theological lenses provided, and to do so in a prayerful manner, asking—and indeed *expecting*—God to illuminate your own cultural and theological assumptions and spiritual blind spots in order that you might be blessed by the voices of the global communion of the saints.

In a book that is global in scope and diverse in content and contributors, there is often a desire for theological coherence, but this desire is not often achievable. We asked the contributors to follow a prescribed format as they composed the chapters. We think that this has resulted in a high degree of literary and theological coherence that will greatly benefit the reader. We have organized this book into three main sections. These sections explore (1) the inherently spiritually formative nature of biblical and theological study, (2) the various acts and elements of worship that function as catalysts for spiritual formation, and (3) the way in which Christian engagement in

---

[12]See Kenneth E. Kirk, *The Vision of God: The Christian Doctrine of the Summum Bonum, The Bampton Lectures for 1928* (London: Longmans, Green, 1932); Vladimir Lossky, *The Vision of God*, trans. Asheleigh Moorhouse, 2nd ed., Library of Orthodox Theology 2 (1963; repr., Leighton Buzzard, UK: Faith, 1973).

contemporary culture spiritually forms believers and contributes to the spiritual health of society.

We will now briefly introduce the content of the book to provide a snapshot of the book's main themes and to increase the reader's ability to make connections between the various chapters and cultural/theological perspectives.

Biblical and theological study as spiritual formation. It is fitting to begin a theological book on the topic of spiritual formation with a chapter that invites us to conceive of the task of biblical and theological study *itself* as spiritually formative. Michael J. Gorman's chapter, "New Testament Theology and Spiritual Formation," confronts the bifurcation that is commonly encountered in the West that separates "spiritual" and "academic" readings of Scripture. Gorman, a United Methodist and renowned Pauline scholar and theologian, rejects this bifurcation, arguing instead that Scripture understands itself to be formative; therefore, spiritual and intellectual engagements with Scripture should be vitally integrated and are, in fact, inseparable. For Gorman, New Testament theology is formational theology, and it only meets its intended end when it leads to spiritual formation. Through a detailed engagement with Matthew 5, Luke 6, and 1 John 4, Gorman shows how Scripture moves seamlessly from theological affirmations to formational implications. He then moves to consider how the christological passages of 1 Corinthians 15, Romans 6, and Philippians 2 display Paul's inherently formational theology, inviting us to see and live our lives through the cruciform lens of Jesus Christ. Spiritual formation is not just about the imitation of Christ but participation in and with Christ in his life, death, and resurrection.

Sammy Alfaro's chapter, "Theological Education and Spiritual Formation," looks at how spiritual formation occurs in the context of Latina/o Pentecostal Bible institutes. Like Gorman, Alfaro, a pastor and theology professor in Phoenix, Arizona, argues that theological education and spiritual formation are not "at war with each other" and that academic study and spirituality are not mutually exclusive. While Gorman's chapter investigates the formational theological substructure of various New Testament texts, Alfaro makes this point by noting that many prominent Old and New Testament figures, like Daniel and the apostle Paul, would have received their education, in part, from prestigious pagan teachers. Thus, Alfaro argues, the biblical authors did not conceive of academic study as something that was devoid of spiritual value. He also traces this pattern through luminaries of the church, such as Thomas Aquinas, ultimately making the case that we should understand the task of theology as a spiritual discipline. It is interesting to consider that Alfaro and Gorman both arrive at this conclusion from completely different cultural and denominational contexts, and without having corresponded with each other during the composition of their respective chapters. Thus, it is evident that theological study, while having sometimes been forced into a dichotomous battle between the head versus the heart, is being recalibrated and reintegrated as it comes to be seen not as a set of polar opposites but as two inseparable elements of a robust approach to spiritual formation. Alfaro then provides a case study, demonstrating how the Latina/o Pentecostal church has utilized the approach of Bible institutes to form its leaders with both academic and spiritual vigor.

This focus on the formative power of biblical study as both a spiritual and intellectual act is then situated within the realm of the formation of missional leaders in the following chapter: "Biblical Faithfulness and Spiritual Formation," by Alfred Olwa, an Anglican Bishop of Uganda. Bishop Olwa focuses his work on the formative results of holding a high view of Scripture, arguing that it is only *faithful* intellectual engagement with Holy Scripture that leads to spiritual growth and formation. Faithfulness to the Bible as the Word of God spiritually forms ministers who subsequently become agents of the spiritual formation for their own congregants. Olwa articulates a biblical-theological rationale for missional leadership and formation and then explores the role of the Holy Spirit in leadership development. He uses the Bishop Tucker School of Divinity and Theology in Uganda as a case study for biblically faithful and spiritually formed theological foundations, faculty, curriculum, and community. It is interesting to note the overlap between the Latina/o Pentecostal theological distinctives of the Bible Institute approach to ministerial formation and the Ugandan approach articulated by Bishop Olwa.

The conversation then shifts to the topic of spiritual theology, an interdisciplinary method of theology that integrates academic study and spiritual living, reinforcing that theological study is itself spiritually formative. John H. Coe, a professor of spiritual theology and leading figure in the field of

spiritual formation, suggests that spiritual theology is an integrative endeavor that seeks to bring together the study of Scripture with the study of
the work of the Holy Spirit and spiritual growth in the experience of human
beings. It is thus a discipline that combines biblical study with empirical
study. The focus here on empiricism and experience is what makes this
chapter unique and highly significant to the volume. Coe demonstrates that
spiritual theology is a theological discipline that allows for contextualized
cultural expressions and personalized dimensions, hence the title of the
chapter: "Spiritual Theology and Spiritual Formation." There is no spiritual
theology that is the same for everyone; rather, Christians *in their own
contexts* must practice it in order to understand how spiritual formation
takes place. God's spiritual work, while having similarities across cultures as
seen in Scripture (e.g., the fruit of the Spirit) will not be the same, for
example, for someone in Zimbabwe as it is for someone in Thailand. That is
to say, precisely how the fruits of the Spirit are expressed will differ de-
pending on the cultural and spiritual experiences of diverse people in diverse times and places. In this way, spiritual theology helps to provide the
global church with a meaningful method to foster understanding about how
the Spirit works in different contents. Coe concludes by suggesting that a
return to a robust spiritual theology would help believers to learn from other
indigenous global believers while also recognizing and appreciating their
own cultural limitations.

Acts and elements of worship as spiritual formation. With the conclusion
of the first section of the book on biblical and theological study as spiritual
formation, we move into the second major section on the relationship between various elements of worship and spiritual formation. Though there
are many areas that can be included in a spiritually formative theology of
worship, these chapters focus on the formational power of prayer,
Communion, confession, and the ultimate telos of worship, namely the
beatific vision.

This section begins with Robyn Wrigley-Carr's chapter, "Liturgy and
Spiritual Formation." Wrigley-Carr, an ecumenical Christian, is a lecturer
in theology and spirituality at a Pentecostal liberal arts college in Sydney,
Australia. She discusses the significance of liturgy to spiritual formation
through an analysis of *Evelyn Underhill's Prayer Book*. Evelyn Underhill

(1875–1941) was a British Anglican laywoman and a prolific author, spiritual director, and lecturer of theology at the University of Oxford. Her collected prayer book, which also contained some of her own prayers, demonstrates the role of prayer and liturgy in our spiritual growth to Christlikeness. Wrigley-Carr's chapter concludes that God is the initiator in our spiritual formation and that we cooperate with his formation through, among other things, engagement in corporate liturgical prayer. She then shows the helpfulness of praying liturgy aloud as it engages our senses. Corporate liturgical prayer also helps us to focus on God rather than on ourselves. It increases our awe of and devotion to God instead of relying on our own pursuit of religious experiences characterized by raw emotionalism. Finally, she demonstrates the significance of this method for global theology. Liturgy, she argues, grounds us in the historical and corporate church as we join in the prayers of the people that have gone before us and worship with us by the power of the Spirit.

Next, Markus Nikkanen, director of a seminary of the Evangelical Free Church in Finland, explores the relationship between holy Communion and spiritual formation in "The Eucharist as Spiritual Formation." Nikkanen argues that the Eucharist is a ritual that exists to transform our perception of ourselves—that is, our identity—in relation to Christ and to others who are in Christ. Receiving the elements, therefore, acknowledges our dependence on Christ; thus, by taking part in Communion, we remember ourselves in Christ and participate in his death and resurrection. However, this remembrance is not a mere cognitive recollection of past events. Rather, through an exegesis of 1 Corinthians 5:1-13, 10:14-22, and 11:17-34, Nikkanen invites us to see participation in the Eucharist as a form of covenantal *transformative remembrance* that is spiritually formative. This means that participating in the Eucharist signifies the obligation of exclusive worship to God in Christ alone and of equal covenantal access for all those in the covenant.

This focus on transformative participation in God as part of his covenant community continues as a key theme in "Sacrifice and Surrender as Spiritual Formation," by John Frederick and Jonathan K. Sharpe. In this chapter, Frederick and Sharpe, both theology professors and evangelical Anglicans (Anglican Church in North America) explain how grace-empowered acts of love contribute to the process of sanctification and spiritual formation. Working together across continents (Australia and the United States, respectively), they explore the sacrificial nature of works in Ephesians in conversation with the theological perspectives of Aquinas and Bonhoeffer. The chapter begins by demonstrating that references to "works" in Ephesians are neither part of a polemic against works-righteousness nor a reference to Jewish works of law (like in Galatians or Romans). Rather, "works" in Ephesians are shown to refer specifically to grace-empowered works of ecclesial love that function as God-ordained acts of transformative surrender to Christ in his body, the church. Frederick and Sharpe argue that participation in acts of ecclesial love are not merely *evidential* (demonstrating that one has been saved) but *instrumental.* They reapply and appropriate the perpetually efficacious benefits of Christ's once-for-all sacrifice and resurrection. This theology is then applied to the practice of confession. The authors conclude by providing a theological rationale for a retrieval of the practice of confession in global evangelical contexts.

Ryan Brandt's chapter, "The Beatific Vision as Spiritual Formation," continues the theme of retrieval for the purposes of a global theology by exploring the close connection between the anticipation and actuality of the vision and spiritual formation here and now. Brandt, a theology professor in Phoenix, Arizona, suggests that a retrieval of Augustine's distinctions between sign and thing, and use and enjoyment, helpfully frame the spiritual life as a pilgrimage toward the vision. In this pilgrimage one perceives the teleological connection of all of creation to God (and a perfected vision of God) as well as the means, form, and end of him who changes us—Father, Son, and Holy Spirit. Brandt's argument, then, is that a robustly developed understanding of the beatific vision (as the end of theology and life) is a necessary linchpin for healthy spiritual formation. The vision changes us relationally as we are in Christ and thus empowered by the Spirit; we are thereby able to perceive and appreciate the "thing" behind the "signs," that is, God in the midst of creation. This is the context of spiritual formation generally and the spiritual disciplines specifically. The chapter's subject— that all created reality is a sign of God, and thus proleptically points forward to the beatific vision—nicely transitions the book to the final topic involving the larger body of issues in culture, society, and the world and its relation to spiritual formation.

Christ, contemporary culture, and spiritual formation. As the book moves into its third section, the chapters examine how the mission of the gospel makes a spiritually formative impact on contemporary culture and society. In other words, the final chapters center on the way in which Christian engagement in contemporary culture spiritually forms believers and contributes to the spiritual health of society.

S. Min Chun, a Korean scholar writing and teaching in Vancouver, Canada, provides a biblical framework for holistic holiness in his chapter "Old Testament Ethics and Spiritual Formation." Through a detailed exploration of Leviticus 19, Chun demonstrates how the concept of holiness is conceived by the biblical author in a threefold manner consisting of theological, economic, and social aspects. This exegetical and theological foundation is then applied to issues pertinent to contemporary Korean Christianity, which are also relevant and beneficial to the life and vitality of the global evangelical church more broadly. Spiritual formation, Chun argues, is never merely an individual enterprise meant to be undertaken for one's own personal spiritual enrichment and growth. Rather, biblically faithful spiritual formation is characterized by a holistic form of holiness that exists for the sake of the world. Chun agrees with systematic theologians and New Testament exegetes whose definitions of spiritual formation often revolve around the concepts of the *imitatio Dei* and the development of Christlike character. Yet, he rightly shows that the most comprehensive and biblical approach to pursuing the transformative way of Jesus Christ is by consulting the Scriptures that informed Jesus' own life and spirituality, namely the Old Testament. When we do this, we find a framework and corrective for our own individualistic appropriations of Jesus' teachings on spiritual formation, and we set sanctification in the context of the public square for the purpose of the common good rather than in the confines and comfort of the privacy of our own hearts.

Shifting to a Taiwanese cultural context, in "Second Peter, Postmodernity, and Spiritual Formation," Le Chih Hsieh, a New Testament professor at a seminary in Kaohsiung City, Taiwan, makes the case that Taiwan, in its current democratic form, struggles with a cultural phenomenon known as "little happiness." This is, essentially, a contemporary form of Epicureanism. "Little happiness," as Hsieh calls it, operates according to the same basic elements as classical Epicurean thought, such as the idea that there is no god or afterlife and that, therefore, the pursuit of joy in the comforts of one's present condition constitutes the ultimate goal of contemporary life. This, of course, contrasts starkly with the message of biblical Christianity. Hsieh's evaluation of contemporary society in Taiwan parallels Ryan Brandt's focus earlier in the book. In both the North American and Taiwanese assessments of this phenomenon, to place one's ultimate desire and happiness on something other than God amounts to a form of idolatry that hinders one's spiritual formation and diminishes one's access to the fullness of fellowship with God. In Brandt's piece, it is argued that we must ultimately enjoy God through the *use* of created things rather than enjoying the created things as ultimate goods and ends in themselves. For Hsieh, the emphasis is different but complementary. He begins by arguing that adopting modern Epicureanism is incommensurate with Christianity. Instead, he suggests, through an exegetical focus on the pertinent texts of 2 Peter, that Christians ought to live for the purposes of the kingdom, which causes us to recognize that we exist for the sake of others. In concert with the work of Frederick and Sharpe on the spiritually formative power of ecclesial life together, Hsieh points Christians away from consumeristic and individualistic forms of Christianity in favor of a corporate view of the church that finds happiness in the common pursuit of the kingdom purposes of God. North American readers will instantly resonate within the current trajectory of the Taiwanese culture, which has many parallels to a similar form of "little happiness" that exists within contemporary American culture.

Next, in "The Holy Spirit, Supernatural Interventionism, and Spiritual Formation," J. Kwabena Asamoah-Gyadu, professor of African Christianity and Pentecostal Theology at a seminary in Ghana, shows how global Christians can learn from the African Pentecostal traditions of divine interventionism and spiritual warfare. Western Christians live within the heritage of the Enlightenment, which tends to downplay and even reject certain aspects of the supernatural, thereby marginalizing the work of the Spirit in spiritual formation. However, African Christians are uniquely positioned to discern the nature of biblical and spiritual reality as they live in a world that reflects the frequent supernatural experience of the work of the Holy Spirit. Whereas all Christians believe in the Spirit, Asamoah-Gyadu suggests that his heritage more tangibly lays hold of the power and experience of the Spirit, giving a more crucial role to the Spirit in spiritual formation, something that is well reflected in the book of Acts as well as other biblical texts. His major argument concerning spiritual formation is that when people are not flourishing or enjoying abundant life, there may be supernatural evil at work that is impeding their spiritual well-being. Because the world is more than a physical reality, spiritual warfare is real, and it may be that one's life is being afflicted by negative cosmic elements, including the oppression of demonic beings and powers. In articulating the contour of these phenomena in an African context, the chapter proves extremely illuminating to Western Christians. It challenges all Christians to take the reality of evil spirits seriously. Furthermore, it provides a framework within which believers can examine the potential "demonic doorways" that invite evil to take root in our own lives. Supernatural interventionism in spiritual formation involves the deployment of the power of the Holy Spirit as a means of healing, deliverance, and spiritual formation. In the African context, with its plausibility structure governed by a cosmology that expects spiritual forces to be actively involved in the lives of all people, interventionist ministries have proven to be a central contributing factor to the growth of the church and to the church's evangelistic mission.

Finally, in "Spiritual Formation Through Failure and Faithful Perseverance," Korean pastor, scholar, and professor HaYoung Son shows how a Korean cultural distinctive, namely the impulse to hide or ignore one's own emotions (which is a common virtue in shame/honor cultures), is actually a weakness that applies to all Christians. To the Western reader, it is immensely helpful to see this gospel truth through a Korean cultural lens, and then to allow this viewpoint to challenge one's own unique cultural and theological perspectives and assumptions. Once this area of sin is detected, Son helps us to course correct our own views with those of Holy Scripture. She does this by expositing two episodes in the life of the apostle Peter, which are then used as case studies for the integration of inevitable failure into the redemptive providential purposes of God for our spiritual formation. The basic idea is that our instances of momentary failure are instrumental in the process of spiritual formation. For the apostle Peter—and for us all—failures that are reframed within the framework of the faithfulness of Jesus Christ allow us to rest upon God's sovereign wisdom and goodness. This gives us strength to persevere and progress in the process of our own spiritual growth by means of the power and energy that God provides.

The authors of this book believe that the very act of reading Scripture and engaging in theological reading and discourse is itself an act of spiritual formation, an inseparable fusion, so to speak, between the pursuit of God with the head and the heart. It is, therefore, fitting to invite you to join with us in prayer as we embark on this journey together. Let us pray that we might see God more clearly by arriving at a deeper sense of our unity as participants in the life of God and the communion of the saints—one mystical body in Christ—brought together by a love from which nothing can separate us across cultures, continents, and time. To God be the glory: the Father, the Son, and the Holy Spirit. Amen.

> Almighty God, to you all hearts are open, all desires known, and from you no secrets are hid: Cleanse the thoughts of our hearts by the inspiration of your Holy Spirit, that we may perfectly love you, and worthily magnify your holy Name; through Christ our Lord. Amen.[13] (The Collect for Purity)

---

[13]The Collect for Purity in *The Book of Common Prayer and Administration of the Sacraments with Other Rites and Ceremonies of the Church. According to the Use of the Anglican Church in North America. Together with the New Coverdale Psalter* (Huntington Beach, CA: Anglican Liturgy Press, 2019), 106. http://bcp2019.anglicanchurch.net.

PART ONE

BIBLICAL
and
THEOLOGICAL
STUDY
as
SPIRITUAL FORMATION

CHAPTER ONE

NEW TESTAMENT THEOLOGY AND SPIRITUAL FORMATION

MICHAEL J. GORMAN

CHURCHES AND STUDENTS OF THE BIBLE—whether lay, clergy, or academics—in the West have often manifested certain perspectives with respect to the relationship between Scripture and spirituality. These include the following:[1]

Group 1

1. understanding both Bible reading and spirituality in individualistic and self-centered ways;

2. understanding spirituality in "otherworldly" ways;

3. creating a disjunction between spirituality, on the one hand, and mission and ethics, on the other;

Group 2

1. regarding academic biblical studies as superior to, and in conflict with, spirituality;

2. regarding serious study of the theology (or theologies) in the New Testament to be an appropriate academic discipline (sometimes called "New Testament theology") but regarding study of that theology with a faith commitment, for theological and spiritual purposes (sometimes

---

[1]I present these in two groups for reasons that will become apparent below.

called "theological interpretation" and "spiritual reading"), to be inherently nonacademic and even nonintellectual;

3. regarding spirituality as superior to, and in conflict with, academic biblical studies, including the study of New Testament theology— either because academics is thought to be dangerous to one's spiritual health or because Christianity is said to be about knowing a Person, not doctrine.

Space does not permit an elaboration of these various perspectives except to note that what they have in common is bifurcation: inappropriately separating that which (we might say) God has joined together. Each of them, I contend, misunderstands both Scripture and spirituality/spiritual formation. In my view, these sorts of bifurcated perspectives are misguided and, indeed, dangerous, both intellectually and spiritually.

The fundamental claim of this chapter is that New Testament theology is *formational* theology. The chapter will be devoted to looking at selected passages from the New Testament that demonstrate two things. First, we will briefly consider how the New Testament takes a "both-and" rather than an "either-or" approach to certain key topics hinted at in the list above. Second, and at greater length, we will see how the New Testament itself joins theology and spiritual formation. These two topics are, I believe, significant for spiritual formation both in churches of the West and in the global church.[2] Furthermore, it may be necessary for the global church both to avoid the bifurcations noted above (often inherited from the West) and to assist churches in the West in recovering from these misunderstandings.

UNDERSTANDING THE NEW TESTAMENT'S "BOTH-AND" DYNAMIC

We can divide the six sorts of bifurcated approaches to reading Scripture noted above into two major categories: the vertical versus the horizontal (group 1: bifurcations 1–3),[3] and the spiritual versus the intellectual (group 2: bifurcations 4–6). We may respond to each of these two major categories with two simple phrases: "God and neighbor" and "heart and mind."

---

[2]My own denominational affiliation is United Methodist, a global church with its roots in England and the United States.

[3]I am using spatial language to distinguish between our relationship with God ("vertical") and our relationships with others ("horizontal").

God and neighbor. We begin with the vertical versus horizontal bifurcations (1–3). The terms *spirituality* and *spiritual formation* are sometimes misunderstood to refer to a private experience of God that has no relationship to life in the real world and no necessary relationship to how we engage with others. What we find throughout the New Testament, however, is that our relationship with God is inseparable from our relationship with our neighbor. We find this inseparable connection expressed in various ways. A few samples will have to suffice.

- Like many ancient Jews, Jesus summarized the requirements of the Law and the Prophets as love of God and love of neighbor: "The first [commandment of all] is, 'Hear, O Israel: the Lord our God, the Lord is one; you shall love the Lord your God with all your heart, and with all your soul, and with all your mind, and with all your strength.' The second is this, 'You shall love your neighbor as yourself.' There is no other commandment greater than these" (Mk 12:29-31; cf. Mt 22:37-40; Lk 10:27-28).[4]

- "But when you thus sin against members of your family [lit. "your brothers"], and wound their conscience when it is weak, you sin against Christ." (1 Cor 8:12)

- "When you come together, it is not really to eat the Lord's supper. For when the time comes to eat, each of you goes ahead with your own supper, and one goes hungry and another becomes drunk. What! Do you not have homes to eat and drink in? Or do you show contempt for the church of God and humiliate those who have nothing?" (1 Cor 11:20-22)

- "For he is our peace; in his flesh he has made both groups into one and has broken down the dividing wall, that is, the hostility between us . . . for through him both of us have access in one Spirit to the Father." (Eph 2:14, 18)

- "Religion [or "devotion"; CEB] that is pure and undefiled before God, the Father, is this: to care for orphans and widows in their distress, and to keep oneself unstained by the world." (Jas 1:27)

---

[4]Unless otherwise indicated, all scriptural quotations are taken from the NRSV.

- ♦ "But no one can tame the tongue—a restless evil, full of deadly poison. With it we bless the Lord and Father, and with it we curse those who are made in the likeness of God. From the same mouth come blessing and cursing. My brothers and sisters, this ought not to be so." (Jas 3:8-10)

- ♦ "We know love by this, that he laid down his life for us—and we ought to lay down our lives for one another. How does God's love abide in anyone who has the world's goods and sees a brother or sister in need and yet refuses help?" (1 Jn 3:16-17)

- ♦ "No one has ever seen God; if we love one another, God lives in us, and his love is perfected in us. . . . Those who say, 'I love God,' and hate their brothers or sisters, are liars; for those who do not love a brother or sister whom they have seen, cannot love God whom they have not seen." (1 Jn 4:12, 20)

All of these texts demonstrate that theology has consequences for how we treat our neighbor; that spirituality is about a relationship with both God and neighbor—simultaneously and inextricably. New Testament spirituality is personal, but it is not private.

What is fascinating about this brief selection of texts is how it shows the God-neighbor link in connection with various spiritual topics: love of God, relationship with Christ, experience of Christ in the Lord's Supper, peace with God, devotion to God, blessing of God, experiencing love from God, and having God within. Many people would refer to these topics as in some sense "mystical." Yet they are all also concerned about other people. There is no New Testament mysticism, or spirituality, without a connection to others; no vertical without the horizontal.[5]

Considering the goal of loving God and neighbor together, inseparably, leads us next to consider another inseparability in spiritual formation according to the New Testament: loving God with our minds as well as our hearts.

Heart and mind (and more). We turn next to bifurcations 4–6. It is sometimes thought that Christians do not need theology or rigorous, academic

---

[5]See further my essay "The This-Worldliness of the New Testament's Other-Worldly Spirituality," in *The Bible and Spirituality: Exploratory Essays in Reading Scripture Spiritually*, ed. Andrew T. Lincoln, J. Gordon McConville, and Lloyd K. Pietersen (Eugene, OR: Cascade, 2013), 151-70.

study of the Bible, since all that matters for spiritual growth in Bible reading is having a prayerful attitude, an openness to the Spirit. However, while prayerfulness and openness are always *necessary* for spiritual growth through Scripture study, they are not always *sufficient*.

A creative and helpful way to think about this matter was offered by N. T. Wright at the Synod of Roman Catholic bishops on the Word of God, which occurred in Rome in October 2008. Wright was, at the time, Bishop of Durham in the Church of England and an invited special guest at the Synod. Titled "The Fourfold *Amor Dei* [Love of God] and the Word of God," Wright's brief message drew on the words of Jesus (quoting the Shema; Deut 6:5) that we should love God with all our heart, soul, mind, and strength (Mk 12:29-30).[6] Wright suggested that we think of engaging Scripture as employing—and balancing—these four aspects of our humanity.

We read with the *heart*, meaning meditatively and prayerfully, as in the medieval practice of lectio divina ("sacred reading") that has enjoyed a transdenominational comeback in recent years.[7] We read also with the *soul*, meaning in communion with the life and teaching of the church. We read as well with the *mind*, meaning through rigorous historical and intellectual work. And finally, said Wright, we read with our *strength*, meaning that we put our study into action through the church's mission in service to the kingdom of God.

Wright's words remind us that we cannot love God with only part of our being, which means that if we are reading Scripture to better know and love God, it will require the use of our minds. And that further means doing the hard work of rigorous study of the Scriptures. This does not imply that every Christian needs to be a trained New Testament scholar. But it does imply that carefully engaging New Testament theology to the best of our ability is an obligation—and a privilege!—given to all Christians. Loving God with our minds is one aspect of spiritual formation, and one way in which we are able to grow to maturity in Christ. Paul speaks of the need to

---

[6]The brief text of what was actually presented is available at http://ntwrightpage.com/2016/04/25/the-fourfold-amor-dei-and-the-word-of-god/. Wright sent me a copy of the full text, which elaborated on the oral presentation.
[7]Wright draws special attention to "reading in the Eucharist" (Lord's Supper).

"bring every thought into captivity and obedience to Christ" (2 Cor 10:5 NJB). This is doing theology, and when we read the New Testament with this approach (meaning with heart, soul, mind, and strength), we are both studying and doing New Testament theology. New Testament theology is inherently formational.

This last sentence contains a claim that requires a bit more unpacking.

One way of understanding the term *theology* is this: talk about God and all things in relation to God. Such a definition allows the possibility of a purely analytical approach to "doing theology," including studying the theology we find in the New Testament. But the phrase "all things in relation to God" clearly invites us to do more than hold the contents of the New Testament at arms' length. Another, ancient way of understanding theology is as "faith seeking understanding," a phrase that comes from the great theologian Anselm (1033–1109). I would suggest, however, that Anselm's definition needs expanding in light of Scripture's own testimony about what it means to seek to understand God and all things in relation to God: "faith seeking understanding seeking discipleship." That is, theology involves mind and heart and soul and body.

Theologians and other scholars often distinguish the study of New Testament theology from "theological interpretation."[8] The former is allegedly an academic pursuit that does not require a faith commitment, even if it permits one. The latter, on the other hand, exists only when such a commitment is present. My proposed reworking of Anselm's definition of theology challenges this distinction. The New Testament is itself theology, a collection of early Christian theological writings whose focus is Christology and discipleship—and these two dimensions are inseparable. That is, the New Testament writings are meant to proclaim Christ and to form Christians, or what Martin Luther described as "Christs to one another" and C. S. Lewis called "little Christs."[9] The New Testament is *theology seeking*

---

[8]For a recent discussion, see Robert Morgan, "Two Types of Critical Theological Interpretation," *New Testament Studies* 41 (2018): 204-22.

[9]Harold J. Grimm, ed., *Luther's Works*, vol. 31 (Philadelphia: Muhlenberg, 1957), 367-68 (part of Luther's "The Freedom of a Christian"); C. S. Lewis, *Mere Christianity* (New York: HarperCollins, 2001), 199, 226; cf. 178, 193, 194. Lewis sees the mission of God and of the church as making little Christs who share in the character of Christ the Son of God; this is a major theme of the book's fourth part, "Beyond Personality: Or First Steps in the Doctrine of the Trinity."

faith, so to speak; theology seeking spiritual formation in its hearers and readers. And because Christian spirituality must keep the vertical and the horizontal together, this spiritual formation will include formation in Christian ethics and mission.

Since spiritual formation is their purpose, the New Testament writings are best engaged—one might even say only rightly engaged—for that purpose. The "model reader" of the New Testament is an individual or community who pursues this purpose.[10] It will help us to understand the relationship between the New Testament and the goal of spiritual formation by looking at how certain New Testament texts themselves both contain theological claims and have formational purposes.

FORMATIONAL THEOLOGY: THE NEW TESTAMENT'S APPROACH TO THEOLOGY AND SPIRITUAL FORMATION

Since the New Testament is a collection of writings, there is of course no single approach to theology and spiritual formation in the New Testament. There is, nevertheless, a coherence within the various approaches—a pattern, so to speak. This pattern is as follows: theological claims lead to formational claims in such a way that it becomes clear that the formational claims are inherent in the theological claims. This is what I mean by describing the New Testament writings as "formational theology."

Formational theology in the Gospels and 1 John. A simple illustration of this formational theology occurs in the well-known words of Jesus about his heavenly Father:

> You have heard that it was said, "You shall love your neighbor and hate your enemy." But I say to you, Love your enemies and pray for those who persecute you, so that you may be *children of your Father in heaven; for he makes his sun rise on the evil and on the good, and sends rain on the righteous and on the unrighteous.* For if you love those who love you, what reward do you have? Do not even the tax collectors do the same? And if you greet only your brothers and sisters, what more are you doing than others? Do not even the Gentiles do the same? *Be perfect, therefore, as your heavenly Father is perfect.* (Mt 5:43-48, emphases added)

---

[10]"Model reader" is a term from Umberto Eco, *The Role of the Reader: Explorations in the Semiotics of Texts* (Bloomington: Indiana University Press, 1979), esp. 7-11.

In this text from Matthew's Sermon on the Mount, Jesus makes a properly theological claim about God's providential, loving care for the enemies of God, the evil and unrighteous.[11] This is what Jesus, according to Matthew, means in calling his—and the disciples'—heavenly Father "perfect." Jesus' theological claim is not made simply to say something about God, though it clearly does that. But its primary purpose in Matthew's sermon is to assist in the formation of Godlike disciples of Jesus who also love their enemies, not just their friends. As such, they will be disciples of Jesus (because they receive and obey his teaching about God and, it is implied, follow Jesus in loving enemies) and children of their heavenly Father—they will possess the divine DNA, so to speak. In other words, theological teaching about God leads to imitation of God in order to be like God and be Jesus' disciples. That is, theology is inherently formational.

Luke's Gospel makes a very similar point, in slightly different language, in his Sermon on the Plain:

> But I say to you that listen, Love your enemies, do good to those who hate you, *bless* those who curse you, *pray for* those who abuse you. If anyone strikes you on the cheek, *offer* the other also; and from anyone who takes away your coat *do not withhold* even your shirt. *Give* to everyone who begs from you; and if anyone takes away your goods, *do not ask* for them again. *Do to others as you would have them do to you.* If you love those who love you, what credit is that to you? For even sinners love those who love them. If you do good to those who do good to you, what credit is that to you? For even sinners do the same. If you lend to those from whom you hope to receive, what credit is that to you? Even sinners lend to sinners, to receive as much again. But *love your enemies, do good,* and *lend, expecting nothing in return.* Your reward will be great, and you will be *children of the Most High; for he is kind to the ungrateful and the wicked. Be merciful, just as your Father is merciful.* (Lk 6:27-36, emphases added)

Luke's account of Jesus' teaching differs from Matthew's in two main ways. First, it has the divine quality to be imitated as *mercy* rather than *perfection*. On the surface, Luke's requirement of mercy seems narrower

---

[11]By "properly theological" I mean a claim about God the Father, Creator, and sustainer.

than Matthew's demand for perfection—until we note the other difference. Second, then, Luke provides more concrete examples of imitating the Father's merciful character. Such imitation includes blessing abusers; responding without retaliation to physical mistreatment; sacrificing material possessions, either permanently or as a loan; and performing unspecified, imaginative acts of doing good (esp. vv. 31, 35). In other words, the disciples' merciful lifestyle is radical, concrete, and open-ended; there is always some new way to be kind, which means that God's kindness is similarly radical, concrete, and open-ended.

This theological claim about God's character, which is communicated with the adjectives "merciful" (Luke) or "perfect" (Matthew), is fundamentally another way of making the theological claim, with a noun, that we find in 1 John: "God is love" (1 Jn 4:8, 16). As with the claims in Matthew and Luke, this basic theological affirmation about the divine character (as noted briefly earlier) carries with it a moral imperative and thus a formational agenda:

> Beloved, let us love one another, because love is from God; everyone who loves is born of God and knows God. Whoever does not love does not know God, for *God is love*. God's love was revealed among us in this way: God sent his only Son into the world so that we might live through him. In this is love, not that we loved God but that he loved us and sent his Son to be the atoning sacrifice for our sins. Beloved, since God loved us so much, we also ought to love one another. No one has ever seen God; if we love one another, God *lives* in us, and his love is perfected in us. By this we know that we *abide* in him and he in us, because he has given us of his *Spirit*. And we have seen and do testify that the Father has sent his Son as the Savior of the world. God *abides* in those who confess that Jesus is the Son of God, and they *abide* in God. So we have known and believe the love that God has for us. *God is love*, and those who *abide* in love *abide* in God, and God *abides* in them. (1 Jn 4:7-16, emphases added)

A major theological and spiritual image in this passage, as in the texts from Matthew and Luke, is that of being children of God. We have already introduced the contemporary image of DNA above. That seems to be the point here too: those who share in the divine DNA by being born again/ anew/from above (see Jn 3) will manifest the divine trait of love. A related point, stated in the negative, is made in 1 John 3:9, where the NRSV has, "Those who have been born of God do not sin, because God's seed (Gk. *sperma*) abides in them; they cannot sin, because they have been born of God." The CEB, interestingly, renders this verse with the image of DNA: "Those born from God don't practice sin because God's DNA (Gk. *sperma*) remains in them. They can't sin because they are born from God."

The text of 1 John 4:7-16 also makes an important link between theology and spiritual formation that appears frequently elsewhere in the New Testament, sometimes explicitly and sometimes implicitly: the formational expectation associated with a theological affirmation is not just a matter of coming to a logical conclusion and then implementing it. This would mean that Christian formation is simply a matter of imitation, or of obedience to a set of external norms, even if those norms are derived from theological truths. Rather, spiritual formation into Godlikeness, or Christlikeness, is itself the work of God, specifically the work of the Spirit. Spiritual formation is Spirit-ed formation, a divine work from within, as the prophets Ezekiel and Jeremiah especially knew and promised (Ezek 18:31; 36:26-27; 37:1-14; 39:29; Jer 31:31-34). Spiritual formation is a matter of the person or community abiding in God, and vice versa; we see the word *abide* used in our 1 John passage six times (vv. 13-16), plus the synonym *live* (v. 12).

We hear Jesus making a similar connection between theology (specifically, Christology) and spiritual formation in John's Gospel, when he tells the disciples that he is the vine, and they are the branches (Jn 15). In that passage, the verb *abide* occurs eleven times in ten verses (Jn 15:1-10). As in 1 John 4:16, the abiding is mutual: "Abide in me as I abide in you. Just as the branch cannot bear fruit by itself unless it abides in the vine, neither can you [bear fruit] unless you abide in me" (Jn 15:4). The meaning of bearing fruit has been much discussed, but it is probably best to understand it rather broadly, openly, as signifying both Christlike virtues (like Paul's "fruit of the Spirit" in Gal 5) and Christlike missional practices. The latter is implied in the reference to "doing" in John 15:5: "Those who abide in me and I in them bear much fruit, because apart from me you can do nothing." It is made more explicit in the commissioning of the disciples near the end of the "I am the vine" discourse: "You did not choose me but I chose you. And I appointed you to go and bear fruit, fruit that will last, so that the Father will give you whatever you ask him in my name" (Jn 15:16). The formational fruit of mutual abiding is both going out (v. 16) and staying put (v. 17: "love one another").[12]

Mutual abiding in Christ/the Spirit is also prominent in the theology and spirituality of Paul, as we will see below. But before considering that aspect of Paul, we turn first to how he, like the Gospels and 1 John, moves seamlessly from theological affirmations to formational implications.

Formational theology in the letters of Paul. To consider the nature of formational theology in Paul's letters, we will look briefly at two dense christological narratives: 1 Corinthians 15:3-5 and Philippians 2:6-11. These texts are universally recognized as central to Paul's theological agenda, even though the 1 Corinthians text was *definitely* pre-Pauline in origin (see 1 Cor 15:3), and the Philippians text may have been pre-Pauline.

The text of 1 Corinthians 15:3-5 has the appearance of a mini-creed in narrative form that Paul was given and then passed on. This mini-creed has four principal phrases, each beginning with the word "that" (Gk. *hoti*). They are set out here to show that structure, with the four main affirmations italicized:

> For I handed on to you as of first importance what I in turn had received:
> that *Christ died for our sins* in accordance with the scriptures, and
> that *he was buried*, and
> that *he was raised on the third day* in accordance with the scriptures, and
> that *he appeared* to Cephas, then to the twelve.[13]

This dramatic story in four brief acts narrates two main saving events, each of which is said to be "in accordance with the scriptures": (1) that Christ died for our sins and (2) that he was raised (i.e., by the "glory" of God the Father [Rom 6:4][14]) on the third day. Throughout his letters, Paul focuses on the death and resurrection of Christ as the means of salvation. Supporting

---

[12]See further Michael J. Gorman, *Abide and Go: Missional Theosis in the Gospel of John* (Eugene, OR: Cascade, 2018).

[13]The following two verses, detailing more appearances, may have been part of the original "creed," or (more likely) may have been supplied by Paul as additions to the fourth phrase ("appeared").

[14]Perhaps indicating the Spirit.

these two main events in this text are two events that establish the reality of the death and the resurrection: that he was buried (verifying his death) and that he appeared (verifying his resurrection).

This mini-creed makes some critical theological claims, offered in narrative form as a truthful account of what Christ has done, and God the Father has done, for our salvation. But although it may not be immediately apparent when one reads this text, these are theological affirmations with inherent formational consequences. In the context of 1 Corinthians 15, the most obvious consequences have to do with the "doctrine" of Christ's resurrection. Not only is this the basis of Christian hope, as much of chapter 15 attests, but it is also the basis for Christian praxis and mission in the present. Negatively, Paul puts it this way:

> and if Christ has not been raised, then our proclamation has been in vain and your faith has been in vain. . . . If Christ has not been raised, your faith is futile and you are still in your sins. Then those also who have died in Christ have perished. If for this life only we have hoped in Christ, we are of all people most to be pitied. . . . If with merely human hopes I fought with wild animals at Ephesus, what would I have gained by it? If the dead are not raised, "Let us eat and drink, for tomorrow we die." (1 Cor 15:14, 17-19, 32)

Positively, he says this: "Therefore, my beloved, be steadfast, immovable, always excelling in the work of the Lord, because you know that in the Lord your labor is not in vain" (1 Cor 15:58).

There is still more to this story, however. Paul is not done with this traditional creed-with-consequences. When he writes to the Romans a few years later, he will instruct them about the significance of their baptism (as he may have also done with the Corinthians orally) by returning to the dramatic story of salvation. Paul tells the Romans that in baptism they have been narrated into this story, immersed into its reality. Table 1.1 shows the parallels between the main theological affirmations in the creed and their formational implications for the baptized:[15]

---

[15]This table combines and abridges tables in Michael J. Gorman, *Apostle of the Crucified Lord: A Theological Introduction to Paul and His Letters*, 2nd ed. (Grand Rapids, MI: Eerdmans, 2017), 81, 310, 489-91.

Table 1.1. Creedal affirmations and implications

Narrative Reality	Christ, according to the Creed (1 Cor 15)	Believers in their baptism (Rom 6)
Death	Christ died for our sins in accordance with the scriptures (1 Cor 15:3)	We ... died to sin ... were baptized into his death (Rom 6:2-3)
		We have been united with him in a death like his (Rom 6:5)
		Our old self was crucified with him so that the body of sin might be destroyed, and we might no longer be enslaved to sin. For whoever has died is freed from sin (Rom 6:6-7)
		We have died with Christ (Rom 6:8)
		Dead to sin (Rom 6:11)[16]
Burial	He was buried (1 Cor 15:4)	We have been buried with him by baptism into death (Rom 6:4)
Resurrection	He was raised on the third day in accordance with the scriptures (1 Cor 15:4)	*Present:*
		So that, just as Christ was raised from the dead by the glory of the Father, so we too might walk in newness of life (Rom 6:4)
		Alive to God in Christ Jesus (Rom 6:11; cf. Rom 6:13)
		Future:[17]
		We will certainly be united with him in a resurrection like his (Rom 6:5)
		If we have died with Christ, we believe that we will also live with him (Rom 6:8)
Appearance	He appeared to Cephas, then to the twelve (1 Cor 15:5)	Present yourselves to God as those who have been brought from death to life (Rom 6:13)[18]

Paul's use of the creed in the context of explaining the significance of baptism is clearly formational; Paul wants the Roman believers to recognize the reality of their co-crucifixion and co-resurrection with Christ and to "walk" appropriately in the new, resurrected life. To be sure, this resurrection is not the bodily resurrection of 1 Corinthians 15; that resurrection is

---

[16]With many other interpreters I have altered the NRSV by spelling "sin" as "Sin" (uppercase "s") because Paul is portraying Sin as an apocalyptic power from which people need to be liberated and are liberated in Christ.

[17]These two texts are most probably only about the future resurrection, although the logic of crucifixion leading to resurrection applies as well to the present reality of newness of life.

[18]Paul does not use the verb "appear" in Romans 6, but the overall narrative parallels are such that it is all but certain that Paul sees a parallel between Christ's appearances and the post-baptismal, postresurrection "presentation" of the self to God. On this self-presentation, see also Romans 6:16, 19; 12:1.

reserved for the future. Nonetheless, there is already a real resurrection: "newness of life" (Rom 6:4); it is a resurrection *in* the body that involves the bodily members (see Rom 6:12-23) and anticipates the future resurrection *of* the body.

This way of interpreting the creed is not supplemental or optional. The significance of the creed's theological claims is only fully understood and realized when they become the framework of people's lives—when the baptized are immersed in the narrative. This is how Paul's formational theology "works."

We see a similar pattern of theology-to-formation in another Pauline creedal text, Philippians 2:6-11. This passage has often been understood to be a pre-Pauline text—perhaps a hymn, a poem, or another creed of sorts—that Paul adapts and presents to the Philippians. Recent scholarship, however, has suggested that Paul's use of the poem (as I would classify it) both in Philippians and throughout his correspondence indicates that it is quite possible that Paul wrote it. Whether he received it from others or composed it himself, Paul clearly found it to express some of his core beliefs about Christ—and about the life of those who are in Christ and in whom Christ lives by the Spirit. I would go so far as to call Philippians 2:6-11 Paul's *master story*.

Here is that story, with its introduction (v. 5), set out to show (once again) the principal phrases and main verbs:

Let the same mind be in you that was in Christ Jesus, who,
though he was in the form of God,
did not regard equality with God as something to be exploited,
but *emptied himself*, taking the form of a slave, being born in human
    likeness. And being found in human form,
he *humbled himself* and became obedient [lit. "becoming obedient"] to the
    point of death—even death on a cross.
Therefore *God also highly exalted him and gave him the name that is above*
    every name,
so that at the name of Jesus *every knee should bend*, in heaven and on earth
    and under the earth, and *every tongue should confess* that Jesus Christ
    is Lord, to the glory of God the Father. (emphases added)

Once again we have a narrative, a succinct epic drama. The basic sequence is one of humiliation followed by exaltation. Verses 6-8 narrate

Christ's downward mobility from the height of divinity—which he chose not to exploit for selfish advantage (by remaining in that state)—not merely to the depths of humanity (self-enslavement = incarnation) but also to the deepest depths of human existence in crucifixion (self-humiliation = obedience to the point of death on a cross).[19] Verses 9-11 narrate God's reversal of that humiliation and the gifting of the obedient slave with the divine name "Lord" (see Is 45:23).

It is clear from the introduction (v. 5) that Paul intends this poem to speak to the Philippians, to form them in Christ.[20] Like Christ in his incarnation and death, they are to exemplify humility and concern for others, rather than self, in their life together:

> If then there is any encouragement in Christ, any consolation from love, any sharing in the Spirit, any compassion and sympathy, make my joy complete: be of the same mind, having the same love, being in full accord and of one mind. Do nothing from selfish ambition or conceit, but in humility regard others as better than yourselves. Let each of you look not to your own interests, but to the interests of others. (Phil 2:1-4)

Elsewhere I have demonstrated in detail the parallels between Philippians 2:6-11 and 2:1-4, the rest of Philippians, and other places in Paul's letters in which the apostle speaks of his own ministry in Christ or his expectations of particular communities in Christ.[21] Space permits us only to note a few briefly, focusing on echoes of verses 6-8 elsewhere in Philippians, where Paul describes others in terms of the Christ-poem, and in 1 Corinthians, where he describes himself in those terms; I have included the transliteration of key Greek words so that the echoes are presented as clearly as possible.

---

[19]I refer to this narrative as a pattern of "although [x] not [y] but [z]," meaning "although [status] not [selfish exploitation] but [self-giving/sacrifice]." See, e.g., Michael J. Gorman, *Cruciformity: Paul's Narrative Spirituality of the Cross* (Grand Rapids, MI: Eerdmans, 2001).

[20]In my view, Philippians 2:5 is best translated in a way that reinforces the motif of participation begun in 2:1: "Cultivate this mindset—this way of thinking, feeling, and acting—in your community, which is in fact a community in the Messiah Jesus." See Michael J. Gorman, *Participating in Christ: Explorations in Paul's Theology and Spirituality* (Grand Rapids, MI: Baker Academic, 2019), 77-95.

[21]For summary tables with more detail, see Gorman, *Apostle*, 81, 310, 489-91.

Table 1.2. Parallels in Philippians and 1 Corinthians

Philippians 2:6-8	The Philippians in Philippians	Paul in 1 Corinthians
Though he was in the form [*morphē*] of God (Phil 2:6); form [*morphēn*] of a slave (Phil 2:7)	Becoming like him in his death [*symmorphizomenos;* lit. "being conformed to his death"] (Phil 3:10) That it [the body of our humiliation] may be conformed [*symmorphon*] to the body of his glory (Phil 3:21)[22]	For though I [Paul] am free with respect to all . . . though I myself am not under the law (1 Cor 9:19, 20)
Did not regard [*hēgēsato*] equality with God as something to be exploited (Phil 2:6)	Regard [*hēgoumenoi*] others as better than yourselves (Phil 2:3) Yet whatever gains I had, these I have come to regard [*hēgēmai*] as loss because of Christ. I regard [*hēgoumai*] everything as loss because of the surpassing value of knowing Christ Jesus my Lord. For his sake I have suffered the loss of all things, and I regard [*hēgoumai*] them as rubbish, in order that I may gain Christ (Phil 3:7-8)	Nevertheless, we have not made use of this right. . . . But I have made no use of any of these rights . . . so as not to make full use of my rights in the gospel (1 Cor 9:12, 15, 18)[23]
Emptied himself [*heauton ekenōsen*], taking the form of a slave [*doulou*] . . . humbled himself [*etapeinōsen heauton*] (Phil 2:7-8)	Do nothing from selfish ambition or conceit [*kenodoxian;* lit. "empty/vain glory"] (Phil 2:3) Regard others as better than yourselves [*heautōn*]. Let each of you look not to your own interests [*ta heautōn*], but to the interests of others (Phil 2:3-4) All of them are seeking their own interests [*ta heautōn*] (Phil 2:21) In humility [*tapeinophrosynē*] regard others as better than yourselves (Phil 2:3)	I have made myself a slave [*emauton edoulōsa;* lit. "enslaved myself"] to all, so that I might win more of them (1 Cor 9:19)
To the point of [*mechri*] death [*thanatou*] (Phil 2:8)	[Epaphroditus] came close to death [*mechri thanatou*] for the work of Christ (Phil 2:30)	I die [*apothnēskō*] every day! (1 Cor 15:31)

As with 1 Corinthians 15 in conversation with Romans 6, it is clear from table 1.2 that Paul's theological affirmations in Philippians 2 are inherently

---

[22]This verse reminds us that it is not just Christ's humiliation that is paradigmatic for Christians but also his resurrection and exaltation, which is the subject of Philippians 2:9-11. Our focus here, however, is on 2:6-8.

[23]Paul is referring the apostolic rights to receiving financial support and bringing a spouse along on the mission.

formational—in this case, both for general Christian living and for Christian ministry.[24] The story of Christ is inherently formational; his story has become, and must continue to become, our story.

Furthermore, we should stress that, as with the Gospel of John and 1 John, this formational theology/spirituality in Paul's writings is not merely about imitation, but participation—*koinōnia* in the Spirit and living in Christ (Phil 2:1), which also means having Christ and the Spirit within.[25] To be in Christ and to have Christ within is like our relationship with the air: it both surrounds and infuses us, enabling us to live, to grow, and to be active in the world.

THE BENEFIT OF THE TRADITION FOR OTHER GLOBAL EVANGELICALS

The argument I have been making in this chapter comes from my context in the West. It is primarily here that I have seen the bifurcations described early in the chapter: the vertical versus the horizontal and the spiritual versus the intellectual. Yet I know that these bifurcations can and do exist elsewhere, especially the spiritual-versus-intellectual types.

The church in the West is at least partly responsible for exporting its spiritual deficiencies around the world. At the same time, as the global church eyes the churches in the West (which can be perceived as being full of intellectually sophisticated people who have often abandoned, or at least watered down, their biblical faith and the spirituality that goes along with it), it is probably wise not to discard the goal of serious study out of fear for one's spiritual existence. As a New Testament scholar, in fact, I have been impressed time and time again by the way in which even doctoral dissertations by scholars from Africa, Asia, and Latin/South America unite the most rigorous intellectual work with equally impressive spiritual reflection.[26] And such spiritual reflection almost always displays the unity of vertical and horizontal that the West has too often broken apart by favoring one or the other.

The global church, in other words, has something to teach the churches of the West even as all Christians, whatever their context, must struggle

---

[24]For passages similar to 1 Corinthians 9, see 1 Thessalonians 2:1-12 and 2 Thessalonians 3:6-13.
[25]On mutual indwelling according to Paul, see especially Romans 8:1-11.
[26]I am thinking of the work of the Langham Scholars, among others. See https://langham.org /what-we-do/langham-scholars/.

to balance the spiritual and the intellectual as well as the vertical and the horizontal.[27] The New Testament is theology, and it is formational theology. If we fail to engage the New Testament as such, our individual and communal formation will be much weaker than it ought to be. And that does not contribute to a healthy, vital church, wherever that church happens to be.

CONCLUSION

We began this chapter by looking at two kinds of bifurcations, the vertical versus the horizontal and the spiritual versus the intellectual. We saw how the New Testament undermines such bifurcations, offering us the both/and approach of God and neighbor, and of heart and mind. We then looked at two dense christological passages, from 1 Corinthians 15 and Philippians 2, and saw how New Testament theology is inherently formational; theological claims lead inevitably to formational goals. In other words, the theological affirmations, or "doctrines," found in the New Testament ("New Testament theology") cannot be properly engaged at a distance, for they are also theological claims about us; indeed, they are theological claims *on* us. That is the very nature of New Testament theology.

The New Testament's theological claims and their spiritual implications require us to use our minds as well as our hearts; careful study is necessary even to discern, and much more, to fully understand them. Such study may require learning the original languages, reading the master interpreters past and present, and engaging in serious discussion with other students of the Word. It is especially important to hear the voices of readers from cultures and perspectives that are different from our own. The results of such study, when undertaken prayerfully, will be to grow in love of God but also in love of neighbor, both within the Christian community and outside of it. Such is the nature of the New Testament's formational theology.

---

[27]My research assistant, Michelle Rader, notes the following from her own experience in the majority world: "We learn so much from, and are encouraged by, the spiritual depth and discernment and prayer life of our fellow believers. But our partners also ask for teaching about how to read Scripture, as a lot of them do not have access to training, especially for women" (personal communication, February 25, 2019).

STUDY QUESTIONS

1. In your own context, where have you seen evidence of the sorts of bifurcation that are noted in this chapter (vertical versus horizontal and spiritual versus intellectual)? Where have you seen evidence of their opposite, the sorts of "both-and" approaches advocated in this chapter?

2. How might recognizing and correcting false bifurcations in our churches, ministries, and personal lives help to encourage and develop spiritual life in your own context? Be as specific and tangible as possible.

3. How might N. T. Wright's fourfold approach to reading Scripture speak to your context? Which of the four approaches do you overlook? Which do you overemphasize?

4. Why is it important to think of spiritual formation as participation and not merely imitation or obedience?

5. What insights have you gained from considering the texts 1 Corinthians 15 and Philippians 2 as examples of the New Testament's formational theology?

6. Can you think of other important New Testament texts that are highly theological in character and yet have inherently formational implications?

CHAPTER TWO

THEOLOGICAL EDUCATION AND
SPIRITUAL FORMATION

SAMMY ALFARO

FOR THE LAST DECADE, laboring for the advance of theological education within Latina/o Pentecostal churches has often placed me in the uncomfortable position of needing to defend the importance of the academic task over against groups of people who sought to establish the supremacy of spirituality in the formation of ministry leaders. It still shocks me that anyone would think theological education and spiritual formation are somehow at war with each other. For this reason, it is crucial to understand how academic training of lay leaders, pastors, and church educators needs to intentionally prioritize the role of spiritual disciplines as tools and sources for doing ministry and theology.[1] This chapter aims to glean insights from my experience within grassroots theological education in the Latina/o Pentecostal context in order to envision a healthy marriage between theological education and spiritual formation. Primarily, it focuses on the Bible institute

---

[1]Another helpful companion volume for this conversation would be Jeffrey P. Greenman and George Kalantzis' edited book *Life in the Spirit: Spiritual Formation in Theological Perspective* (Downers Grove, IL: IVP Academic, 2010). Addressing the issue from the perspective of frenetic activism in the church, Greenman comments: "the [evangelical] activist impulse, when blended with our culture's thoroughgoing pragmatism, can devolve into a lazy anti-intellectualism that seeks little beyond a handful of prepackaged 'simple steps to spiritual success.' Unchecked activism typically encourages a bare-bones instrumental rationality that ignores or diminishes God's call for the *renewal of our minds* (Rom 12:1-2) and Jesus' command for us to love God with all of one's heart, soul, *mind*, and strength (Mk 12:30)." See "Spiritual Formation in Theological Perspective: Classic Issues, Contemporary Challenges," in *Life in the Spirit*, 31 (emphasis added).

model, which is a unique approach to theological education of lay leaders and future pastors in the local church and regional levels.

ACADEMIC SCHOLARSHIP AS A SPIRITUAL TASK

The strange divorce between academia and spirituality, which at times has occurred in the history of the church, should truly baffle academic readers. Considering the intellectual production of the theological giants of old, we should be convinced that spiritual academics is not an oxymoronic term. Since the apostolic era, the great thinkers of the church have distinguished themselves as scholars with a robust spirituality. Thus, it is unthinkable to consider academic theological training as somehow devoid of processes of spiritual formation. In short, the two go hand in hand.

I do not pretend to say something new about the rupture between academic education and spirituality that sadly on occasion exists in the formal training of Christian leaders and ministers. Without a doubt at the local church level, we sometimes still hear echoes of the often-misguided use of Tertullian's words: "What does Athens have to do with Jerusalem? Or the academy with the church?"[2] But, one should note that in its context, Tertullian does not announce the need for a total renunciation of academic tools in the task of interpreting the biblical text. Instead, Tertullian refers to the incongruence between the teachings of philosophy in his time and the doctrines derived from Scripture. Seeking to correct misunderstandings of Tertullian's dictum, Justo L. González writes: "What he is really arguing for is the use of reason in a 'reasonable' fashion, so that it does not lose its bearings and arrive at senseless conclusions. To him, then, the question is not one of reason versus faith as sources of authority but is rather a question of two different sorts of reason. One is the reason of 'Athens'; the other is the reason of 'Jerusalem.'"[3] In other words, Tertullian had no problem with the intellectual approach of philosophy; he simply disagreed with the philosopher's conclusions, which were heretical on the basis of content, not method. Nevertheless, some still posit the need to divorce academic study and spirituality, as if the two were mutually exclusive.[4]

---

[2] A modern paraphrase of Tertullian, *De praescriptione* 7.
[3] Justo L. González, "Athens and Jerusalem Revisited: Reason and Authority in Tertullian," *Church History* 43, no. 1 (1974): 22.
[4] Some recent and significant studies on the topic of the life of the mind include Mark Noll, *The Scandal of the Evangelical Mind* (Grand Rapids, MI: Eerdmans, 1994); John G. Stackhouse, "Why

On the one hand, spiritual fanaticism on a popular level points to the perceived insufficiency of academic studies, judging it as lacking life and power and accentuating the need for the sole dependence on the anointing of the Spirit.[5] But it should be pointed out that even within the guild of ministers in the biblical record, the importance of academic training can be established. Although it is true that some leaders like Peter might have been "uneducated and ordinary men" (Acts 4:13) at the beginning of their ministries, we need not think of them remaining in that state. What is more, the Bible provides many examples of men and women who were well-trained and educated for their ministerial vocation in the secular and religious ambient. God used people like Moses, Joseph, Daniel, and Esther, who received the highest formal training at their time under the tutelage of pagan teachers.[6] Moreover, Paul, the most prolific writer of the New Testament who gave the church elaborate doctrinal and practical teachings that form the essence of our faith, was a Pharisee, a doctor of the Law, who studied with Gamaliel, a

---

Johnny Can't Produce Christian Scholarship," in John G. Stackhouse, *Evangelical Landscapes: Facing Critical Issues of the Day* (Grand Rapids, MI: Baker, 2002); Eric Miller, "Anti-Intellectualism and the Integration of Faith and Learning," *Christian Scholar's Review* 47, no. 4 (Summer 2018): 329-33; Alister E. McGrath, "The Lord Is My Light: On the Discipleship of the Mind," *Evangelical Quarterly* 83, no. 2 (2011): 133-45; Michael Jinkins, "Loving God with Our Minds: The Vocation of Theological Education in the Life and Leadership of the Church," *Journal of Religious Leadership* 2, no. 1 (2003): 1-22; D. Merrill Ewert, "Faith and the Life of the Mind," *Direction* 46, no. 2 (2017): 148-63; Richard J. Mouw, *Called to the Life of the Mind: Some Advice for Evangelical Scholars* (Grand Rapids, MI: Eerdmans, 2014); T. M. Crisp, Stanley L. Porter, and E. G. Ten, *Christian Scholarship in the Twenty-first Century: Prospects and Perils* (Grand Rapids, MI: Eerdmans, 2014).

[5]Space is lacking to mention the many times I have heard this type of arguments against academic ministerial education from the Pentecostal pulpit. A favorite text used out of context to ridicule the inadequacy of academic training in biblical studies is 2 Corinthians 3:6, where Paul states: "The letter kills, but the Spirit gives life." Clearly, though, the context of the passage contrasts the old and new covenants, the law and the Spirit. A couple of studies from much broader perspectives within Pentecostal scholarship would help to substantiate how anti-intellectual attitudes continue to pervade the Pentecostal movement. See Shane Clifton, "A Response to Paul Lewis' 'Why Have Scholars Left Pentecostal Denominations?'," *Asian Journal of Pentecostal Studies* 11, nos. 1-2 (2008): 87-90; Denise A. Austin and David Perry, "From Jerusalem to Athens: A Journey of Pentecostal Pedagogy in Australia," *Journal of Adult Theological Education* 12, no. 1 (2015): 43-55; Nel Marius, "Rather Spirit-Filled Than Learned! Pentecostalism's Tradition of Anti-Intellectualism and Pentecostal Theological Scholarship," *Verbum et Ecclesia* 37, no. 1 (2016): 1-9.

[6]I know I am preaching to the choir here, but it is significant to note Daniel and his three Hebrew friends' Babylonian training. They are described as young men "showing aptitude for every kind of learning, well informed, quick to understand, and qualified to serve in the king's palace," and they had become experts in "the language and literature of the Babylonians" (Dan 1:4 NIV). What is truly significant in this account of their intellectual training is that "God gave [them] knowledge and understanding of all kinds of literature and learning" (Dan 1:17 NIV). They were learning about Babylonian religion and theology, and God helped them excel! Surely it was not a waste of time.

leading scribe of his day (Acts 22:3). This suggests that although it might not have been a requirement, academic training for ministry was considered extremely useful in the hands of God.

On the other hand (and what honestly should worry us most), we academics must also take responsibility for the counterproductive disassociation between the academy and the church. We live in an epoch where academic study of Scripture and spirituality do not always inhabit the same spheres of thought; where sermon preparation and biblical studies at times do not have a significant connection with the theological task at an academic level.[7] Are we not guilty ourselves of building that wall of separation with our own intellectual arrogance and lack of appreciation for leaders who happen to be less educated? Is it not true that on occasions the leader who left a church to attend university or seminary returns having shed her or his spiritual inheritance, having been converted to a form of dispassionate antisupernaturalism?

Truth be told, at times church leaders who have opted to go the road of higher education are seduced by the "greater" opportunities and comforts that academic diplomas naturally create. After being commissioned, and perhaps even anointed with oil and/or by the laying on of hands, they return to their home parishes with a sense of academic superiority, thinking they are now better preachers and teachers of the Word. The spiritual convictions and the love for the church they previously professed were forgotten when titles and church positions became more important. Could it be that spiritual ministerial dispositions were put aside when the love for academic studies replaced spiritual disciplines, which at the beginning helped the ministerial candidate to identify her or his calling? These ministerial realities should motivate us to change the way we envision academic theological preparation.

---

[7]This sort of separation is most prevalent in local church settings. I realize that in the higher echelons of church leadership this might never be the case. However, many times advancement in denominational leadership does not trickle down to the local church level, and negative attitudes persist against ministerial education. Perhaps this is due to the simple reason that some churches continue to only have a few leaders aside from the pastor who have advanced degrees in theology or ministry. Speaking from my own Latina/o Pentecostal context, it is even rare to find a pastor who possesses an MDiv, and much less a doctorate. Sadly, this often results in the critical comparison of seminaries with cemeteries; where supposedly callings and anointings go to die. Without a doubt, academics who are passionate about the life of the mind and spirit need to be more intentional about dispelling this false dichotomy.

The history of the church teaches us that academic ministerial training should not be considered an enemy of spiritual disciplines and ministerial labors. Indeed, the opposite is true. Not only should biblical writers like Moses and Paul (among others) be considered like persons who combined academic work with a profound spirituality, but we can also point to examples from church history. From the time of the apostolic church fathers to the Enlightenment, spiritual disciplines were an indispensable component of the theological task. In his analysis of the origins of theology as an academic discipline, Simon Chan comments: "The division of theology (as spiritual, dogmatic, biblical and so on) was quite unknown before the rise of rationalistic philosophy in the eighteenth century, a period commonly known as the Enlightenment. Before then theologians conceived of their task as a profoundly spiritual exercise, even when they used scholastic methods."[8] In fact, it was inconceivable that it could be otherwise. The great thinkers of the church combined a robust spirituality with a rigorous academic study.

As an example of this spiritual approach to the theological task, Thomas Aquinas commences his *magnum opus* with this prayer: "Merciful God, I ask that Thou wilt grant me, as Thou pleasest, to seek earnestly, to investigate carefully, to know truthfully, and to present perfectly, to the glory of Thy name, Amen."[9] What is significant here is that this introductory prayer is not mere lip service for the sake of providing a superfluous spirituality to his writing. On the contrary, from beginning to end, Aquinas's theological method incorporates a reverent attitude and genuine worship that celebrates with wonder the greatness of God and his work in the created order. For this reason, Karl Barth commenced his first course on church dogmatics with a meditation on the devotion of Aquinas and the need for theologians to imitate him: "The manner in which Thomas pursued dogmatics leaves the impression of a holy, lofty, beautiful, and joyful work of art. . . . We are a generation that has to learn again, sometimes even by name, what are the presuppositions that a Thomas, an Augustine before him, and a Calvin after

---

[8]Simon Chan, *Spiritual Theology: A Systematic Study of the Christian Life* (Downers Grove, IL: IVP Academic, 1998), 16.

[9]Ashley Cocksworth, *Karl Barth on Prayer*, T&T Clark Studies in Systematic Theology, vol. 26 (London: Bloomsbury, 2014), 7.

him could quietly take for granted."[10] Following Barth's lead, we must opt for exercising the theological task by understanding it as a spiritual discipline.

Furthermore, since the university was birthed in the cradle of the church, we should never create a false dichotomy between the academic and the spiritual.[11] Perhaps we need to revisit Tertullian's question from an ecclesial perspective: What does the church have to do with Harvard? Or the Bible Belt with the theological seminary? First, we must recognize the truth that a theology that lacks spirituality is not useful for a community who desires to grow in relationship with God and each other. But what if the questions were inverted? What does the seminary or Bible college have to do with the church? What is the relationship that must exist between academic ministerial preparation and the practice of spiritual disciplines? Simon Chan provides a response to this line of questioning: "True theology arises from personal experience of God in Jesus Christ, and reflecting on that experience leads to a deeper experiential knowledge of God. The one who is engaged in 'an exact tracing of the glory of God' will be affected by that glory, which inevitably elicits praise. True theology is always doxological."[12]

In light of this, we should opt for reestablishing the academic study of the Bible and ministry to what it was in its origins: a spiritual quest for the divine truth contained in the sacred text of the biblical writings. But how do we begin to shift the tide of Christian academic study devoid of spirituality that often operates against the mission of the church? I believe a response could be found in a new way of understanding the academic task by focusing on the mission of the church, which in my circles is modeled by the grassroots educational efforts of local Bible institutes.

THE BIBLE INSTITUTE: A MODEL FOR SPIRITUAL THEOLOGICAL FORMATION

As a case study of how the Latina/o Pentecostal church has sought to form its leaders with both academic rigor and spiritual vigor, I will explore the Bible institute model and demonstrate its potential for producing biblically

---

[10]Karl Barth, *The Göttingen Dogmatics: Instruction in the Christian Religion*, vol. 1, ed. Hannelotte Reiffen, trans. Geoffrey W. Bromiley (Grand Rapids, MI: Eerdmans, 1991), 4.

[11]For an insightful history of the birth of the university, see chapter 8 of Justo L. González, *Breve Historia de la Preparación Ministerial* (Barcelona: Editorial Clie, 2013), 62-75.

[12]Chan, *Spiritual Theology*, 16-17.

equipped leaders who are Spirit-led in their life and approach to ministry. This section will evaluate studies focused on the effectiveness of Bible institutes in the Latina/o Pentecostal tradition and my own experience as both a student and instructor over the last twenty years.

The subtitle of a paper where I first presented these ideas in seminal form ("My Journey from the Bible Institute to the PhD"[13]) highlights my intention to recognize the success Bible institutes have had in the formation of Pentecostal ministers. I can proudly admit that I am a product of the Bible institute. Elizabeth Conde-Frazier states that according to the National Survey of Hispanic/Latino Theological Education, approximately 47 percent of religious leaders within the Latina/o church in the United States were formed in a Bible institute.[14] Considering the reality of these statistics, it can be said that among Latina/o Pentecostals the Bible institute has been in many ways the pinnacle of theological education.

In her landmark study of the history of Latina/o Bible institutes within US Protestantism, Conde-Frazier surveys their origin noting they consist primarily of "grassroots or community-based training programs for church leaders."[15] Among the factors that have made Bible institutes the principal means for educating leaders within the Latina/o community has been their affordable tuition, adult-learner models, night schedules, Spanish-language priority, focus on laity, Bible-based curriculum, and foundational spirituality, among other characteristics.[16] In many respects, the greatest innovation of the Bible institute model was perhaps its approach to theological education in which pastors teach future pastors. Conde-Frazier summarizes

---

[13]Sammy Alfaro, "Building Bridges: My Journey from the Bible Institute to a Ph.D." Unpublished paper presented at the First Summit of Hispanic Young Scholars, May 1, 2008, Church of God Theological Seminary, Cleveland, Tennessee.

[14]Elizabeth Conde-Frazier, "Bible Institutes," in *Hispanic American Religious Cultures*, ed. Miguel de la Torre (Santa Barbara, CA: ABC-CLIO, 2009), 73.

[15]Elizabeth Conde-Frazier, *Hispanic Bible Institutes: A Community of Theological Construction* (Scranton, PA: University of Scranton Press, 2004), x.

[16]It must be noted the remnants of the precursors to the Latina/o Bible institute model can still be seen in the namesakes of two historic evangelical universities: Biola University ("Bible Institute of Los Angeles") and Moody Bible Institute. The origins and histories of these two institutions point to a time when evangelicals were seeking to reinvent theological training due to the perceived threats of modernism. Among revivalists like Dwight L. Moody, church-based training was made available to laypeople through Sunday School teaching, Bible conferences, "and the Bible institute, which became a training school for persons who would carry out ministries in local congregations and on the urban streets" (Conde-Frazier, *Hispanic Bible Institutes*, 46).

the purpose of Bible institutes like this: "to train consecrated men and women, both lay and clergy, for qualified ministry" within a grassroots organization "headed by leaders indigenous to the community they serve" in an atmosphere where "a spiritual fellowship and relationship between teachers and students is cultivated."[17]

Arlene Sanchez-Walsh identifies Bible institutes as the principal resource for forming ministerial identity and theological thought within the Latina/o Pentecostal church.[18] Thus, it is significant to make the connection between the type of theological training received in the Bible institute and the type of ministries their alumni embarked on. For example, today the Latina/o Church of God in the United States owes a great debt to pioneering men and women who were formed in Bible institutes. Therefore, pastoral training within the Bible institute model needs to be recognized as a formidable contribution, especially in regard to spiritual formation and practical theological education.[19] Moreover, while recognizing the formative role of the Bible institutes in the development of church leaders, one must also recognize that they primarily arose as the educational arm of the church.

As was my experience, the local church congregation served to identify ministerial candidates and make sure they had received a genuine call of God to ministry. Having witnessed the candidate's spiritual dispositions and initial ministerial proficiencies, the local pastor and church would send the lay leader to the Bible institute, where more solid biblical and theological training would be received. In other words, in the Pentecostal setting, the

---

[17]Significantly, Conde-Frazier's analysis of Bible institutes yields a threefold typology: (1) independent Bible institutes, which focus on particular theological or doctrinal emphases; (2) denominational Bible institutes, which focus on a church movement's doctrine and preparing ministry candidates for ordination; and (3) local congregation institutes, which focus on preparing leadership for the local church. In all three models, pastoral experience within the administrative leadership and faculty is an indispensable characteristic. Though academic excellence and degrees are valued, pastoral experience is much more highly valued for an educational community whose intent is to form pastors and leaders for the church (Conde-Frazier, *Hispanic Bible Institutes*, 50-51).

[18]Arlene Sanchez-Walsh, *Latino Pentecostal Identity: Evangelical Faith, Self, and Society* (New York: Columbia University Press, 2003), 70-71.

[19]Elizabeth Conde-Frazier's Hispanic Theological Initiative lecture given at Princeton Theological Seminary in acceptance of the 2002 HTI Dissertation Series Award provides a great summary of these contributions. See her "Religious Education in an Immigrant Community: A Case Study," in *Hispanic Christian Thought at the Dawn of the 21st Century: Essays in Honor of Justo L. González*, ed. Alvin Padilla, Roberto Goizueta, Eldin Villafañe (Nashville: Abingdon, 2005), 187-200.

church helps the future ministerial candidate to identify his or her call and spiritual gifting, and even to provide ample opportunities to preach, teach, and lead at the local church level. Though this is not always the case, for the most part, candidates who attend the Bible institute from a local church already have some ministry experience, but what they lack is more formal doctrinal, academic, and ministerial training.[20]

Focusing more directly on how the Bible institutes traditionally trained ministers, it could be said that everything revolved around spiritual formation. For example, the narratives of the pioneers of the Pentecostal movement in Mexico provide a great window into the formational aspect of ministry and spiritual disciplines as practiced in the Bible institute. Angel D. Santiago-Vendrell comments, "The purpose of the institutes was not only to transmit Christian theological knowledge, but also for the teacher to model to new workers the vision and conduct of a Christian minister."[21] In order to fully appreciate the process of spiritual formation developed through the Bible institute model, let me provide a typical description of the program and activities during the usual two years of study from my own personal experience.

From August of 1995 to May of 1997, I attended the Hispanic Institute of Ministry (HIM) located in Dallas, Texas. The school was founded in 1994 by the Hispanic ministries department of the Church of God (Cleveland, Tennessee) in order to provide a space where future pastors and church leaders would be trained in response to the growth of the Hispanic population in the United States. I first heard of HIM at a youth summer camp just prior to my decision to enroll in the Bible institute. I had been serving at my local church for a few years prior, and the local pastor had given me many opportunities

---

[20]Summarizing an interview with Jesse Miranda where he is asked to evaluate the progress of the Latin American Bible Institute (LABI), Sanchez-Walsh points to the need for developing a more rigorously academic curriculum, affirming that this is something that has only taken place in more recent times. It cannot be denied that, characteristically, Bible institutes have provided educational resources to those for whose lack of finances, deficiency in the English language, and even an undocumented immigration status limited their desire to be trained for the ministry. But, if we are to retain and reach the second, third, and fourth generation of Latinas/os in the United States, we need a ministerial body of clergy and laity that is academically trained to respond to and engage with the difficult modern questions that pervade our culture. See Sanchez-Walsh, *Latino Pentecostal Identity*, 59.

[21]Angel D. Santiago-Vendrell, *Tales of Mutual Influence: Biography as Missiology in Latin American Pentecostalism* (Cleveland, TN: Centro de Estudios Latinos Publicaciones, 2017), 70.

to preach, teach, and lead in our small Latina/o Pentecostal congregation. However, it was not until I met and heard a couple of professors who had been invited to that fateful summer camp that I knew God was calling me to full-time ministry. After an altar call on the last night of camp, the preacher asked if anyone would make the decision to serve God by deciding to attend the Hispanic Institute of Ministry. I made my decision that night in July, and the next month I left my home, family, and church to start my ministerial preparation at our denomination's regional Bible institute.

Perhaps the best description I could give for the ministry program at HIM is that of a residential, co-ed Bible college where everyone was enrolled in the same cohort courses and had similar cleaning/maintenance or clerical responsibilities for our life together. Single women and men were assigned a roommate and separated in different halls; married couples had their own apartment. In addition, everyone attended a daily, one-hour, mandatory chapel and were assigned to a church in order to complete the supervised ministry component. As Bible institute interns, we had ample opportunities for individual and communal prayer given that the chapel was open from early in the day until late at night.

More specifically, chapel time was organized almost exclusively by and for students. All of the worship band members were students. Moreover, because we had daily chapel experiences, every student had at least one opportunity to preach during the academic year. The reasoning behind this design was basically to create space for future ministers to practice the art of preaching among fellow students. All in all, the chapel and designated prayer time produced an organic atmosphere of spiritual pursuit. As I reflect elsewhere, "although my time in the Bible institute certainly gave me a taste of the academic study of the Bible, it was these moments of experiencing God's presence through worshipful meditation that made my ministerial formation more Pentecostal."[22]

In hindsight, though it might seem like selective romanticizing of my institute experience,[23] my formation as a Pentecostal minister and future

---

[22] Sammy Alfaro, "Author Meets Critics: Responding to Daniel Castelo's Pentecostalism as a Christian Mystical Tradition," *Pneuma* 40 (2018): 549.

[23] I must admit that along with the formative spirituality that continues to inform my theology, I also experienced denominational indoctrination and legalistic practices, which over the years I have come to leave behind. Angel D. Santiago-Vendrell hints at this in his description of the

theologian is much indebted to this period of Spirit-filled academic training. It was a time of intentional, spiritually infused theological education. Looking back at this formative period of my intellectual ministerial preparation, I am extremely thankful for the leadership, professors, staff, and fellow classmates who made that community of spiritual formation possible. For two years of my life, I imbibed from a Pentecostal ministerial ethos modeled by the leadership and faculty. Together with fellow students, we studied, wrote, preached, sang, prayed, fasted, and worshiped—all part of our curricular activities. In many ways, this was pretty much an extension of my Pentecostal spiritual upbringing with the added dimension of formal theological education.[24]

As Justo González rightly notes, the historical purpose of the seminary was to create a seedbed where ministry leaders would be formed.[25] One must wonder if in the historical transition from the monasteries to universities and eventually to seminaries, we somewhere lost the full significance of the monastic life and spirituality in the making of the church minister and scholar. We need educational models that do not subordinate the spiritual under the academic and vice versa. One that recognizes both disciplines as necessary for a holistic formation of ministers.

Considering this issue pastor and Pentecostal theologian, Darío López Rodríguez comments:

Bible institutes founded by Rev. Hiram Almirudis in the 1950s and 1960s. In many ways, the Instituto Preparatorio Internacional (IPI) was a precursor to many other Church of God (COG) Bible institutes that would follow. I was enrolled in one of the last reincarnations of this model where Almirudis was a Bible professor. Santiago-Vendrell comments: "The purpose of the school was to allure young students interested in a ministerial vocation. The curriculum of the institution focused on the doctrines of the [Church of God (Cleveland, TN)] and the missionary mandate as understood by the denomination. . . . One of the things that Almirudis modeled for his students was how to dress 'properly' as ministers of God meaning a suit and tie or long-sleeved white shirts with a tie. The process of acculturation went beyond the doctrines of the COGCT to a process of Americanization. New Christians needed to follow the clothing style of the [American] missionary and evangelism was apologetics or the defense of the gospel of Jesus Christ against its enemies, meaning other religions and Mexican culture" (Santiago-Vendrell, *Tales of Mutual Influence*, 253-54).

[24]Personally, these years have become my own Pentecostal spiritual plumb line. As I continued in my academic pilgrimage completing a BA, an MA, and then a PhD, I began to read more and more theological treatises outside of my Pentecostal circles. Eventually, I found an intellectual home in Latin American liberation theology, and then more keenly focused on Latina/o theologies. However, like a plumb line, the spiritual formation received in those early days when I studied at the Bible institute have helped me to stay grounded in my Pentecostal faith.

[25]For a more complete history of how the church has trained pastors and leaders, see Justo L. González, *The History of Theological Education* (Nashville: Abingdon, 2015).

Although the years have passed and the social composition of our local congregations has been changing and the pastoral needs of our members have diversified, a good part of the centers of theological formation continue repeating the theological discourse of the decades of the seventies and eighties of the 20th century, and they don't seem to realize that the world has changed dramatically in the past few decades. They also have not realized that members of their local congregations need to learn to think critically about their faith in order to adequately respond to the diverse and complex ethical, social, and political challenges, in which they find themselves in the collective spaces they inhabit as citizens, whose duties and rights are the same of the non-Christian citizens.[26]

In similar fashion, it should be our goal to educate ministry leaders with the dual objectives of spiritual and academic formation. Recognizing this reality, more recently, the Association for Hispanic Theological Education (AETH) has begun to focus more diligently in developing the Bible institute model within Latina/o church structures. Whereas before efforts focused on creating bilingual Latina/o seminaries, the socioeconomic and immigration realities of potential students have led AETH to focus on what seems like a more fruitful endeavor: accrediting Latina/o Bible institutes. The main reason for this is simply because the Bible institutes seem to be doing more for preparing church-minded leaders and pastors, and not just scholars interested in advancing toward a PhD. Both are needed; however, the increasing lack of ministry candidates for ordination has led AETH to step in the breach to provide a remedy with certification programs for Bible institutes, which would allow them to thrive as they continue to grow their student population and finances.[27]

Conclusion

One of the main dilemmas experienced at the local church level is the discouragement in the long and economically costly process of ministerial higher education. At times, the argument is made that as evangelicals we need to focus on completing the Great Commission rather than postponing

---

[26]Darío López Rodriguez, *Pentecostalismo y Misión Integral: Teología del Espíritu, teología de la vida* (Lima: Ediciones Puma, 2008), 85.

[27]For a full history and explanation of these realities, see Edwin I. Hernández et al., *Spanning the Divide: Latinos/as in Theological Education* (Orlando: AETH, 2016).

it to prepare academically. As a middle way for local lay leadership to prepare for ministry, the Bible institute model has provided avenues for equipping leadership in connection to the local church's mission. I believe the Bible institute model can be a viable option for creating certificate programs at the local church. Academic preparation does not have to be disconnected to the life of the church and absolutely needs to focus on the spiritual formation of the leader; these two are not contradictory but rather complimentary.

I have to confess that in the past decade I have struggled with the ambivalence of attempting to establish my own scholarly theological credibility as a Pentecostal academic who is firmly positioned within an experiential Pentecostal worship community. Today I realize I do not need to sacrifice one for the other because the most important contribution Pentecostal theology can make is precisely its reflection from the lived experience of a community saturated in the presence and activity of the Spirit. As a Latino Pentecostal theologian, I understand the most significant contribution I can make to the greater academy community and the church is my theological reflection focused on a genuine experience of God through his Spirit.

Considering the millennial urge to step out into the local and global mission field now, it is imperative for universities and seminaries to work hand in hand with local churches to assist in the preparation of their leadership and future clergy. Certificate programs offered at a lower cost and shorter time frame might yield a better harvest of leaders who will continue to prepare for ministry at the undergraduate and graduate levels.

STUDY QUESTIONS

1. Consider Tertullian's inquisitive dictum: "What has Athens to do with Jerusalem?" What exactly did Tertullian mean by this? How have you experienced anti-intellectualism in your local church, denomination, or parachurch movement?

2. We have all heard the comparison of a seminary to a cemetery. It is assumed that spiritual fervor and vision die at the hand of theological education. Is this really the case? Does the Bible teach that ministers of the gospel need to beware the folly of wisdom and rely exclusively on the guidance of the Spirit? Or can we see it otherwise?

3. Reflect on the secular and religious education of Moses, Daniel, and Paul as evidenced by Scripture. What are the advantages of having a broader education for anyone who seeks to serve the church? Does the reading of many books kill the anointing of the Spirit, or can the two work together in the spiritual formation of church leaders?

4. What contribution might the Bible institute model of theological education and ministerial formation make to your denomination or network?

5. What are some ways that the church has contributed to the perceived contradictory split between the academic and spiritual study of the Bible? Can you think of some tangible ways to bring the two back together in the life and learning experiences of the local church?

CHAPTER THREE

BIBLICAL FAITHFULNESS AND SPIRITUAL FORMATION

ALFRED OLWA

THE BEST ENTRY POINT FOR EXAMINING OUR TOPIC, "Biblical Faithfulness and Spiritual Formation," is to consider the following questions:

- How is faithfulness to the Word of God—Holy Scripture—central to and inseparable from spiritual growth?

- How does faithfulness to the Word of God contribute to the spiritual formation of ministers of the gospel?

- And, in turn, how will ministers form faithful congregations by their preaching of the Word of God?

To begin, I will demonstrate how biblical faithfulness informs and directs an approach to spiritual formation that results in missional activities that grow the church. The relationship of biblical faithfulness to spiritual formation will be demonstrated by (1) articulating a biblical-theological rationale for missional leadership and formation; (2) applying this rationale to the topics of missional leadership and theological education; and (3) exploring the role of the Holy Spirit in leadership development. I will then present the Bishop Tucker School of Divinity and Theology (also at times known as Faculty of Theology; hereafter BTSDT) as a case study. This will serve to highlight an approach to spiritual formation for Anglican church leaders in Uganda and, more broadly, in East Africa, which will also be beneficial to evangelicals across the globe.[1] Biblical faithfulness will be shown to be the common thread in the appointment of faculty, the development of curriculum, and the formation of graduates at BTSDT.

My background as a Bishop in the Church of Uganda (Anglican Church) forms the basis of my own ministerial experience and the focus of the content of this chapter. In particular, I minister and worship in the Diocese of Lango within the Anglican Diocese in Uganda, which has existed for forty-five years as a diocese, having earlier been included within the jurisdiction of the Northern Uganda Diocese. The diocese has a population of 320,000 believers in 1,200 congregations spread across 66 parishes. I have been in a full-time vocational capacity as a priest since 1990.

A BIBLICAL-THEOLOGICAL RATIONALE FOR MISSIONAL LEADERSHIP AND FORMATION

Robert Banks, in his focus on practical application, calls for a return to a more biblical model of leadership development shaped by examples of the Old and New Testaments.[2] In the Scriptures, national leaders like the priests and the prophets as well as the later, more formalized roles occupied by the scribes and the Pharisees all relied on the same model: (1) they learned at the feet of a key figure who initiated them into the service of God;[3] (2) they accompanied him and attended him in service, at times living with him and even temporarily breaking with their normal relationships and surroundings;[4] and (3) the learning occurred in different settings through participant observation, nonformal discussion, action-reflection, and direct instruction.[5]

This kind of model, as will be seen in later paragraphs, is being rediscovered not only for theological education but also for leadership development in other domains. Furthermore, and most important, this model is

---

[1] Of course, BTSDT has trained ministers of the gospel from other countries outside the East Africa region within Africa—Egypt, Sudan, South Sudan, Democratic Republic of Congo (DRC), Rwanda, Burundi, Nigeria, Zimbabwe, and Malawi. They have also trained ministers in the UK and America.

[2] Robert Banks, *Re-envisioning Theological Education: Exploring a Missional Alternative to the Current Models* (Grand Rapids, MI: Eerdmans, 1999).

[3] Banks, *Re-envisioning*, 85-89, 122-24.

[4] Banks, *Re-envisioning*, 92, 126.

[5] Banks, *Re-envisioning*, 92.

well-exemplified in the way Jesus trained his own disciples. Mark puts it in a succinct way when he writes: "Jesus went up on a mountainside and called to him those he wanted, and they came to him. He appointed twelve— designating them apostles—that they might be with him and that he might send them out to preach" (Mk 3:13-14).[6]

Robert Coleman expounds this model of leadership development into seven steps.[7] Jesus first started with (1) the "selection" of a few committed disciples that he called to live with him, thus learning by (2) "association," fellowship, and daily contact. He called them to (3) "consecration," asking them to count the price of their calling and to commit to sacrificial obedience. He influenced them by (4) "impartation," giving himself to them, inoculating them with his love of the lost, his own holy life, and the presence of the Holy Spirit. He trained them by (5) "demonstration," showing them how to live through his practice of prayer, the use of the Scriptures, winning souls, and teaching. He then empowered them by (6) "delegation," first giving them tasks to accomplish and correcting them when they reported their achievements. After his resurrection, he left them the whole work, a clear mandate for (7) "reproduction," that is, doing the same as they saw him doing with them.

It is clear from the readings of Paul's letters, especially 1 and 2 Timothy and Titus, that Paul applied the same model of spiritually formative leadership development. As a master teacher and strategist, Paul reveals in clear terms his leadership formation strategy when he tells Timothy, "The things you have heard me say in the presence of many witnesses entrust to reliable men who will also be qualified to teach others" (2 Tim 2:2). This summarizes the whole strategy: first, the selection of individuals, then the impartation of the skills and character, and finally the commissioning to train others in order to expand the kingdom.

The challenge remains for contemporary Christians to rediscover this model of leadership formation that is faithful to Scripture and to apply it to our own unique ministerial contexts around the globe. Many paths have been explored in terms of the identification of leaders and the methods of ministerial training. The contemporary approach has, by and large, focused

---

[6]All the Bible references in this chapter, unless otherwise indicated, are taken from the NIV.
[7]Robert Coleman, *The Master Plan of Evangelism* (Westwood, CA: Fleming H. Revell, 1964).

mainly on the various pragmatic methods and approaches to the development of spiritually formed leaders. Yet, strikingly, one key element is often left out in the conversation about the spiritual formation of the leaders who will *spiritually* form the future *spiritual* life of their disciples, namely, *the role of the Holy Spirit* in this process!

The Holy Spirit and the Formation of Spiritually Formed and Spiritually Formative Leaders

Most of the discussions covered above are about the theology of mission and even the methods of training missional leaders, but it is rare to see a focus on the role of the Holy Spirit. However, a simple survey of leadership practices in the Bible reveals that, from the very beginning in Genesis up to Revelation, it is the Holy Spirit who forms and empowers the people of God for mission. It is my firm contention that without a return to the "fellowship of the Holy Spirit" (2 Cor 13:14), the church will continue to operate as "orphans" (John 14:18), even if the people of God are led by the skilled leaders trained by people using successful methods. What is required for transformative gospel ministry, theological training, and spiritual formation is not *merely* a skilled leader using a successful methodology but a spiritually formed leader who ministers and leads by the empowering presence and agency of the Holy Spirit. This pneumatic emphasis in the approach to and practices of spiritual formation is not something that exists *in addition to* the scriptural patterns and practice. It is not, so to speak, one among many potential methodologies. Rather, the Holy Spirit's agency in the formation of leaders who form others by means of the Spirit is a matter of faithfulness to the Spirit-inspired patterns and practices that are derived from Holy Scripture itself. Biblical faithfulness does not exist as an addendum to spiritual formation, and it does not exist alongside it; faithfulness to the Bible, when properly pursued by the Spirit, is the *source* of the power, practices, and patterns of a spiritually formed life.

When God created the earth, it was formless, but the Spirit of God was hovering above that formless place. When God spoke, life sprouted out because the Spirit had generated it (Gen 1:1-3). Likewise, when Joseph planned the economy of Egypt and saved the world of his time from hunger, this was a direct result of the inspiration and agency provided by the Holy Spirit (Gen 41:38). Furthermore, when God told Moses to recruit leaders to help him, God made it conditional that these leaders be filled with the Spirit before they go into action (Num 11:16-17). Even the artisans that God recruited to make the Tent of Meeting were first filled with the Spirit (Exod 31:1-6). Moreover, it was only when the Spirit of the Lord had come on the judges that most of them stood up and fought for Israel (Judg 3:10; 6:34; 11:29; 13:25; 14:6; 14:19; 15:14). The same phenomenon occurs with various kings in the Old Testament (1 Sam 10:6; 10:10; and 16:13). All the prophets, in both the Old Testament and New Testament, spoke under the inspiration of the Holy Spirit (1 Pet 1:10-12). Most important, even Jesus Christ himself had to be filled with the Spirit before he started his ministry (Mt 3:16). And Jesus taught his disciples this fundamental pneumatic principle of empowerment for transformational leadership and discipleship as well. Jesus expounded the Scriptures to the disciples, teaching them about himself in the Law of Moses, the Prophets, and the Psalms, but he recommended to them to "stay in the city until you have been clothed with power from on high" (Lk 24:45-49). It is not surprising, then, to find that when the disciples taught and baptized their own converts, they always made sure to pray for them to be filled with the Spirit (Acts 2:38; 8:14-16; 9:17; 19:4-6.).

This is a pattern that is worth taking into consideration when we study the formational dynamics of missional churches and missional leadership that derive their fundamental patterns and practices from biblical principles. Spiritual formation not only leads to biblical faithfulness. Spiritual formation not only grows as a result of biblical faithfulness. *Spiritual formation is itself a form of biblical faithfulness.* The indispensable presence of the Holy Spirit in the missional context has not so much been denied as it has confused. The main problem in regard to the role of the Holy Spirit in Christian formation comes from the false assumption that every believer is automatically filled with the Holy Spirit, but I suggest that his is not always the case. No. Being filled with the Holy Spirit is the work of God. This comes through the Spirit and results in the cultivation of Christ's character in us. And it is our calling to cooperate with God in the process of sanctification as we share in the divine life given to us (2 Pet 1:4). To this end,

Eugene Peterson succinctly states that "spiritual formation is primarily what the Spirit does, forming the resurrection life in us."[8] Consequently, participation in the life of Christ, by the Spirit, reproduces the character of Christ in his followers.

Theological courses on pneumatology should be taken beyond the discursive domain into ministry application, and the Holy Spirit should not be put under the academic microscope to be dissected but rather loved and surrendered to. As Christopher Duraisingh puts it,

> A leader in a mission-shaped church needs to be constantly attuned to the Spirit who goes ahead of the church in mission, rather than relying on precooked strategies and projects, at the same time he/she needs to seek the prophetic gift of the Spirit to nurture, nourish, and evoke a consciousness and perception alternative to consciousness and perception of the dominant culture.[9]

A CASE STUDY IN BIBLICAL FAITHFULNESS FOR SPIRITUAL FORMATION: BISHOP TUCKER SCHOOL OF DIVINITY AND THEOLOGY

In this section, I will apply the biblical/theological rationale above together with an emphasis on the Holy Spirit to demonstrate an application of this approach through the theological seminary of the province of the Church of Uganda: Bishop Tucker School of Divinity and Theology. This will serve as a case study, derived from my own ministerial setting, which will provide an example of a contextualized appropriation of a spiritually empowered approach to the formation of ministers of the gospel—both clergy and lay— in the light of a much-needed focus on faithfulness to the Word of God.

Biblically faithful, spiritually formed foundations. Many prominent African leaders, including Stephen Kazimba Mugalu (Archbishop of the Church of Uganda), Henry Luke Orombi (retired Archbishop of the Church of Uganda), and Emanuel Kolini (former Archbishop of the Province of Rwanda) received their theological education at Bishop Tucker School of Divinity and Theology at Uganda Christian University. The complete list of BTSDT alumni who are prominent in Uganda and elsewhere in Africa (and beyond) in the fields of biblical and theological scholarship, church

---

[8]Eugene Peterson, *Christ Plays in Ten Thousand Places* (Grand Rapids, MI: Eerdmans, 2005), 237.
[9]Christopher Duraisingh, "From Church-Shaped Mission to Mission-Shaped Church," *The Anglican Theological Review* 92, no. 1 (Winter 2010): 7-28.

leadership, education, overseas mission, public life, and sociopolitical action is an extensive one.[10]

Whose responsibility is it to train church leaders who are faithful to the Word of God? Is it the singular role of the BTSDT? Or is it the responsibility of the church to think seriously about what theological and ministerial education must look like? The training of biblically faithful church leaders who are spiritually formed through the biblical patterns of faithful formation must be the priority above all other endeavors. In this task, the responsibility is on both the church and the theological institutions to work from and within this faithful framework under the empowerment of the Holy Spirit.

In 1913 BTSDT was founded for one important reason: to produce church leaders who faithfully uphold the centrality of the authority of the Word of God, seeing to it that Christ and his gospel is proclaimed faithfully to his people. Thus the intention—then and now—was that everyone in our country, Uganda, might hear what God has done in Christ and be saved. Put differently, we want everyone to have an opportunity to respond with repentance and faith, and to experience new life in the Spirit. We desire to see all people knit into local churches, built up in the faith, and conformed to the image of Christ by the Spirit. Thus, our aim is for all people to be shaped in the way they think and live, by means of the Bible's message about God and his purpose, with its focus on his Son, Jesus Christ.

Our vision, however, is not limited to one country or one denomination. In fact, we are the first seminary in East Africa whose reach extends as far as Madagascar in the Indian Ocean. God's message about his Son, Jesus Christ—the gospel—is the transformational message that informs the seminary's twin priorities of mission and ministry. The very particular role we have as a school—as well as a faculty of theology—is to help prepare men and

---

[10]BTSDT was formally called Bishop Tucker Theological College. Other prominent clergy who attended BTSDT include Justin Badi (Primate of South Sudan Province), Misaeri Kauma (former Bishop of Namirembe diocese), Joel Obetia (Bishop of Madi/West Nile diocese and former Chairman Uganda Christian University Governing Council), Bishop Sheldon Mwesigwa (Bishop of Ankole Diocese and current Chairman Uganda Christian University Governing Council), Henry Okullo (former Bishop of Maseno South Diocese, Kenya), William Bahemuka (Bishop of Boga Diocese, Congo), William Nagenda (one of the leading East African revival evangelists), Alex Kagume (former Deputy Vice Chancellor Academic Affairs, Uganda Christian University and current Deputy Director, Uganda National Council for Higher Education), and Medard Rugyendo (Dean, Faculty of Education, Uganda Christian University).

women for that mission and ministry. Biblical principles and biblical faithfulness, therefore, must be central to the formation of men and women who are disciple-making disciples. The goal is formation: formation for gospel ministry by people who know Christ and are committed above all else to making him known. This impulse is itself, of course, rooted in Holy Scripture.

Paul's words to Timothy immediately come to mind: "You then, my child, be strengthened by the grace that is in Christ Jesus, and what you have heard from me in the presence of many witnesses *entrust to faithful men who will be able to teach others also*" (2 Tim 2:1-2 ESV, emphasis added). This is, in many ways, a charter for theological education and a biblically faithful formational ministry. It is a call to Timothy, and in time to others, to recruit and train and send out men and women to share "the faith once for all delivered to the saints" (Jude 1:3).

Biblically faithful, spiritually formed faculty. Increasingly with the kind of theological liberalism experienced within the Anglican Communion, people often ask me, "What is *the most important thing to look for* when thinking about enrolling in a good theological college?" Of course, what they are thinking is about biblical faithfulness and spiritual formation. Without a doubt my answer is simple: first, look at the faculty, and then I typically add, "Don't just ask whether they are clever, well-qualified, skilled in teaching, with a long list of publications to their name, and all of that." No doubt, at least some (if not all) of these things are important. It is certainly desirable to be taught by people who have been taught the Word of God, formed by the Word of God, and who can do so with rigor and evangelical excellence as experts in their field. Surely, biblically faithful faculty of this caliber will assist students in building theological muscle and growing in the knowledge of God.

Most important, however, is the theological orientation of the faculty. Are they gospel men and women first and foremost? Do they know themselves to be undeserving sinners who have received the kind of grace and mercy that takes your breath away? Do they highly value the forgiveness of sins because they know that without it, they would be lost? Are they Bible people? When they teach, is their inclination to go to the Bible first—whether the subject is Old Testament, New Testament, doctrine, ethics, ministry, mission, or even church history?

Are they mission-minded people? Do they see all they do in the service of Christ and his mission? Instead of being preoccupied with academia and intellectual prestige and international reputations, are they preoccupied with making Christ known throughout the entire world through their teaching, writing, and ministry? Are they people who—like Jesus Christ— exist for the sake of others, both inside and outside of the church? Do they care about unbelievers who, without Christ, have no hope in the world? And do they care for Christ's people, the church? Do they have the heart of a shepherd, caring for Christ's sheep, wanting to protect, guard, and guide those who are placed in their care but actually belong to another, namely the triune God?

While most of the faculty at BTSDT are leaders in their respective fields, more important, they are deeply Christian, servant-hearted men and women. These are people who have, as the Anglican collect says, heard, read, marked, learned, and inwardly digested the Word of God.[11] The faculty seek to live under the Word of God and to walk alongside students, seeking to encourage them and to provide pastoral as well as educational help on the journey. This is part of the fabric of BTSDT because a biblically faithful, spiritually formed faculty is necessary to the formation of missional leaders and disciple-making disciples. The biblical model for Christian formation takes place not in the stale and dusty ivory towers of academia but in the warm solidarity of biblically faithful, spiritually empowered Christian fellowship. It is a model in which the faculty do not rule as lords but walk with students as brothers and sisters in Christ, and experience the powerful presence and love of God through the Spirit as he speaks, corrects, trains, and transforms believers through the community he himself superintends and sovereignly guides with the Father.

Biblically faithful, spiritually informed curriculum. The second most important thing for a biblically faithful, spiritually formative seminary experience is the curriculum. The foundational component of this is a comprehensive, transformational immersion in the Scriptures that permeates and marks the entire curricular design. In order to spiritually form leaders

---

[11]See Collect of Sunday Closest to November 16, Year A, Proper 28, *Book of Common Prayer,* www .lectionarypage.net/YearA/Pentecost.

who will in turn spiritually form others, ministers must learn the biblical languages and spend extensive time in the biblical texts of both the Old and New Testaments. Since the biblical text is itself inspired by and illuminated by the Holy Spirit, this biblical focus is itself a spiritual exercise and a spiritual discipline rather than a merely cerebral and intellectual exercise. As Michael Gorman has argued in this volume, serious study and spiritual devotion ought not to be separated in biblical exegesis and interpretation. Rather, the spiritually formative study of the biblical text is a matter of both the head and the heart.

Therefore, students must be trained to think theologically, since the task of theology is, like biblical study, a *spiritual*—and therefore a *spiritually formative*—discipline. Theological thinking—when it is biblically faithful—refers not simply to the development of a familiarity with historical, literary, or systematic approaches to the Bible. Rather biblically faithful, spiritually formative theological thinking functions on the basis of a biblical theology that operates from the understanding that, from Genesis to Revelation, the Bible is the inspired, authoritative, and infallible Word of God. Theological thinking that is formative draws together all that the Bible has to say on a topic in a way that is comprehensive and coherent.

A healthy, formative approach to theological thinking does not distort or manipulate the biblical witness in order to provide politically correct answers to the hard questions that we inevitably bring with us to the Bible. Many seemingly clever and falsely comforting claims are made, and these claims often come with an appeal to the biblical text. Of course, not everything that is claimed on the basis of the Bible is actually consistent with a robust biblical theology, faithful exegesis, and surrender to the Word of God. A spiritually formative curriculum for future formational leaders must enable students to be so spiritually and biblically attuned to the Word of God that they can easily recognize a false trail and thus be able to stand firm against every wind of doctrine. This attentiveness to a formative, biblical-theological framework for formation will naturally generate and nurture a missional ethos in the students and the institution. Students and faculty will be driven to make decisions through the matrix of a faithful theological framework rather than as a result of worldly pragmatic patterns.

Biblically faithful, spiritually formed community. A great deal of thought over the years has gone into the relationship between curriculum and community at BTSDT. We have sought to maintain a strong focus on the Scriptures and a commitment to original language study, along with a robust study of doctrine, ethics, apologetics, church history, ministry, and mission. In this regard, we rejoice in being a part of the classic evangelical approach to theological education that is bearing fruit in many other institutions across the world. But more than that, there is the wider curriculum, namely, opportunities for ministry and chaplaincy groups.

Most importantly in regard to formation, a biblically faithful curriculum should take place in the midst of a spiritually formative community. At BTSDT community life happens over meals together in the dining hall, worship in chapel, and through missional outreach opportunities. The approach of a biblically faithful, spiritually formative community—whether a church, seminary, or parachurch organization—is not merely to provide theological information but to generate spiritual transformation. Information only becomes transformative in the midst of a community surrendered to and empowered by the Holy Spirit. Only then does the functional purpose of orthodox theological propositions finds its telos, namely, the formation of Christians who live in the presence and power of the triune God. Doctrine and biblical fidelity exist to produce spiritually formed leaders who will in turn empower the spiritual formation of others through faithful gospel ministry. In a biblically faithful seminary, formation happens when students grow in Christian character by being strengthened in evangelical conviction for the development of the skills of pastoral ministry.

Benefits for Global Evangelicals: A Summary

In my context in Uganda, we live in a land that is discarding its Christian heritage at an alarming rate. People are lost. Some of those who are not lost are also frightened. The need for transformational gospel ministry is greater than ever. Is this not much more the case when you look outside of Uganda to the world? Continental Europe, the United Kingdom, and the United States essentially need to be re-evangelized all over again. It is tragic, but it is true.

Rapidly growing churches in Uganda, and more broadly in Africa, are suffering from a lack of biblically faithful, spiritually formed pastors who teach God's Word rather than their own ideas. A case in point recently: a pastor of a Pentecostal church made sections of his congregation drink Jik (a product meant for removing stains on clothes), and over forty people died! Students need to hear the gospel from those who know it is true and love to tell it, because what they typically hear from their professors is a ridicule of the Christian faith. In our primary and secondary schools in Uganda—and I imagine throughout the world—our children need an opportunity to hear the truth. We need to watch out for education that may introduce an anti-Christian agenda. There is no limit to the opportunities.

We need more gospel workers today than we have ever had before. In the last few months alone, I have had an Archbishop in the neighboring country contact me, asking whether I knew of any theologically trained people who could come to assist in ministry. The need is exceedingly great, and it continues to grow. And in order for our brothers and sisters in ministry to stand firm in the midst of hostile missional and cultural realities across the globe, they need to be spiritually formed through the framework of biblical faithfulness. Only then can we expect the spiritual power of the gospel to have its transformative effect on our communities. Without leaders who are both faithful and formed, we will preside over the baptism of the post-Christian status quo and will become chaplains of cultural complacency—as indistinguishable from our cultural contexts as we will be irrelevant. By forming leaders who form others, however, we are investing in the world-transforming mission of the church. For it is through the church, conformed by the Spirit to the image of the Son, that the world comes face to face with the glory of God in the face of Jesus Christ in his people, in his body, and in his one, holy, catholic, and apostolic church.

STUDY QUESTIONS

1. Explain how biblical faithfulness informs and directs spiritual formation that results in activities that grow the church.

2. How would you answer someone who asked, "Why is fellowship with the Holy Spirit indispensable in church ministry?"

3. What are the four main areas that seminaries and churches must emphasize in the course of dispensing biblical faithfulness and spiritual formation?

4. Explain the benefits for the church of having leaders who are both biblically faithful and spiritually formed.

5. What is your experience of the greatest needs in the church today? What sorts of needs do you perceive in your own context?

CHAPTER FOUR

SPIRITUAL THEOLOGY AND SPIRITUAL FORMATION

An Integrative Methodology for a Global Approach

JOHN H. COE

THERE EXISTS A SERIOUS PUZZLE in the minds of many believers about the nature of their spiritual growth, especially for those who have been believers for a while.[1] The puzzle has to do with the gap that they see between where they should be in their growth, where they know they really are in their life, and how to close that gap. The goal or spiritual ideal is readily understood, at least intellectually, and desirable: to be conformed to Christ, to love God with all our hearts and our neighbor as ourselves, to exhibit the fruits of the Spirit, to pray without ceasing, and to be filled with the Holy Spirit. And we hear preaching on these things. But the frustration begins right there. While we may not always be aware of this gap, when we hear good preaching or perceive the lack of holiness in our lives, the awareness emerges. There is a distance between where we know we should, could, or ought to be spiritually and where we in fact are—a huge gap that some have called the "sanctification gap."[2] This gap is less experienced by the young believer and more by the one who has heard the ideal before, has said "yes"

---

[1]This chapter contains material adapted from "Spiritual Theology: When Theology and Psychology in the Spirit Service Faith" by John H. Coe in *Psychology and Spiritual Formation in Dialogue: Moral and Spiritual Change in Christian Perspective*, eds. Thomas M. Crisp, Steven L. Porter, and Gregg A. Ten Elshof (Downers Grove, IL: IVP Academic, 2019).
[2]For example, Richard Lovelace, "The Sanctification Gap," *Theology Today* 29, no. 4 (1973): 363-69.

to God to growth, and yet still seems to remain where they are. And they wonder how the gap can be closed; that is, they wonder about the process of getting to the ideal.

This sanctification gap exists in the understanding of many Christian leaders as well. A pastor once confided to me, "I know how to preach, teach, and administrate a church. But when people tell me their spiritual problems—that they don't pray enough or that they struggle with anger or worry—and I quote to them the Bible that they should pray more, put off anger and not worry, they often respond, 'I know that pastor, so what is wrong with me?' The truth is, I don't know what to say or do from there. I have said everything I was trained to say, and I don't know what else there is to say." I do not think the problem is unique to this pastor. Those of us who teach and preach would love to see transformation just by speaking the Word: "Pray more; love God; put off anger!" "Lord, give us wisdom as we care for souls."[3]

Consequently, one of the most pressing questions for the church is how to close this sanctification gap and how to understand the process of growth that is from God and not from mere human strength and fortitude (Col 2:19). I have been part of the evangelical "spiritual formation movement" in the latter twentieth and early twenty-first centuries, which emerged primarily in America to help close this sanctification gap. However, a criticism of this movement is that its theories and prescribed practices sometimes seem theologically thin, uninformed, or even misguided by legalism or religious ecstatic experiences foreign to the Christian faith. Moreover, theological training in the West, in general, though being rich in its theoretical under-standing of the Scriptures, God, and God's work in salvation remains vul-nerable to the charge that it has failed to provide pastors with deep insight and meaningful application to the struggles of the spiritual journey.[4] The

---

[3]For more on this "sanctification gap," see Richard Lovelace, "The Sanctification Gap," *Theology Today* 29, no. 4 (1973): 363-69.

[4]For example, William Shedd in his *Dogmatic Theology* spends over fifty pages on "Divine Decrees" and six pages on "Sanctification" (William G. T. Shedd, *Dogmatic Theology,* ed. Alan W. Gomes [Phillipsburg, NJ: P&R, 2003]); Louis Berkhof in his *Systematic Theology* spends over a hundred pages on the "Nature of Dogmatic Theology" and seventeen pages on "Sanctification" (Louis Berkhof, *Systematic Theology,* rev. ed. [Grand Rapids, MI: Eerdmans, 1996]); Grudem in *Systematic Theology* spends over a hundred pages on the "Doctrine of the Word" and seventeen pages on "Sanctification" (Wayne Grudem, *Systematic Theology* [Grand Rapids, MI: Zondervan, 1994]);

absence of this in our training in the West has been largely due to the fact that research, training, and preaching has focused on correct interpretation of the text (a very needed thing) but to the neglect of an in-depth understanding of how the text applies to life.

The result of this situation is a church—at least in the context in the West and, particularly, in evangelicalism in America—that is either theologically thin or existentially anemic about the growth of the believer. Thus, the question of how to close this sanctification gap in a theologically grounded, theoretically rich, and practically meaningful way becomes a pressing question for the church, pastors, and theological training of pastors. I will argue that the pressing need for leaders is to develop a deep understanding of this *process* and to help realize this growth in one's life and those in the church community, an understanding that will also assist the church globally. This will involve developing a robust spiritual theology that seeks to understand the nature, process, and directives for spiritual growth that is both integrative with special and natural revelation and that is culturally sensitive to the particular group of people being addressed. As a result, spiritual theology will serve both the church and the academy by bridging the biblical content of the faith and the practice of the faith by providing a theory of the *process* of growth (which is spiritual theology).

SPIRITUAL THEOLOGY AS AN INTEGRATIVE METHODOLOGY FOR A GLOBAL APPROACH TO SPIRITUAL FORMATION

The general thesis of this chapter, then, is that the church would better be able to address this "sanctification gap" if pastors and theological schools were more interested in and given to the task of working out a theoretical and existential understanding of the process of transformation in real life, which is the task of spiritual theology. This particular branch of theology has the unique method of study that combines and integrates (1) the scriptural teaching on sanctification and growth from a biblical and systematic theological perspective with (2) observations and reflections (an empirical study)

Erickson in *Christian Theology* spends over a hundred pages on "Revelation" and eighteen on "Sanctification and the Christian Life" (Millard Erickson, *Christian Theology*, 3rd ed. [Grand Rapids, MI: Baker Academic, 2013]).

of the Spirit's actual work in the believer's spirit and experience.[5] And it is this empirical element that is the peculiar and unique task of the spiritual theologian. I will argue that spiritual theology is that branch of theology that asks both the existentially and culturally relevant questions about spiritual growth that are needed for the church local and global. In fact, as I will argue later, spiritual theology by definition can only be answered by the church in its own milieu. This is the heart of spiritual theology.

In the most general sense, all theology is "spiritual" insofar as it encompasses the minimal task of bringing out the spiritual implications and application of theology to real life. However, spiritual theology goes beyond this in terms of scope and rigor to include an in-depth understanding of spiritual growth by combining both observation and reflection on the Scripture as well as the actual work of God in the lives of believers. In that sense, spiritual theology is pastoral theology. However, the absence of this in our pastoral training has been largely due to (1) the belief that this is the task of someone other than the theologian or pastor or (2) the incorrect assumption that understanding the process of sanctification and spiritual growth is solely a textual study that involves no reflection on human experience. This is unfortunate for the church of the twenty-first century.

Sadly, I had no acquaintance with the methodology of spiritual theology in my theological training at a Bible college and seminary. As I reflect now on the nature of theological education in America, it is clear that much of the training in conservative evangelical education is geared more toward academic understanding of theology and Scripture and less on the actual caring for souls and understanding the process of spiritual growth in the lives of people. And while I have little firsthand experience of global theological education, I have heard from some of my Majority World colleagues and students that theological training in other parts of the world have too often followed this Western model of "intellectualizing" the faith.

Consequently, I want to address the nature of spiritual theology, including an example that is relevant and meaningful for the work we do in the church. And though this is an academic model that is developed here

---

[5]For examples of thoughtful Roman Catholic spiritual theologies, see Reginald Garrigou-Lagrange, *The Three Ages of the Interior Life*, 2 vols. (Rockford, IL: Tan, 1991), and Jordan Aumann, *Spiritual Theology* (New York: Continuum, 2006).

for theological training, it would be a mistake to think it is for professionals only.[6] I believe that all believers need to do spiritual theology to some degree if they are to understand the dynamic process of growth in Christ and participate in life in the Spirit. In that sense, spiritual theology is pastoral theology and implicitly the task for all believers who desire to integrate the truths of the Word of God into the reality of how the Spirit works in our everyday lives.

The data of spiritual theology: Scripture and observation of life in the Spirit. On this model of spiritual theology, the Scriptures are the central datum for the content and understanding of the process of spiritual transformation (a theological task). The Word of God is just what it claims: God's mind revealed, providing an authoritative understanding of those areas that it addresses. However, this textual study needs to be combined with the pastoral task that involves an empirical study of understanding how these realities discussed in the Bible actually work in real life (a psychological, observational, and reflective task). And it is both the theologian and pastor who must stretch themselves to ask the question of how the Spirit of God works transformation in real life. I cannot overestimate the significance of this point—one that is sometimes difficult for the pastor and theologian to recognize until they are confronted with their own struggles or the struggles of their congregants. After all, it is a real question regarding how we put off anger in the Spirit and how we become filled with the Holy Spirit. Perhaps these questions can be avoided or ignored in seminary for more theoretical and intellectually interesting conundrums. However, real life and real disciples cannot ignore these issues when the spiritual and psychological struggles ensue, when anger and fears persist, when prayer is dry, when one wonders whether one's life is filled with the Spirit and what this means, or when one's marriage is struggling for survival. And when I say there is a need for empirical study, I am not talking about the dogma of empiricism held by certain scientific thinkers who restrict knowledge to what only the senses provide. By "empirical" I refer to the God-given use of observation, reason, experience, reflection, and common sense to understand certain dimensions of reality, namely, growth in life in the Spirit. In some sense, this

---

[6]I am indebted to Jim Wilhoit for this type of concern at our roundtable discussion at the Center for Christian Thought, Biola University, 2014.

is the job of every Christian, but it is the specific and unique task of spiritual theology. And the pastor cannot avoid it.

This empirical or observational element in spiritual theology will focus on two fundamental dimensions: the Holy Spirit and the human person. First, because spiritual growth involves the work of the Holy Spirit in the believer's life—something that takes place in real life—if we are to have a full understanding of his work in sanctification, it is insufficient to limit our study of the work of the Spirit to a textual study of the Scriptures. Rather, it is necessary to actually study the Spirit's work in human experience. This would involve observation and reflection on the lives of the saints in order to understand the phenomena of the Holy Spirit at work in their lives. It would also involve the development of new theological methodologies of integrating reflection on Scripture with reflection on the work of the Spirit in human lives.

Second, because the Spirit does the work of transformation in the human person, the pastor as spiritual theologian will also need to study the dynamic processes of the human spirit, sin, psychopathology, and response to the Spirit. Again, few of us have had training in this kind of reflection outside of textual studies of theology and Scripture, so it will require new training in developing keen observation skills on ourselves and others in relation to patterns of human development, sin, and being sinned against. These empirical tasks of observation and reflection are the work of spiritual theology and need to be done in schools of theology if pastors are to have a robust understanding of the dynamics of spiritual growth. In this case, it is clear how much theologians need those from other academic disciplines such as psychology, neurobiology, and philosophy, if they are to do spiritual theology in the most complete manner. This is overdue, but the possibilities are great.

This approach to spiritual theology raises the fundamental epistemological question of whether we can even do empirical work to provide information on the spiritual life.[7] Of course, a number of epistemological issues will arise regarding the justification of truth claims in spiritual theology.[8]

---

[7]For a more in-depth understanding and defense of Spiritual Theology, see John H. Coe, "Spiritual Theology: A Theological-Experiential Methodology for Bridging the Sanctification Gap," *Journal of Spiritual Formation & Soul Care* 2, no. 1 (2009): 4-43.

[8]Some may object that this view of spiritual theology contradicts the Reformation commitment to *sola Scriptura*—or at least to some peoples' interpretation of this doctrine—that the Scriptures

Spiritual theologians will need to develop a thoughtful methodology and adjudicating procedures by which to scrutinize the study and findings of a spiritual theology insofar as they need to be informed, governed, and judged by a study of the Word of God. Great care will need to be given in developing the criteria and guidelines for this study as it integrates theology and knowledge from observation and other academic disciplines. Much could be said and needs to be said on this important topic. I have argued elsewhere that we have a biblical model for gaining wisdom from an empirical study of nature so that spiritual theology has a biblical justification in the integrative model of the Old Testament Wisdom literature. Proverbs, for example, insists there is an important extrabiblical source of wisdom for living that God has provided, and that it is discernible by observing and reflecting on (1) the created world (6:6; 30:24-28) and especially (2) persons and their complex situations (24:30-34; 30:21-23). This serves as a kind of biblical model for doing spiritual theology.[9]

Definition of spiritual theology. Spiritual theology is that theological-empirical discipline, with its own unique data and methodology, that brings together (1) a study of the truths of Scripture (a historical-literary discipline) with (2) a study of the ministry of the Holy Spirit and spiritual growth in the experience of human beings (a broadly empirical discipline involving

---

alone contain all that we need for understanding the spiritual life, and that all wisdom for living is contained in the Bible and no wisdom for spiritual growth can be discovered outside the Bible. Let me say briefly here that spiritual theology is consistent with the Protestant view of *sola Scriptura*. The important use of *sola Scriptura* by the Reformers is a very subtle and complex matter that takes us beyond the scope of this chapter. Suffice it to say that its original intent was not so much to mean that the Scripture alone provides *all* information or wisdom for spiritual growth. Rather, it was employed to affirm that Scripture alone, and not some Pope or council, provides the *constitutive tenets of the faith*, that is, those central doctrines that define the faith and are essential for faith to which the believer must assent. It was also used with reference to providing a boundary condition on practice, so that no spiritual practice could be required of a believer that was not explicitly taught in the Scripture. Of course, this does not preclude the possibility of finding wisdom outside the Bible that may assist in our understanding of spiritual growth. Spiritual theology is that theological discipline that is interested in determining whether there is any extrabiblical wisdom that we can discover, which is helpful for understanding and participating in the process of spiritual growth. For more on this, see John H. Coe and Todd W. Hall, *Psychology in the Spirit* (Downers Grove, IL: InterVarsity, 2010), chaps. 6–9.

[9]For an in-depth discussion of how the Old Testament Wisdom literature and the Old Testament wise man are biblical models for doing spiritual theology, see Coe and Hall, *Psychology in the Spirit*, chaps. 6–9.

observation, reflection, and integration with other relevant disciplines). By its very nature it is an integrative endeavor. The purpose or goal of this study is threefold: (1) to define the nature of supernatural life in Christ (which is derived from the Bible and theology as the primary data); (2) to explain the process of growth by which persons move from the beginning of the spiritual life to its full perfection in the next life (which is derived from the data of the Bible, theology, and experience); and (3) to formulate directives for spiritual growth and development (which are derived from the data of the Bible, theology, and experience). The notion of "data" for study is important to spiritual theology, for this branch of theology is integrative and multidimensional in nature. In that sense, spiritual theology's task is to study all relevant data regarding spiritual growth.

As stated before, though the Bible is the central datum, the peculiar and unique task of spiritual theology—in comparison to other kinds of academic theological disciplines (such as systematic theology and biblical studies)—is to integrate a theology of sanctification within a broadly empirical study of what is relevant to understanding spiritual growth in the real world. With God in heart and Scripture in hand, the unique and peculiar task of spiritual theology is to go into the church and the Spirit's work in believers' lives to study and understand all one can about the nature, process, and directives for spiritual growth.

In its most robust sense, this biblical and empirical study of life in the Spirit would include integrative and interactive dialogue between various academic disciplines of the university and knowledge gained from common human experience and from the Scriptures. The spiritual theologian in fact is a kind of generalist. Whether in the seminary or pastorate, the spiritual theologian seeks to glean from study of and interaction with specialists in Scripture and theology, as well as Christian psychologists, philosophers, sociologists, and anthropologists in order to better understand the person, human psychological-relational-cultural dynamics, and the nature of the ministry of the indwelling Holy Spirit. In particular, this methodology blends the work of the theologian and the Christian psychologist in a robust synthesis. And though the work of spiritual theology can be captured by an academic discipline, it also has a general application in the life of any believer who attempts to understand how to obey and integrate truth and the

Scriptures into real Christian existence and life in the Spirit. In its simplest sense, spiritual theology is a form of pastoral and everyday theology.

The unavoidable need for doing spiritual theology. Though pastors may not have been overtly trained in spiritual theology, it should be obvious that the theologian, pastor, and ordinary believer should, at least implicitly, engage in spiritual theology. Indeed, it is inevitable and unavoidable that a believer, when confronted by the truth of Scripture, has reflected on how this works in actual life and experience. This takes us right into the heart of spiritual theology. The question is not whether we will do spiritual theology; rather, the question is whether we will do it explicitly and well. There is a *necessity* to doing spiritual theology.

In the first place, spiritual theology is necessary in any context if we are to apply Scripture to our lives. In some sense, all believers implicitly do spiritual theology in the sense that they seek to understand how the truths of Scripture apply to our everyday lives in the Spirit. Regardless of the culture we live in, one cannot seek to obey the commands to "put off anger" or "be filled with the Holy Spirit" or "be anxious for nothing" without asking how to accomplish these things. In seeking to attend faithfully to these biblical imperatives, we must ask, What is the process by which we can obey these commands in real life? It is clear, then, that there is a need in the church for a meaningful theory-praxis of transformation (i.e., spiritual theology) that will be helpful to believers—a *practice* of formation that is *theoretically* connected to theology and human experience. The question of the universality or contextual particularity of a spiritual theology will be discussed later in this chapter.

Second, spiritual theology is important so that we might better understand how the Holy Spirit actually works in the believer's life. As stated before, the Bible is the sole or at least primary datum for expounding most doctrine (employing exegesis, biblical theology, and systematic theology).[10] However, there is a need to employ observation and reflection on the Spirit's work in human affairs if we are to understand all that can be known about

---

[10]When I say that the Bible is the primary datum for "most" doctrines, this takes into account the fact that the church throughout its history has employed reason and philosophical categories to assist in theological precision, understanding, and expression, as in the case of the doctrine of the Trinity or the dual nature of Christ.

the doctrines of sanctification and spiritual growth. The reason for this is the fact that the locus of formation by the work of the Holy Spirit is in the human soul and the church. This is an activity of God that takes place in the Holy Spirit that the Scriptures themselves affirm (2 Cor 4:7; Col 1:27). If we are to understand the totality of the Holy Spirit's work, we will need to study his work in human lives and the church.

Third, and along a similar line, spiritual theology and its empirical work of observation and reflection are particularly important to understand more fully the interpretation of biblical passages having to do with the Holy Spirit. This point relates to the issue of meaning and reference in biblical interpretation. In order to properly interpret or understand the *meaning* of the biblical texts having to do with the Spirit's work in transformation, we need to also understand the *referent* of the texts that relates to human experience of the Spirit. That is, we need to understand what those texts refer to in our present experience of the Spirit in real space and time. In that sense, exegesis is not merely a literary investigation but depends on empirical observation and reflection to understand fully the phenomena referred to in the text. In order to understand as fully as possible what Paul is saying about the ministry of the Holy Spirit in the person, we will need to begin empirical observation of and reflection on the church's and our own present experience with the Spirit. That is, to understand what it is to be filled with the Holy Spirit (Eph 5:18), what is involved in walking and living by the Spirit (Gal 5:16, 25), being led by the Spirit (Rom 8:14), or being filled with all the fullness of the Spirit in love (Eph 3:17-18) will require understanding something of the meaning and referent to which Paul is referring in these biblical texts. This raises deep epistemological and cultural questions and issues that will touched on in the next section.[11]

Thus, it is clear that spiritual theology services the church and the academy by bridging (1) the biblical and theological content of the faith and (2) the practice of the faith by providing (3) a theory of the *process* of growth (which is spiritual theology). There is a need in the church for a meaningful theory of the process of transformation that will be helpful to all believers, which

---

[11]The epistemological questions are various regarding adjudicating between interpretations that to some degree depend on one's experience of the Spirit or lack of experience, which is beyond the purview of this chapter.

assists in theoretically connecting the *practice* of formation to theology and to what is going on in human experience. Thus, a robust spiritual theology theoretically and experientially connects a purely biblical theology of sanctification with an *understanding* of the nature of growth in Christ, the developmental *processes* involved, and the *practical directives* for growth, resulting in application and praxis.

THE BENEFIT OF SPIRITUAL THEOLOGY FOR THE GLOBAL CHURCH

Though it is clear that this approach to spiritual theology may be helpful in a particular local context, some may argue that any one particular approach to spiritual theology will be unduly ethnocentric and unhelpful to people of other cultures and milieus. The same argument has been raised by those doing systematic theology in general, namely that it is often too ethnocentric in its orientation and has blinders to other parts of theological and spiritual realities. I will argue that there is something quite correct about this critique. Yet, instead of being a criticism of spiritual theology, this actually highlights the global genius of spiritual theology.

In the first place, it is true that a systematic theology may be uncritical and ethnocentric insofar as the questions and issues that are brought to the biblical text are grounded in a particular culture's concerns and issues. As a result, the systematic theologies of one culture may not be very helpful to the theological questions and contexts of another culture. Furthermore, it may altogether miss what the biblical text may be addressing regarding a particular subject. Systematic theologians need to be self-understanding and critical of this issue. However, this "particularity" is precisely what the spiritual theologian will predict about his or her robust spiritual theology. That is, because spiritual theology is, in part, empirical insofar as it observes and reflects on the human and spiritual situation *in a particular concrete context* (*my* life, *our* church, *our* culture, *our* context), one's spiritual theology will to some degree be explicitly narrow and psycho-ethnocentric. This, in fact, is the brilliance of spiritual theology—it is relevant to *me*, to *this* people, and *this* context. It is why each pastor, each people group, each church, and each training must *do* spiritual theology for itself and not merely rely on another tradition and official "text" for their understanding of the spiritual life. We certainly *learn* from other spiritual theologies, both present-day and in the history of the church, but we *do* them for ourselves and our community as well. A grave mistake of contemporary spiritual formation studies is to rely solely on spiritual theologians of the past and fail to *do* spiritual theology now.

Having said that, however, a particular spiritual theology will not be *merely* subjective or ethnocentric, and thus unhelpful to other peoples and cultures. Spiritual theology attempts to understand something that is universal to personhood, to the soul, to understanding how the Spirit works in and transforms the soul, and how we can help one another in this process. The Scriptures seem to assume that beneath the obvious and not-so-obvious cultural idiosyncratic elements of our lives, there is also something universal and species-wide regarding the human and spiritual dimensions in which we share as the universal body of Christ. Consequently, our particular, concrete spiritual theologies done in Southern California in 2020 will be in some ways different to and some ways similar to that which is done in Bangladesh or Kiev or by St. John of the Cross in the sixteenth century. But in the differences and similarities, we may discover that the pastor and spiritual theologian have hit on something we did not see that is truly human and species-wide in the spiritual life. Thus, we should expect each concrete spiritual theology to differ due to its relevant observations and reflections but provide something that is worth learning from that we might miss in our observations and reflections on the Scriptures and the spiritual life.

It turns out, then, that spiritual theology is that branch of theology that at its very essence does the kind of work and asks the kinds of existentially and culturally relevant questions about spiritual growth that are needed for the global church. Spiritual theology inescapably contextualizes spiritual formation for a particular people in a particular location. By its definition, spiritual theology is a culturally relevant enterprise insofar as its task concerns the work of theoretically understanding the work of the Spirit here and now, in *this* people, in *myself* as the spiritual theologian. There certainly will be some universal, generalized principles of spiritual growth from our biblical and systematic theologies related to sanctification. That is clear from the history of the church. However—and this is the genius of spiritual theology—by definition it does not stop with general, universal principles but works from these and always pushes on to what is going on in *this* people at *this* place and time. This is the implication of the empirical nature of spiritual theology, which involves observation and reflection on human beings and believers in this place at this time.

In that case, no one society, culture, church, or academic group can do all the work of spiritual theology that is sufficient for another group or culture. Each group or culture must take universal principles from Scripture and insights from others and then drive these into the hard empirical work of what the Spirit is doing here and now with us. To drive this point home even further: no one group or culture can do the work of spiritual theology for every person. Even this contextualized spiritual theology, in turn, must be applied by each person. In the ideal situation, each informed person has the opportunity to take these universal principles from the Scripture, insights from others, and contextualized insights from spiritual theology, and then integrate these with personal observation and reflection on what the Spirit is doing here and now. In the most general sense, doing spiritual theology is unavoidable if one is to be a Christian who is open to and cooperating with the work of the Spirit in one's life. This is the existential and empirical heart—and genius—of spiritual theology, of a faith that is living and must be understood by opening oneself to what the Spirit of God is doing here and now.

Perhaps it would be helpful to provide an example from the history of spiritual theology in order to demonstrate how this might be both helpful and complex as we look at a more global context. Specifically, spiritual theology has been particularly helpful in providing thoughtful reflections on the developmental processes of growth related to consolation, desolation, and what some spiritual formation writers have termed the "dark night of the soul" phenomena, and the different stages of our spiritual growth. Whereas the Scriptures address this subject of a developmental spirituality and spiritual experience somewhat cursorily (e.g., 1 Jn 2:12-13; 1 Cor 3:1-5; 2 Cor 12:1-10), theologians, pastors, and spiritual writers of the church have given much attention to this.[12]

---

[12]For more on this developmental spirituality regarding the process of growth, see John Coe, "Musings on the Dark Night of the Soul: St. John of the Cross on a Developmental Spirituality," *Journal of Psychology and Theology* 28, no. 4 (2000): 293-307. See also St. John of the Cross, *Dark Night of the Soul*, trans. E. Allison Peers (New York: Image, 1959). For a thoughtful and historical account of various developmental approaches to spirituality, see Bruce Demarest, "Reflections

The ancient spiritual writers noticed, both in themselves and many of their committed disciples, different seasons of experiencing God. They observed that the convert or young believer (the "beginner" in 1 Jn 2) at some point often experienced a strong sense of the felt presence of God. On the other hand, they also noticed that the same believer at a later time (when more mature) often experienced a sense of spiritual dryness or the felt absence of God (an empirical observation). They came to call these times, respectively, "consolation" or the felt presence of God, and "desolation" or the felt absence of God. As they observed and reflected on these phenomena in light of a theology of sanctification (the integrative work of doing of spiritual theology), they developed a number of hypotheses about the felt presence of God.

First, at least at the beginning of the spiritual life, the felt presence of God (consolation) or felt absence of God (desolation) is not necessarily correlated to maturity of character. This is a truth from observation and reflection. This phenomenon is contrary to what one might expect, namely, a pure correlation between character maturity and experience of the presence of God. We know that the Spirit is always present relationally in his people, which is a truth from Scripture: we are all "partakers of the divine nature" (2 Pet 1:4 ESV), and Paul refers to "Christ in you" (Col 1:27). Thus, since God is always present, they reasoned (doing spiritual theology) that the *felt* presence or absence of God (consolation and desolation), at least at some times and perhaps in the beginning of the spiritual life, are more *gifts* from God than the causal result of our actions, more the result of differing ways the Spirit works in the soul at different stages of our growth. Notice that this is a hypothesis from integrating both theological and empirical (psychological) reflections in spiritual theology. In that case, it is hypothesized that consolation, for the beginner, is often a filling of the Spirit ahead of one's character with a purpose to encourage faith and reinforce the practice of spiritual disciplines.[13] Desolation, on the other hand, may be a sign of God withdrawing from the young believer "infant consolation" or spiritual pleasure

---

on Developmental Spirituality: Journey Paradigms and Stages," *Journal of Spiritual Formation and Soul Care* 1, no. 2 (2008): 149-67.

[13]As an aside, there is a "filling of the Holy Spirit" that is of consolation but in a deeper sense, more congruent with character and maturity.

in order to reveal one's character and one's reliance on a sensual spiritual experience. This arid experience acts as a mirror to show the reality of one's heart and one's true motivations. This is not a withdrawing of the *presence* of the Spirit but rather the Spirit *drawing near* in truth apart from a feeling. This happens to show the person the true state of some of the vice elements of the character, how the person is not truly filled with the Spirit in those places of the heart but filled with oneself, the places in the heart that are dry and "cool" toward God, how the person has come to depend on a sensual spirituality of pleasure and consolation, and how God can slowly wean us from this and ultimately meet us in love in those dark places of the soul.

Notice that in each of the cases above, the kernel insight for this developmental model was initiated from observation and reflection on experience (the *consolation* experience in the immature and the *desolation* experience of the more mature believer). This was then brought into dialogue with theological truth, namely, that God is always with the believer, original sin's effect on the heart, the need to put off the former vices of the heart, and the need to not rely on sensual spirituality. From this integration of doctrine and observation/reflection emerges a set of spiritual-theological-psychological hypotheses regarding how to explain this experience of early consolation and later desolation given what we know (spiritual theology).

As insightful as this spiritual theology of the dark night of the soul has been in my life and the lives of many saints throughout church history, this may be quite complex and problematic to apply to all believers everywhere and at all times. There is always a question of the degree to which a particular spiritual theology will apply to others in other circumstances. The spiritual theologian must have the humility to realize that while some elements of theology and praxis may have universal validity, these very same elements may be empirically applicable only in certain situations. On one hand, there is plenty of dark-night phenomena in the Psalms, particularly the lament or psalms of disorientation, such as Psalms 13, 22, 77, and 88. It is interesting, however, that dark-night phenomena typically do not emerge in Christian literature until after the early church persecutions and during the times of peace and safety after Constantine. The reasonable explanation for this is that times of circumstantial trials such as persecution do the same spiritual or purging work of the heart that dark nights do, so that the spiritual trials are often unnecessary when undergoing circumstantial trials. However, when the church enters a time of circumstantial peace and prosperity, the dark-night literature of the church emerges. Likewise, it may be that dark-night literature may not be relevant to parts of the global persecuted church as it is in the West. Thus, parts of the church may not relate to this phenomena at all, though it may have related at different times in its history and may relate in the future. But, again, this variance is what a spiritual theology would predict due to its inherently empirical nature.

CONCLUSION

While the contemporary church has struggled with providing a theoretically and practically relevant understanding of spiritual formation, it can alter this trajectory by developing a robust spiritual theology. Doing spiritual theology to some degree is at the heart of each believer's life in the Spirit. Because the whole of our spiritual life is a kind of dependence, response, and openness to the indwelling Spirit of God (Jn 14:16-17; Gal 5:16; Rom 8:15-16; Eph 5:18; 3:16-19), the Christian life is a form of doing spiritual theology. Perhaps not all will engage in this discipline in its more robust academic form in schools of theology. However, all believers are involved at some level in the common-sense practice of observing their lives, trying to apply Scripture, discerning the ways of the Holy Spirit, watching for the work of God, and asking how the truths of Scripture apply to everyday life. This is the work of spiritual theology, which is inescapable for every believer in every context to some degree.

Moreover, the contemporary church has also struggled to provide a *globally relevant understanding* of spiritual formation due to its failure to develop a robust spiritual theology. What one Christian community has thought to be central to the spiritual life might be entirely ignored by another Christian community. Furthermore, some Christian communities have critiqued other Christian communities' experience of the Christian life without really understanding or studying the other's spiritual experiences and lives at all. The contemporary church and theology in general have been non-empirical in their orientation.[14] This is precisely what spiritual theology can

---

[14]I recall coming to the Lord in a Word-oriented community in which it was taken for granted that God does not speak to us personally apart from his Word. To seek to "hear" from him or

provide. Thus, the ethnocentricity of our spiritualities is either the failure of the academy and the church to do spiritual theology or the failure to realize that spiritual theology must be done by all people groups and all people, for each people and church group and even each person must discover and understand the Spirit's work in their own life. A robust return to doing spiritual theology would help ecclesiastical and theological bodies of believers to open up to and learn from the global context of doing spiritual theology. By its nature, spiritual theology will seek to provide the church with a meaningful understanding of spiritual formation for the church in its particular contexts. Spiritual theology is a global methodology for understanding spiritual formation for the global church.

Finally, spiritual theology should be a main element in Christian theological training. If spiritual theology is necessary for the church to understand spiritual formation and how it actually works in the believer's life—in this place and time—then it is clear that this theological-empirical first-order discipline needs to be within the purview of theological and pastoral training. To put it simply, spiritual theology is pastoral theology. This is where Scripture, theology, and preaching interface with the questions and existential needs of this people in this place and time. It is one thing to preach "be filled with the Holy Spirit," and it is another thing to help a believer who asks the pastor, "How am I to be filled with the Spirit, and what do I do to obey this?" This is the work of spiritual theology. If spiritual theology were to be taken seriously by schools of theology, it would go a long way toward training pastors to understand spiritual formation for their own context throughout the world. This would radically transform priorities for schools and for pastors in addressing the spiritual needs of the church. I think the main hindrance to this process of bringing spiritual theology and formation into theological education and the church will be the professor and pastor. Our own experience or lack of experience of the Spirit and

---

discern God's voice in some internal fashion was nonsense. However, there are other traditions of Christian spirituality that take for granted God's desire and intention to lead and speak to his people inwardly. Over time, I have now come to benefit from both of these traditions and have learned much from both. I see now the failure of my tradition to take others' religious experiences seriously to empirically investigate what others experience. So there is much to learn from one another's spiritual theology. But what is most important is for each community, each person, to do spiritual theology and open up to the Spirit's work here and now—and then to learn from one another and be open to one another.

transformation, personal and corporate, will be the limiting horizon of our teaching. May God expand our vision for walking in the Spirit!

STUDY QUESTIONS

1. Do you agree that there is a need for the church to do spiritual theology? Why or why not? To what degree has your church context done spiritual theology, that is, to what degree have they developed a deep understanding of how spiritual growth takes place and how to participate in this? Has your church been able to assist others in their spiritual development? To what degree do you personally have a developed spiritual theology, and how has this helped or hindered your understanding of and participation in growth and life in the Spirit?

2. Why do you think most schools of theology and pastoral training do not have a department of spiritual theology? Why do you think this might be controversial to some theologians or pastors?

3. To what degree do you think that the theology and scriptural interpretation you have learned have been too ethnocentric or egocentric? That is, to what degree has the Bible teaching you have experienced been overly influenced by one's surrounding culture or overly influenced by the person teaching? Is this a bad thing? Why or why not? What would be the benefit of a spiritual theology that addresses other cultural contexts?

4. Are there universal principles of spiritual formation and spiritual theology that apply to all believers? What are some of these? What might be some insights of spiritual theology that may be particularly applicable to your context and your life but not necessarily universal to all believers? Can you think of something you have heard from a fellow Christian from another denomination or culture or faith community different to yours that you found insightful for understanding spiritual formation?

5. Is it possible that your cultural or Christian cultural experience limits your understanding of the Scriptures and spiritual formation? Do you think this is true for other Christians that you might disagree with?

6. If you are interested in doing an experiment, take some time to study another denomination or Christian faith community that is foreign to you and your understanding of spiritual growth and the spiritual life in general. Then go to its worship service and interview an informed believer of that tradition. From there, seek to write a brief spiritual theology for them of what is universal between you and them, what might be unique for their spiritual life, and how this impacts your understanding of the Christian life.

7. What could you do to begin to be a "spiritual theologian" in your own right? What common-sense observations and reflection could you begin to make in this development? What kinds of studies could you begin to do?

PART TWO

ACTS

and

ELEMENTS

of

WORSHIP

as

SPIRITUAL FORMATION

CHAPTER FIVE

LITURGY AND SPIRITUAL FORMATION

Engaging with Evelyn Underhill's Prayer Book

ROBYN WRIGLEY-CARR

I AM AN ECUMENICAL CHRISTIAN, that is, a christocentric, trinitarian, biblically centered Christian with wide sympathies and allegiances with many branches of the Christian church. The varied influences on my spiritual formation over many years have led me to own this position. I was brought up in the Churches of Christ, a fairly "low" denomination that does not use liturgy. However, from the age of twelve, I have put the Psalms to music. I used to sit at the piano, with my Bible on the music stand, and sing the Psalms. It was only when I was studying at Regent College, Vancouver, with Eugene Peterson that I realized I had been praying! All those years as I sang the Psalms, I was praying liturgy.

I encountered Anglican churches as a university student. It was there that I learned about the Book of Common Prayer. Then two decades ago, while studying spiritual theology at Regent College, my horizons were further expanded. I was introduced to Catholic spirituality and Catholic mystics who were passionate lovers of God.

I am now a lecturer in theology and spirituality at a Pentecostal tertiary Christian liberal arts college in Sydney, Australia. *Pentecostal* and *liturgy* are not usually two words you would expect to find in the same sentence, as Pentecostal worship tends to not be liturgical. However, in my formation of

Pentecostal students, I engage them in some ecumenical liturgy: *Evelyn Underhill's Prayer Book.*[1]

In this chapter we explore the role of liturgy in spiritual formation through the writings and prayer book of Evelyn Underhill (1875–1941). I give examples from using liturgy in spiritual retreats for students and for faculty and as an assessed spiritual practice.

THE ROLE OF LITURGY IN SPIRITUAL FORMATION

Liturgy is not usually at the forefront of discussions about spiritual formation. However, in this chapter, the role of liturgy in our spiritual growth to Christlikeness is outlined in relation to *Evelyn Underhill's Prayer Book*. Eugene Peterson argues that prayer is "fundamentally liturgical."[2] He continues:

> Left to ourselves, we are never more selfish than when we pray. . . . Liturgy defends us against the commonest diseases of prayer: the tyranny of our emotions, the isolationism of our pride. Liturgy pulls our prayers out of the tiresome business of looking after ourselves and into the exhilarating enterprise of seeing and participating in what God is doing. . . . Liturgy breaks us out of the isolation of ego and emotion where we are cut off from the large winds and landscapes of grace . . . pulls us into the great dance of grace.[3]

Liturgies help us engage in the "dance of grace." As well as being drawn into this "dance of grace," liturgies shape our identities by "forming our most fundamental desires and our most basic attunement to the world."[4]

Evelyn Underhill engaged in what she called "care of souls" and repeatedly encourages her spiritual directees to pray the liturgical prayers of the "greats" of church history. She sees formal prayers such as the Psalms and the prayers of the saints as "educative to the soul which wants to learn to pray" and a means of "enter[ing] into their atmosphere."[5] Underhill states, "The best way of knowing God is to frequent the company of His friends."[6] It is no

---

[1]*Evelyn Underhill's Prayer Book* was published in 2018. All book royalties are donated to the House of Retreat, Pleshey, where Underhill led her spiritual retreats.

[2]Eugene. H. Peterson, *Answering God* (London: Marshall Pickering, 1989), 83.

[3]Peterson, *Answering God*, 91-92.

[4]James K. A. Smith, *Desiring the Kingdom: Worship, Worldview, and Cultural Formation* (Grand Rapids, MI: Baker Academic, 2009), 25.

[5]Charles Williams, ed., *The Letters of Evelyn Underhill* (London: Longmans, Green, 1944), 84.

[6]Williams, ed., *Letters*, 84.

wonder that she collected prayers from lovers of God from the fourth to twentieth centuries to lead her spiritual retreatants in prayer.

In her letters of spiritual direction, Underhill repeatedly instructs her directees to engage with formal, vocal prayer,[7] even if it means reciting prayers "mechanically."[8] She writes that those whose prayers "tend to dreaminess" should use vocal prayer.[9] Liturgical prayer is also recommended for those who are suffering,[10] or are experiencing spiritual dryness[11] or "spiritual convalescence."[12] From personal experience, Underhill knows the "curious [positive] effect of a daily Office."[13] The Lord's Prayer is also recommended as it helps us engage in the "attitude of the human Christ."[14]

Engaging with the prayers of women and men of faith who have preceded us reminds us that "there are others to whom God speaks. . . . I am neither the only nor the favourite child."[15] One example of liturgy that includes prayers written over 1,700 years is *Evelyn Underhill's Prayer Book*. We now turn to hear the backstory of this liturgical text.

EVELYN UNDERHILL'S PRAYER BOOK

In 2016 I discovered two books of prayers that Evelyn Underhill collected for leading spiritual retreats in the 1920s and 1930s at The House of Retreat at Pleshey, near Chelmsford in England. Researchers had assumed that these prayer books Underhill used for retreat leading had been lost many decades ago. However, an Anglican priest had discovered one of them long ago in an Oxfam shop and had used the prayers to nurture his private devotion. He donated this prayer book to The House of Retreat in 2004, where it was carefully placed in a suitcase for safekeeping. Sadly, it lay forgotten for twelve years. The earlier prayer book, with identical red calligraphy headings, also mysteriously emerged around the same time, both in the seventy-fifth anniversary year of Underhill's death.

---

[7]Williams, ed., *Letters*, 120-21, 195, 247.
[8]Carol Poston, *The Making of a Mystic* (Urbana: University of Illinois Press, 2010), 312-13.
[9]Williams, ed., *Letters*, 132.
[10]Williams, ed., *Letters*, 90.
[11]Williams, ed., *Letters*, 190, 194.
[12]Poston, *Making*, 312-13.
[13]Williams, ed., *Letters*, 264.
[14]Williams, ed., *Letters*, 133.
[15]Peterson, *Answering God*, 85.

Evelyn Underhill (1875–1941) was a British, Anglican laywoman who wrote nearly forty books and hundreds of articles, and was a spiritual director and retreat leader. She was the first woman to lead spiritual retreats for Anglican clergy and the first woman to lecture in theology at the University of Oxford. As well as receiving an honorary doctorate from the University of Aberdeen, she was made a fellow of Kings College, London. The Church of England commemorates Underhill liturgically on June 15 each year, and the Episcopal Church in the United States honors her with a yearly feast day.

Evelyn Underhill's Prayer Book contains prayers written by women and men from the fourth to the twentieth centuries from all branches of the church—Protestant, Catholic, and Orthodox. We find prayers written by early theologians such as Augustine, Ambrose, Pope Gregory VII, and Anselm; later theologians such as Edward Pusey and John Henry Newman; writers in Christian spirituality such as Thomas à Kempis, Francois Fénelon, Ignatius of Loyola, and Teresa of Avila; and poets such as John Donne, Christina Rossetti, and Margaret Cropper. The greatest historical concentration clusters in the sixteenth century. Evelyn Underhill also contributes her own prayers, with the majority of these in the second half of the published volume.

One might wonder if such a lot of historical and ancient prayers would be accessible to a twenty-first century audience. First, I need to mention that I modernized the English to make the prayers more accessible and relevant to contemporary readers. Second, Underhill chose prayers that are often passionate and poetic; such prayers tend not to "date" but are timeless and draw in the reader. Charles Williams tells us that Underhill gathered the prayers that "specially delighted" her from her varied and eclectic reading and that each prayer was placed "on probation" for some time before being admitted into her collection.[16] Here are a few examples of the prayers, to give you a taste of some of the liturgy used to aid in the spiritual formation of my students:

- ◆ *Passionate* prayers: "Let our lives run to Your embrace . . . and breathe the breath of Eternity. O God Supreme! Most secret and most present, most beautiful and strong. Constant yet Incomprehensible, changeless

---

[16]Williams, ed., *Letters*, 333.

yet changing all! What can I say, my God, my Life, my Holy Joy . . . You are the only reality."[17]

♦ *Poetic* prayers: "Beyond us are the hills of God, the snowfields of the Spirit, the Other Kingdom."[18]

♦ Prayers about *union* with God: "Mercifully grant that Your life may be in ours for evermore."[19] "Within Your wounds, hide me!"[20]

♦ Prayers desiring God's *presence*: "O God! . . . Help us to be conscious of Your presence."[21]

♦ Prayers desiring a view of *eternity*: "Give ease to our hearts, by bringing us close to things Infinite and Eternal."[22]

♦ Prayers inviting God to take *initiative*: "Take possession of our souls. So fill . . . our imaginations with a picture of Your love."[23] "Breathe into our souls holy and heavenly desires and make us like our Saviour."[24] "Let our lives run to Your embrace . . . till they . . . breathe the breath of eternity."[25] "The house of our soul is narrow. O enlarge it, that You may enter in!"[26]

I have used *Evelyn Underhill's Prayer Book* in courses I teach in spirituality and theology. I have prayed some of the prayers as part of my prayer at the beginning of classes. I have also had the students engage in praying the prayers as one of two chosen spiritual practices in a student assignment.

LITURGY AND "SPIRITUAL PRACTICES"

In my course "Christian Spirituality," the first of four assessments are experiential. I do not want students to simply learn *about* prayer, I want them to *pray*. So, students are asked to engage in two spiritual practices for weeks two and three of the course and record their experiences in an online forum.

[17]Robyn Wrigley-Carr, ed., *Evelyn Underhill's Prayer Book* (London: SPCK, 2018), 42.
[18]Wrigley-Carr, ed., *Evelyn Underhill's*, 58.
[19]Wrigley-Carr, ed., *Evelyn Underhill's*, 43.
[20]Wrigley-Carr, ed., *Evelyn Underhill's*, 62.
[21]Wrigley-Carr, ed., *Evelyn Underhill's*, 49.
[22]Wrigley-Carr, ed., *Evelyn Underhill's*, 72.
[23]Wrigley-Carr, ed., *Evelyn Underhill's*, 48.
[24]Wrigley-Carr, ed., *Evelyn Underhill's*, 52.
[25]Wrigley-Carr, ed., *Evelyn Underhill's*, 42.
[26]Wrigley-Carr, ed., *Evelyn Underhill's*, 42.

Students can select from a variety of spiritual practices. For example, lectio divina on the Psalms, gazing at religious icons, labyrinth walking/praying, or Ignatian meditation on Gospel narratives. Another possible spiritual practice is prayerful engagement with liturgy: *Evelyn Underhill's Prayer Book*. Students are asked to pray aloud some prayers from this prayer book for twenty minutes a day, for seven days. Praying aloud slows down their reading and helps them to engage more of their body in their praying (e.g., seeing, hearing). As they pray the prayers, they are asked to take note of any phrases that especially resonate with them and ponder them further, repeatedly praying those meaningful, short phrases throughout their day.

While participating in their two chosen spiritual practices, students keep a daily journal, recording their experiences and outlining their responses to the practice. They subsequently write a post in the online forum, reflecting on the value of the practices, any benefits or detriments experienced, and how the practices might be best utilized in their churches. Students read each other's posts and thus get to hear about spiritual practices that they did not get to try. This assessment is deliberately only worth a small amount of the students' overall grade, but it provides students with the opportunity of engaging in the practice of prayer and other spiritual practices.

One student who chose the spiritual practice of praying the liturgy in *Evelyn Underhill's Prayer Book* recorded in his post that this was his first experience of praying liturgy. He wrote, "At first it felt strange," but gradually he found it "exciting and challenging." He went as far as encouraging his fellow students to "read it daily." He then proceeded to write about seven phrases from the prayers that deeply impacted him. He reflected that the phrase "forgetting ourselves" affected him. He began to recognize that his prayers tend to be all about *him* and *his* desires. He reflected that forgetting himself in God's presence means "I let him do what he wants to do. Sometimes I just should keep quiet and stop talking." In another reflection about aligning his will with God's, he wrote, "My prayer is that God changes the way I think to the way he thinks. I pray that God changes the desires of my heart into his desires." In another rumination he wrote, "Wow, what a prayer. From now on this is going to be one of my favourite prayers. I want to live a clean and holy life because I don't want to offend God but please him." This student's prayers were enriched and deepened by engaging with the prayers of Underhill.

LITURGY AND RETREATING

I have also used *Evelyn Underhill's Prayer Book* when leading a spiritual re-treat for the students at my college. The retreat's theme was "Darkness and Dawn," and we explored the biblical image of darkness and light through engaging prayerfully with the Psalms as well as from the liturgy chosen by Underhill in her prayer book. As the students arrived at the retreat house and headed off to unpack their bags, they were greeted with a copy of *Evelyn Underhill's Prayer Book* on their bed pillow. This became a memento to take with them following their retreat, so they could continue engaging with the prayers.

In the advertising material for this retreat I wrote the following:

> We are surrounded by the ongoing reality of darkness. This state of being is acknowledged by the Psalmist, who closes one Psalm with the words, "Darkness is my closest friend." But the darkness is always—eventually—followed by the dawn, by "dawning light." Christ is a "fountain of cascading light," our companion and protector in the darkness, and the One who opens our eyes to the light in the midst of the darkness, or when the shadows pass.

The retreat provided a mix of group sessions and times alone for indi-vidual prayer and reflection, so students could listen to God and be revived and refreshed, whatever their current experience of darkness and dawn. Liturgy from *Evelyn Underhill's Prayer Book* was used in group sessions, praying responsive reading of prayers out loud that were related to the retreat theme. Students were also encouraged to pray selected prayers from the prayer book during times alone that would help them be reminded that God is with them, whatever their present experience of darkness may be. Surrender is key in many of these prayers. For example, from à Kempis's *Imitation of Christ*: "If You will that we be in light, blessed may You be; if You will that we be in darkness, blessed may You be."[27]

But it is not just students who can benefit from liturgy at spiritual retreats. This year I also initiated a faculty retreat for lecturers in our theology faculty. We *teach* who we *are*, so I believe that spiritual formation for lecturers of theology, Bible, and ministry courses should be a priority in our theological colleges. The theme I chose for the faculty spiritual retreat was "Living

---

[27]Wrigley-Carr, ed., *Evelyn Underhill's*, 13.

Water." I led four sessions: "Water Cleansing the Soul"; "A Thirst for God"; "Water Refreshing the Soul"; and "The Well-Watered Garden." Several prayers in *Evelyn Underhill's Prayer Book* cluster around the theme of "washing" and "cleansing," so they were prayed in sessions one and three. Once more, retreatants engaged in liturgy from the prayer book through participating in group recitation of the prayers in a responsive fashion. One example of a prayer is "Water from the side of Christ, wash me! . . . Within Your wounds, hide me!"[28] Retreatants were also ushered into other prayer activities such as lectio divina in small groups of excerpts from the Psalms centering on the theme of water, and Ignatian meditation on the Gospel narrative of Jesus walking on the water. The retreat refreshed us spiritually as individuals and enhanced our sense of community as a team. Our corporate engagement in liturgy was key in this process. Having discussed the use of liturgy with students and faculty using *Evelyn Underhill's Prayer Book*, we now consider some of Underhill's thoughts concerning the nature of spiritual formation and the role of liturgical prayer.

THE "PREVENIENCE OF GOD" AND SPIRITUAL FORMATION

The conviction that God is the prime mover in our spiritual formation underlies my practice of leading spiritual retreats and encouraging students to engage in spiritual practices. Like Evelyn Underhill and her spiritual director, Friedrich von Hügel, the concept of the "prevenience" of God is foundational to my work with students. This is the idea that God is the one who goes before us, *initiating* the work of shaping and transforming us to become like Jesus. Spiritual formation is primarily the triune God's work, not ours. In Underhill's words, it is "the Divine Love; God, the Spirit of Spirits, indwelling His creature and moulding it to the pattern of Christ;"[29] "God Himself, His loving energy at work within . . . our souls."[30]

God's ongoing spiritual formation of us is repeatedly stated by Underhill. The image of a "great magnet" inexorably drawing "iron filings" vividly illustrates God's prevenient grace on the soul.[31] Underhill argues that God is

---

[28]Wrigley-Carr, ed., *Evelyn Underhill's*, 81.
[29]Evelyn Underhill, *The Fruits of the Spirit* (London: Longmans, 1960), 42.
[30]Underhill, *Fruits*, 42.
[31]Underhill, *The Spiritual Life* (Manly: Centre for Christian Spirituality, 1976), 34-35.

"pressing us in a certain direction, and moulding us."[32] This "moulding" is like "the invisible lines of force within a magnetic field condition[ing] all the tiny iron filings scattered on it. But now and then it does emerge on the surface and startles us by its witness to a subtle and ceaseless power and love working within the web of events . . . the direct action of God . . . a personal energy, a never-ceasing Presence that intervenes."[33]

And this "moulding action" is constantly ongoing as God "slowly change[s] us."[34] Not surprisingly, Underhill encourages her spiritual directees to "throw the whole emphasis on God—*His* work in your soul. *His* call to you."[35] God is the great initiator, not us. Underhill emphasizes that "we must expect our small action to be overruled and swallowed up in the vast Divine Action."[36] When directees repeatedly asked Underhill what *they* should do to hasten their spiritual growth, she tells them to assimilate the "priceless art of letting *God* make the first move."[37] For God's work on the soul is "infinitely more important" than anything *we* do.[38] One directee is told not to "wriggle" in God's arms in some sort of feeble "effort to help Him along, because you *can't.*"[39]

However, Underhill also makes it clear that they are to *cooperate* with God's work and participate. The "spiritual life," writes Underhill, is "the life of a human creature which is being transformed in God by the joint action of His energetic grace and its own faithful love."[40] Thus we are "like children being taught a job by a loving parent who teaches by allowing us to help with the job."[41] Underhill writes of the necessity of our "vigorous and yet humble co-operation with [the] Spirit's ceaseless action"; however, she explicitly cautions, "all that really matters is indeed done *to* us and not *by* us."[42] Despite

---

[32]Underhill, *Spiritual Life,* 29.
[33]Underhill, *Light of Christ* (London: Longmans, 1960), 73.
[34]Grace Adolphsen Brame, ed., *The Ways of the Spirit* (New York: Crossroad, 1994), 231; Underhill, *Spiritual Life,* 45; Evelyn Underhill, "The Degrees of Prayer," *Collected Papers of Evelyn Underhill* (London: Longmans & Co, 1949), 36.
[35]Williams, ed., *Letters,* 187, italics added.
[36]Evelyn Underhill, *Abba* (London: Longmans, 1960*)*, 31-32.
[37]Williams, ed., *Letters,* 194, italics added.
[38]Williams, ed., *Letters,* 194, italics added.
[39]A. M. Ramsay and A. M. Allchin, *Evelyn Underhill: Anglican Mystic* (Oxford: SLG, 2002), 43.
[40]Evelyn Underhill, *The Golden Sequence* (London: Methuen, 1933), 56-57.
[41]Brame, ed., *Ways,* 189.
[42]Underhill, *Golden Sequence,* 151, italics added.

this, our role in "co-operating with the grace which has been given" is necessary.[43] It is in "trying to work . . . for and with God, that the soul grows."[44] In
the end we need to accept this "paradox moving to and fro between aban-
donment and effort."[45] God's initiative; our participation. And prayers are
the tools for "being and becoming . . . that we use to collaborate in his work
with us."[46]

OUR COOPERATION IN SPIRITUAL FORMATION

Having established that her spiritual directees need to participate in God's
transforming work in their lives, what does Underhill tell them about the
nature of that participation? First, an expectant, attentive posture is recommended to help us try to identify the "traces of grace."[47] She reminds them
that it is difficult to maintain a slow gaze when "anxious to get on to the next
stage and be practical."[48] Another essential aspect of our cooperation is
"self-abandonment" so we become "unresisting agents" who can be "formed
and shaped" under the "gradual pressure."[49] God "gives the conditions," and
our task is to "accept them with humility and . . . adjust our will to His great
rhythm," not waste strength "fighting against the stream."[50] Underhill encourages her directees to "be supple in his hands and let Him mould you . . .
responding with very simple acts of trust."[51] So being "co-workers with God"
involves self-abandonment, placing ourselves "with entire confidence" in his
hands and giving ourselves "for the purposes of His *redemptive love*."[52]

Alongside aligning our will, patient trust and an ability to wait are also essential, as spiritual formation is usually slow. Underhill writes we are "drawn,
at His pace,"[53] so we need to rest in God and wait patiently.[54] Our usual default
is "resisting . . . grasping . . . never lying quiet on the waves." But such

[43]Ramsay and Allchin, eds., *Evelyn Underhill*, 39.
[44]Underhill, *Concerning the Inner Life* (London: Methuen, 1953), 45.
[45]Underhill, *Abba*, 49.
[46]Peterson, *Answering God*, 2.
[47]Eugene Peterson, *The Contemplative Pastor* (Grand Rapids, MI: Eerdmans, 1989), 60-61.
[48]Underhill, *Light of Christ*, 32.
[49]Underhill, *Golden Sequence*, 50.
[50]Underhill, *Fruits*, 25.
[51]Williams, ed., *Letters*, 213.
[52]Underhill, *Light of Christ*, 32; Brame, ed., *Ways*, 187.
[53]Underhill, *Spiritual Life*, 39.
[54]Underhill, *Fruits*, 25.

impatient hurrying is the mark of the amateur.[55] Underhill presents the life of Christ, who took thirty years to grow and only a few years to act as her rebuke to our "spiritual impatience and uppish hurry."[56] God's action is gradual as He "fosters and sanctifies growth."[57] It is not "shooting up in a hurry": we should not strain but gently accept what comes without comparing ourselves to others.[58] We "wait, to grow and change" according to God's "overruling Will and Pace."[59] Using the analogy of plants, Underhill describes healthy growth as "so gentle as to be almost imperceptible."[60] Such growth requires feeding but not forcing.[61] Underhill reinforces this with the image of "the wind's pat," which is unseen.[62] She states that we are each subject to forces we know nothing about,[63] and it is difficult to discern direction.[64] Thus, as we help others grow, we must not be "straining souls" or hurrying to enlighten, but encourage a quiet, humble patience—the "artist's pace."[65] And Underhill encourages her retreatants not to look too far ahead or wonder about their growth but simply "respond bit by bit" and leave the result to God.[66] God does not make clones, and growth does not have "conformity to a pattern."[67] We need to be patient with the process as "growing creature[s]" whom God is completing "in His own time and His own way."[68] And praying liturgy is one means of engaging in this undertaking, given the nature of the spoken word.

THE EFFECT OF SPOKEN WORDS

The spoken word has more suggestive power—reaching and modifying "our deeper psychic levels"—than inarticulate thought, argues Underhill.[69] This is the case, she argues, because "the centres of speech are closely connected

---

[55]Underhill, *Fruits*, 25.
[56]Underhill, *Light of Christ*, 43-44.
[57]Underhill, *Light of Christ*, 44.
[58]Underhill, *Light of Christ*, 45-46.
[59]Underhill, *Light of Christ*, 33.
[60]Brame, ed., *Ways*, 91.
[61]Brame, ed., *Ways*, 92.
[62]Underhill, *Fruits*, 24.
[63]Underhill, *Fruits*, 24.
[64]Underhill, *Fruits*, 24.
[65]Underhill, *Light of Christ*, 50, 51.
[66]Brame, ed., *Ways*, 93.
[67]Brame, ed., *Ways*, 94.
[68]Underhill, *Fruits*, 25.
[69]Underhill, *Degrees of Prayer*, 8.

with the heart of our mental life."[70] Thus people who articulate aloud a daily office or the Psalms are "keeping closer to the facts of existence than those who only talk generally of remaining in a state of prayer."[71] Similarly, the fourteenth century English mystic Walter Hilton states that if we "cease from saying, devotion vanishes away."[72] Underhill goes as far as arguing that some vocal prayer recited aloud should be part of the daily rule of even the most contemplative soul. The reason for this insistence is twofold. Liturgy provides "shape and discipline to our devotions, and keeps us in touch with the great traditions of the Church" and also "qualities of poetry . . . rouse the dormant spiritual sense, and bring us into the presence of God."[73] Underhill argues that as we grow these vocal prayers, they become "slower and more pondered" and we merge into meditation.[74] So as my students engage with liturgy for their spiritual practices assessment or on spiritual retreats, I encourage them to articulate the prayers aloud. This approach recognizes the importance of the body in our prayer. And persevering with humble practices in prayer, such as praying liturgy aloud, regardless of how we feel, keeps us centered and focused on God.

I vividly recall Eugene Peterson describing his morning ritual. He would make his coffee, have a look at the weather outside, then pray the Psalms aloud. Every day. He did not wait to gauge whether he *felt* like praying the Psalms; he just did it as a spiritual discipline. And if he could not find his place in one of the Psalms he was praying, he would think of someone he knew who was experiencing the pain expressed by the psalmist and pray it for them. It was his "long obedience in the same direction" and central to the constancy of his devotional life. Alongside this bodily aspect of spoken words when praying liturgy, Underhill writes that praying liturgy brings us into "the atmosphere of eternity"[75] as we join in "the great corporate prayer of the Church."[76] One means of being enriched by lovers of God from past eras is through actively engaging with their prayers.

---

[70]Underhill, *Degrees of Prayer*, 8.
[71]Underhill, *Degrees of Prayer*, 8.
[72]Underhill, *Degrees of Prayer*, 8.
[73]Underhill, *Degrees of Prayer*, 8.
[74]Underhill, *Degrees of Prayer*, 8.
[75]Brame, ed., *Ways*, 112.
[76]Williams, ed., *Letters*, 190, 194.

THE BENEFIT OF THE TRADITION FOR OTHER GLOBAL EVANGELICALS

There are several benefits of the use of liturgy for the global church today. I mention three here: it leads to (1) enrichment from ecumenical and historical breadth, (2) renewed awareness and practice of the corporate nature of prayer, as well as (3) the "unselfing" of liturgy.

Enrichment from ecumenical and historical breadth. One of the benefits my students have experienced from praying the prayers in *Evelyn Underhill's Prayer Book* is that they have been able to join with prayers from all branches of the Christian church from the fourth to twentieth centuries. Underhill reminds us that our experience is narrow if we are cut off from liturgical history. She emphatically argues, "How raw and thin a religious experience would be which cut itself off from this long liturgical history, refused all this culture, these gifts of the past, . . . it would mean hopeless impoverishment for the average soul."[77]

Too often as contemporary worshipers we forget that we are members of the historical church. As Peterson argues, confining ourselves to "one-generational knowledge" results in us being "impoverished beyond reason."[78] Underhill goes further arguing that gaining a "sense of belonging to a supernatural society committed to the practice of the spiritual life" means we can find our own "difficulties and errors noted and dealt with centuries ago" as well as thoughts we might think of as modern are simply "the discoveries of the mystics" in contemporary language.[79] Alongside learning from past wisdom through ancient prayers, we may even identify our contemporary blind spots. Much wisdom can be gained through joining with the entire "communion of Saints, the living and the dead, in reverent adoring delight in God."[80]

Short quotations from liturgies from different branches of the historic church are included in *Evelyn Underhill's Prayer Book*, for example, the *Leonine Sacramentary*, the oldest liturgical text in the Western Latin tradition, and the *Mozarabic Rite* from the Latin Catholic Church in the seventh century. Another ancient source is "Veni Creator Spiritus," a hymn from the

---

[77]Lucy Menzies, ed., *Collected Papers of Evelyn Underhill* (London: Longmans, Green, 1949), 75.
[78]Peterson, *Answering God*, 117.
[79]Underhill, *Degrees of Prayer*, 7.
[80]Menzies, ed., *Collected Papers*, 65-66.

ninth century sung in Roman Catholic and Anglican Churches. Praying these ancient liturgies from different branches of the church family reminds us that we are part of a historical, ecumenical community.

C. S. Lewis recommends the rhythm of reading a historical book after each contemporary book, stating that "every age has its own outlook," and old books help us see and "correct the characteristic mistakes of our own period."[81] The same can be argued for historic prayers. As Simon Chan argues, "An openness to the Christian past is one important sign of genuine Christian spirituality."[82]

In the Christian spirituality course that I teach, I introduce my students to my "friends from the cemetery," that is, women and men who have now passed but embodied rich lives of prayer. The students are invited to learn prayer practices and postures from the greats from the past, who were often more deeply immersed in prayer and less distracted. Underhill describes the "communion of saints, that Supernatural Society, which both transcends time and indwells it" and how our prayer and liturgy needs to have "an historic sense" so we are engaging with the words of "a living and of an historic society."[83] Similarly when we pray the Psalms, we "join with the long line of Hebrew and Christian saints" in using that poetry so often found on Jesus' lips.[84] The Psalms were the prayer book for Israel and the prayer book for the church until the twentieth century. As well as deepening our lives of prayer, engaging with "friends from the cemetery" and Hebrew and Christian saints can help us to safeguard against the contemporary tendency toward individualism. Intentional relationship with other diverse souls can help us replace "mine" with "ours."[85]

The corporate nature of prayer. Liturgy feeds and fosters the individual by "the corporate life," claims Underhill.[86] In our individualistic, contemporary world, the communal nature of spiritual formation and prayer are not always emphasized sufficiently. But as Peterson argues, the idea of prayer

---

[81]C. S. Lewis, introduction to Athanasius's *On the Incarnation,* 2, www.bhmc.org.uk/uploads/9/1/7/7/91773502/lewis-incarnation-intro.pdf.

[82]Chan, *Spiritual Theology,* 30.

[83]Evelyn Underhill, "Essentials of a Prayer Book," in *The Revised Prayer-Book of 1927* (Cardiff: Western Mail, 1927), 51.

[84]Menzies, ed., *Collected Papers,* 75.

[85]Underhill, *Abba,* 15.

[86]Underhill, "Essentials," 57.

as something we do when "alone—the solitary soul before God—is a persistent error. . . . Prayer begins in community."[87] And our Christian community is larger than the one we can see and touch. It extends across time and denominational boundaries: the body of Christ.

Community is essential to our spiritual formation. As Peterson reminds us, "We are never more ourselves than when we pray, but if we remain only ourselves, we are less than ourselves. Liturgy installs us praying in a community."[88] And if a primary function of prayer is "becoming ourselves . . . we cannot do that alone."[89] Underhill reiterates this arguing the following:

> Dante says that directly a soul ceases to say Mine, and says Ours, it makes the transition from the narrow, constricted, individual life to the truly free, truly personal, truly creative spiritual life; in which all are linked together in one single response to the Father of all spirits, God. Here, all interpenetrate, and all, however humble and obscure their lives may seem can and do affect each other.[90]

Liturgy can help us "interpenetrate" as we voice our prayers together. And Underhill emphasizes God initiating "the conquest of our rampant individualism" through his supernatural power, gradually making each human life "a living part of the Body of Christ."[91] Further, alongside safeguarding against individualism, praying liturgy can help us move beyond our self-absorption, to adoration of God.

The "unselfing" of liturgy. Another benefit of engaging with liturgy is that it helps us not simply to participate in "supernatural shopping-lists" focused on the self. As Underhill argues, people who think the spiritual life centers around themselves need a larger horizon. For "any spiritual view" that "puts the human creature . . . in the centre foreground, is dangerous till we recognise its absurdity."[92] Hence, the necessity to be ushered into a life of prayer that encourages us to focus on *God*, not self. For our natural default tends to be on ourselves, but this

---

[87]Peterson, *Answering God*, 84, 19.
[88]Peterson, *Answering God*, 88.
[89]Peterson, *Answering God*, 84, 19.
[90]Underhill, *Spiritual Life*, 33-34.
[91]Underhill, *Abba*, 35.
[92]Underhill, *Spiritual Life*, 25-26.

"kingdom of self" needs to be undermined so we can focus on the kingdom of God.[93]

By contrast, the ancient prayers of the Psalms and ancient Christian liturgy invariably place the emphasis on *God*, not on us. Even though two-thirds of the prayers voice lament, they take the pray-er beyond their despair to adoration of God.[94] We see a recurring reorientation: "I'm hurting . . . and You are God." We are transported from ourselves into a larger reality. Underhill notes that all through the ancient daily offices from which our morning and evening prayers are drawn is an emphasis on "God's Being" rather than on our needs.[95] Underhill reiterates this, arguing that "joyous adoration . . . obliterates all thoughts of self. . . . The historic liturgies of the Christian Church, whether Latin, Anglican or Orthodox, constantly em-phasise this principle."[96] Also, these liturgies encourage us toward humility and "creatureliness"[97]; "knowing our own size and own place . . . fit[ting] into God's great scheme instead of having a jolly little scheme of our own"— and adoration of God is essential to this process.[98]

In *Evelyn Underhill's Prayer Book* we see repeated prayers of adoration that can help us gain a sense of the supernatural that conquers our "per-sistent self-occupation."[99] Even pious humans are beset by this "cramping tendency": *my* soul, *my* spiritual life, *my* sins, *my* problems, *my* communion with God. But this self-centeredness becomes "disentangled" and "drowned"[100] when the spirit of adoration colors our lives, releasing us from our narrow, selfish outlook so our little affairs can be reduced to proper proportion against God's majesty.[101] The humble upward gaze, our eyes cleansed by adoration,[102] is needed to rescue us from shallow and "cheaply familiar" lives of prayer.[103] Underhill emphasizes the necessity for liturgy to include

---

[93]Peterson, *Contemplative Pastor*, 8.
[94]Psalm 88 is the only psalm that does not have the "reorientation" from self to God but closes with "darkness is my closest friend."
[95]Menzies, ed., *Collected Papers*, 70.
[96]Menzies, ed., *Collected Papers*, 70.
[97]Underhill, *Fruits*, 35.
[98]Underhill, *Fruits*, 35.
[99]Underhill, *Concerning the Inner Life*, 44.
[100]Underhill, *Abba*, 42; Menzies, ed., *Collected Papers*, 77-78.
[101]Menzies, ed., *Collected Papers*, 78.
[102]Underhill, *Abba*, 43.
[103]Underhill, *Golden Sequence*, 159.

"awe-struck adoration."[104] But alongside words voicing the "adoring joy of the soul that has caught a glimpse of the Transcendent," we need the "sudden return to our creaturely status." This "balanced divine and human reference," the two poles of our spiritual life, is required; indeed, "liturgic forms may safely be judged by their ability to introduce more and more souls of every level more and more fully into this balanced mood of humble dependence and disinterested delight."[105] And this sense of our "creaturely status over against the Eternal" is the "salt" of religion.[106] For growth in the spiritual life consists of an "increase of God and decrease of self."[107] This is not marked by emotional reactions but by an increase in our awe and devotion.[108]

Conclusion

God is the initiator in our spiritual formation. We are merely participants in that process who cooperate with God's work in our lives. We need to be attentive to what God is doing, be full of acceptance, and patiently trust in him. One way of participating is through prayerful engagement with liturgy. Praying liturgy aloud can have a powerful impact as we engage our senses. Further, historic liturgy can remind us we belong to the universal church as we join in the faith-filled prayers of women and men of prayer who have gone before us. Liturgy reminds us of the corporate nature of prayer. Further, liturgies that lead us to adoration of God can help reduce our self-focus as we find our place as creatures in humble worship before the Creator.

Study Questions

1. Underhill describes the bodily aspect of praying liturgy. She argues that the spoken word has more "suggestive power"—reaching and modifying "our deeper psychic levels"—than "inarticulate thought." What do you think of Underhill's argument? What is your experience of praying liturgy? In what ways might externally spoken prayers impact you differently than silently thought prayers? Discuss.

---

[104]Underhill, *Abba*, 17.
[105]Underhill, "Essentials," 50.
[106]Underhill, *The Golden Sequence*, ix.
[107]Underhill, *The Golden Sequence*, 82.
[108]Underhill, *The Golden Sequence*, 83.

2. How might you grow to recognize the corporate dimension of prayer? In what ways are we encouraged to think in terms of the self in our churches and culture? What are ways to fight against this tendency?

3. Underhill emphasizes that we are part of a historic community, the living and the dead. How does that concept strike you? What can we learn from the prayers of Christians who have lived in previous centuries?

4. Though Underhill was an Anglican, she was deeply ecumenical and personally gained from Protestant, Catholic, and Orthodox prayers. What is your response to engaging with the prayers of men and women from different branches of the Christian church? Why? Which might be some of the challenges?

5. Underhill argues that adoration of God helps to "unself" us. As we gaze on God in his majesty, we recognize our smallness in comparison and are humbled. What has been your experience of this reality of gaining, in Teresa of Avila's words, authentic, humble "self-knowledge"? How might such humbling impact our lives of prayer?

6. Often our prayers consist of self-absorbed shopping lists? How might engaging with liturgy help us to focus on God and not simply on ourselves?

CHAPTER SIX

THE EUCHARIST AS SPIRITUAL FORMATION

MARKUS NIKKANEN

THIS CHAPTER IS ABOUT THE EUCHARIST as a means of spiritual formation.[1] The apostle Paul describes spiritual formation as a lifelong process in which the Holy Spirit, in cooperation with human agents, conforms the disciples of Jesus to their true identity as God's people who are in Christ.[2] According to Paul, those who have put on "the new self" have "stripped off the old self with its practices" and are continually "being renewed in knowledge according to the image" of their Creator, Christ (Col 3:9-10; cf. 1:15; see also 2 Cor 3:18; 4:4). Paul's definition places a lot of emphasis on the human mind: we are transformed by the renewing of our minds (Rom 12:2) as we come to see ourselves and other disciples in Christ (2 Cor 5:17).

As the process unfolds, the disciples become more and more centered on Christ.[3] As a result, all other things that contribute to the disciples' identity

---

[1]The nomenclature carries no theological weight. The Eucharist is simply one of the most ancient names for the early Christian ritual meal. See Andrew B. McGowan, "Naming the Feast: Agape and the Diversity of Early Christian Meals," *Studia Patristica* 30 (1997): 314-18; Jerker Blomqvist and Karin Blomqvist, "Eucharist Terminology in Early Christian Literature: Philological and Semantic Aspects," in *The Eucharist: Its Origins and Contexts,* ed. David Hellholm and Dieter Sänger, 389-422, WUNT 376 (Tübingen: Mohr Siebeck, 2017), 402.

[2]On identity and participation in Christ, see Klyne R. Snodgrass, *Who God Says You Are: A Christian Understanding of Identity* (Grand Rapids, MI: Eerdmans, 2018). On ethics and participation in Christ, see Grant Macaskill, *Living in Union with Christ: Paul's Gospel and Christian Moral Identity* (Grand Rapids, MI: Baker Academic, 2019).

[3]For the helpful language of de-centering and re-centering, see Miroslav Volf, *Exclusion and Embrace: A Theological Exploration of Identity, Otherness, and Reconciliation* (Nashville: Abingdon, 1996).

are rendered secondary to being in Christ. Paul writes, "There is no longer Greek and Jew, circumcised and uncircumcised, barbarian, Scythian, slave and free; but Christ is all and in all!" (Col 3:11; cf. Gal 3:28). Things like ethnicity, socioeconomic status, and gender—although important in their own right—do not have the ultimate defining power over a person who is in Christ: "if anyone is in Christ, there is a new creation" (2 Cor 5:17; cf. Gal 6:15). According to Paul, the disciples have died and risen with Christ, and this union with Christ has transformed and keeps transforming them (Rom 6:3-5; Gal 2:19-20; Col 2:11-13; 3:1-5). Consequently, Christlike behavior begins to flow freely from the inside out, and Christian ethics cannot remain as a mere legalistic observance of an external standard.

Since God designed human life to flourish in an ordered relationship with himself and in embodied interaction with other human beings, spiritual formation is "an intra, inter and transpersonal experience" that involves every aspect of human life.[4] Spiritual formation is not an independent working of the human spirit nor something that takes place in isolation from other disciples of Jesus. Rather, God the Holy Spirit forms us in interaction with and through the community of believers. It is only fitting, then, that spiritually forming practices are often embodied and communal: we do something tangible together and in cooperation with the Spirit to center ourselves on Christ. One of these tangible things is sharing bread and wine with one another.

In this chapter I will argue that the Eucharist should be understood as a ritual that seeks to transform our perception of ourselves in relation to Christ and to others who are in Christ.[5] In other words, the Eucharist seeks to center us on Christ which is both the starting and end point of spiritual

---

[4]See John Swinton's definition of spirituality in John Swinton, *Spirituality and Mental Health Care: Rediscovering a "Forgotten" Dimension* (Philadelphia: Jessica Kingsley, 2001), 20.

[5]Ritual and ritual theory made their way into biblical studies through Mary Douglas's influential works on purity and natural symbols. While Douglas viewed ritual as a symbolic representation of beliefs, later studies by Catherine Bell and Dru Johnson have emphasized ritual as an embodied practice that transforms its participants by fusing thought and action. Viewed this way, ritual is not lifeless and monotonous repetition, but a means for deeper knowing and understanding. See Mary Douglas, *Purity and Danger: An Analysis of Concepts of Pollution and Taboo* (London: Routledge, 1966); Mary Douglas, *Natural Symbols: Explorations in Cosmology* (New York: Random House, 1973); Catherine Bell, *Ritual Theory, Ritual Practice* (New York: Cambridge University Press, 2009), 19-20, 31, 98-101; Dru Johnson, *Knowledge by Ritual: A Biblical Prolegomenon on Sacramental Theology* (Winona Lake, IN: Eisenbrauns, 2016), 34-41.

formation, and also the point to which we must continually return in order to be renewed.

When we receive the signifiers of "my body that is for you" and "the new covenant in my blood" (1 Cor 11:24-25) at the table, we are led to acknowledge our dependence on Christ. The ritual is not, however, only about recalling our helplessness in sight of perdition and the price that was paid for our salvation. Rather, to "do this in remembrance of me" is ultimately about remembering ourselves in Christ and about participating in his death and resurrection—the two events that constitute the foundation of the believer's identity (cf. Gal 2:19-20; Col 3:1). In fact, the Eucharist does not only remind us of our true identity and status in Christ but also draws us to live our lives in Christ, that is, in conformity with the pattern set before us in Christ's death and resurrection.[6] Furthermore, the act of sharing the Eucharist with other believers declares that we belong to the people of God. Since the table is the Lord's and no one gains access to it by their own merit, all who eat from the table are equally in Christ (cf. Gal 3:28). This means that eating from the same table not only strengthens the believer's identity as one who belongs to the family of God but also presents a challenge to all participants to love one another regardless of ethnicity, socioeconomic status, and gender.

This chapter is written from the perspective of a New Testament exegete whose own spiritual roots lie in a revival movement that swept Finland in the 1870s, culminating in the formation of a new denomination in 1923. Known as a bridge-builder between various theological contexts, the Evangelical Free Church of Finland does not exclude Christians from other denominations from participating in the Eucharist: the table is open to all who profess their faith in Christ regardless of their theological leanings.

The main part of the chapter consists of a close reading of three eucharistic texts: 1 Corinthians 5:1-13, 10:14-22, and 11:17-34. I argue through the exposition of these texts that Paul understood the Eucharist as a ritual meal that was partaken to remember oneself correctly in Christ and as part of God's people. In other words, sharing bread and wine together was about

---

[6]On the pattern, see Michael J. Gorman, *Cruciformity: Paul's Narrative Spirituality of the Cross* (Grand Rapids, MI: Eerdmans, 2001); Michael J. Gorman, "Cruciform or Resurrectiform? Paul's Paradoxical Practice of Participation in Christ," *Ex Auditu* 33 (2017): 60-83; Markus Nikkanen, "Present Participation in Christ—Cruciform, Resurrectiform, or Simply Christ-Shaped? A Response to Michael J. Gorman," *Ex Auditu* 33 (2017): 84-91.

spiritual formation whereby the disciples centered themselves on Christ. It was an act of identification with Christ and participation in his death and resurrection.

THREE EUCHARISTIC TEXTS

The Eucharist and the people of God in 1 Corinthians 5:1-13. In 1 Corinthians 5:1-13 Paul responds to a report concerning a case of sexual misconduct: a man who is part of the community of believers has been having sex with his "father's wife" (5:1).[7] This outrage—by both Jewish and Roman standards—forces Paul to pronounce judgment: the community must "hand this man over to Satan" (5:5) and "drive out the wicked person from among you" (5:13). What does a hard text like this have to do with the Eucharist and spiritual formation? To understand, we need to take a closer look at Paul's argument.

A well-established body of scholarship has highlighted Paul's use of the Deuteronomic extirpation formula, "Drive out the wicked person from among you," in 1 Corinthians 5:1-13.[8] In the book of Deuteronomy, this formula appears in texts that deal with grievous offenses committed by God's covenant people, offenses that require capital punishment.[9] Paul alludes to the formula already in verse two ("so that he who has done this would have been removed from among you"),[10] and his list of cases warranting exclusion from the community in verse eleven resonates with the cases in which the extirpation formula occurs in the book of Deuteronomy.[11]

---

[7]See James N. Adams, *The Latin Sexual Vocabulary* (London: Duckworth, 1982), 186; Bruce W. Winter, *After Paul Left Corinth: The Influence of Secular Ethics and Social Change* (Grand Rapids, MI: Eerdmans, 2001), 227.

[8]Brian S. Rosner, "Temple and Holiness in 1 Corinthians 5," *Tyndale Bulletin* 42, no. 1 (1991): 137-45; Brian S. Rosner, "Written for Our Instruction: Paul's Dependence upon the Scriptures for Ethics in 1 Corinthians 5-7" (PhD diss., University of Cambridge, 1992); Brian S. Rosner, *Paul, Scripture, and Ethics: A Study of 1 Corinthians 5-7* (Leiden: Brill, 1994); Brian S. Rosner, "Deuteronomy in 1 and 2 Corinthians," in *Deuteronomy in the New Testament: The New Testament and the Scriptures of Israel*, ed. Maarten J. J. Menken and Steve Moyise, 118-35, LNTS 358 (London: T&T Clark, 2007).

[9]Cf. LXX Deuteronomy 17:7, 12; 19:19; 21:21; 22:21, 22, 24; 24:7; cf. 13:6.

[10]For definitions of quotation, allusion, echo, and influence, see the methodological discussion in William A. Tooman, *Gog of Magog: Reuse of Scripture and Compositional Technique in Ezekiel 38-39* (Tübingen: Mohr Siebeck, 2011).

[11]Rosner, *Paul, Scripture, and Ethics*, 69-70; Roy E. Ciampa and Brian S. Rosner, *The First Letter to the Corinthians* (Grand Rapids, MI: Eerdmans, 2010), 217.

Moreover, the concluding line of Paul's discussion in verse thirteen reproduces the formula almost verbatim:[12] as the ancient Israelites drove out the wicked person from among God's covenant people, so the Corinthians must also expel the wicked man from the new covenant community.

In verses seven and eight, Paul uses language derived from the Jewish twin festival of Passover and Unleavened Bread to drive home his point about the expulsion of the man.[13] It is here that Paul makes his first reference to the Eucharist. To grasp it, however, we need to understand what the twin festival was all about: "Clean out the old yeast so that you may be a new batch, as you really are unleavened. For our paschal lamb, Christ, has been sacrificed. Therefore, let us celebrate the festival, not with the old yeast, the yeast of malice and evil, but with the unleavened bread of sincerity and truth" (1 Cor 5:7-8).

Paul's commandment to "clean out the old yeast" mirrors the Jewish paschal law that obligated the people of God to get rid of all leavened products once a year, on the Day of Preparation, just before the twin festival began (Ex 12–13; Num 9:1-14; Deut 16:1-8).[14] The paschal law was followed meticulously—no leavened products were present during the twin festival— because the rituals performed were supposed to help the present generation to identify themselves as the people of God who once had left Egypt to become God's holy people. It was important to eat the same food as the first generation ate—the paschal lamb on the night of Nisan 15 and unleavened bread throughout the seven-day festival.

Failing to keep the rituals had serious ramifications: transgressors were cut off from God's people (Num 9:13). Thus, while the ritual did not make

---

[12]See Richard B. Hays, *Echoes of Scripture in the Letters of Paul* (New Haven, CT: Yale University Press, 1989), 97; Rosner, *Paul, Scripture, and Ethics*, 82-83; Richard B. Hays, *The Conversion of the Imagination: Paul as Interpreter of Israel's Scripture* (Grand Rapids, MI: Eerdmans, 2005), 160n30. In light of this evidence, Paul's opening line about the man having sex with his "father's wife" is not an allusion to Leviticus 18:8 or 20:11, but to Deuteronomy 27:20, where the covenant people of God pronounce a curse on "the one who sleeps with his father's wife."

[13]While Passover lasted for just one night, unleavened bread began at the same time but lasted for seven days.

[14]The NRSV attempts to bring out the rising (i.e., corrupting) effect of leaven by translating *zymē* as "yeast" here. The ancients, however, did not have yeast, but a small portion of the old dough that had naturally fermented (i.e., leavened). This portion, when added to the new dough, had the same rising effect as yeast does now. The same baking technique is used now when baking with a sourdough starter.

anyone part of God's people, it "display[ed] and reinforce[ed their] . . . place in the native systems of classification."[15] Those who participated in the ritual were in, others were out.

Paul knew all of this. Nevertheless, when he wrote to the Corinthians, he was not speaking about the twin festival of Passover and Unleavened Bread. Rather, Paul's exhortation to celebrate "the festival" without leaven comes straight after his claim that "*our* paschal lamb, *Christ*, has been sacrificed." In other words, Paul has re-actualized or "Christianized" the Jewish festival so that it points to a feast in the life of the Corinthian community. The feast *is* the ancient Eucharist, a full communal meal far from the modern wafer-like pieces of bread and tiny amounts of wine in individual cups (cf. 1 Cor 11:17-22; *Didache* 10.1).

There is, however, one problem with this interpretation. Exegetically, the strongest reason to reject eucharistic readings of 1 Corinthians 5 has been one Greek word in verse eleven where Paul gives more instructions to the community on what "handing over to Satan" means. Most Bible translations (the NRSV included) translate *mēde* emphatically as "not even" instead of "and not": "But now I am writing to you *not to associate with* [*mē synanami-gnysthai*] anyone who bears the name of brother or sister who is sexually immoral or greedy, or is an idolater, reviler, drunkard, or robber. Do *not even* [*mēde synesthiein*] *eat with* such a one."

According to this translation Paul "adds insult to injury" by prohibiting even the act of eating with the man.[16] This, however, cannot be the case.[17] First, to think that Paul viewed eating with someone as something less than associating with someone does not fit with what scholars know about ancient dining. For example, Jesus was scorned for eating with prostitutes and tax collectors whom the onlookers interpreted as Jesus's friends (Mt 11:19; Lk 7:34; 19:7). Second, translating *mēde* as "not even" does not fit with what grammarians have learned about the Greek particle *mēde* in constructs such

---

[15]Ronald Hendel, "Ritual," in *The Oxford Encyclopedia of the Bible and Law*, ed. Brent A. Strawn, 238-45 (Oxford: Oxford University Press, 2015), 2:238.

[16]Jonathan Schwiebert, "Table Fellowship and the Translation of 1 Corinthians 5:11," *Journal of Biblical Literature* 127, no. 1 (2008): 159-64, 159.

[17]For a technical discussion, see Markus Nikkanen, "Participation in Christ: Paul and Pre-Pauline Eucharistic Tradition" (PhD diss., University of Aberdeen, 2018), 148-52; Jonathan Schwiebert, "Table Fellowship and the Translation of 1 Corinthians 5:11."

as the one present in 1 Corinthians 5:11.[18] If the rules of grammar are followed, the verse should be translated: "But now I am writing to you not to associate . . . *nor* eat with such a one."

This means that eucharistic readings of 1 Corinthians 5 are possible. And since the whole passage is clearly addressed to the community rather than individuals (the plural is used throughout the text), the meal Paul has in mind is the Corinthians' communal meal, the ancient Eucharist. Indeed, verse eleven clarifies Paul's earlier reference to the Eucharist in verses seven and eight: the man's expulsion from the community of believers is enacted in the expulsion from the eucharistic table.[19]

So, what shall we make of this text? While eucharistic origins continue to be debated by scholars, Paul's argument shows that for him the Eucharist carries the same ritual function as the twin festival of Passover and Unleavened Bread. Participating in the Eucharist declares the participant's covenantal status: "I have access to this table; I am part of God's people in Christ." Simultaneously, the fact that other people are at the table, too, forces the participant to recognize their covenantal status as well: "These people have access to the table, they are my brothers and sisters, the people of God in Christ." Consequently, participating in the ritual builds in the believer a sense of being one with God and one with his people, a sense of belonging to God and a sense of solidarity with his people.

The Eucharist, allegiance, and oneness in 1 Corinthians 10:14-22. In 1 Corinthians 10:14-22, Paul addresses the question of eating food offered to idols at pagan gods' tables.[20] In the immediate context, Paul has just drawn a figural correspondence between the Corinthians and "our fathers" (10:1) who perished in the wilderness in spite of having spiritual food and drink from Christ himself (10:4).[21] The fathers perished because they forsook their

---

[18]For details, see Schwiebert, "Table Fellowship and the Translation of 1 Corinthians 5:11"; and Nikkanen, *Participation in Christ*, 148-52.

[19]Similarly, Dennis E. Smith, *From Symposium to Eucharist: The Banquet in the Early Christian World* (Minneapolis: Fortress, 2003), 203.

[20]While there are two competing views about the issue at hand in 1 Corinthians 8–10, all agree that in 1 Corinthians 10:14-22 the issue is food offered to idols eaten in a cultic context. See Gordon D. Fee, "Εἰδωλόθυτα Once Again: An Interpretation of 1 Corinthians 8-10," *Biblica* 61 (1980): 172-97; Jerome Murphy-O'Connor, *Keys to First Corinthians: Revisiting the Major Issues* (Oxford: Oxford University Press, 2009), 114-19.

[21]Grant Macaskill, "Incarnational Ontology and the Theology of Participation in Paul," in *"In Christ" in Paul: Explorations in Paul's Theology of Union and Participation,* ed. Michael J. Thate,

covenant with God. As Paul puts it, they "sat down to eat and drink, and they rose up to play" before the golden calf (1 Cor 10:7; Ex 32:5-6).[22] If the Corinthians continue to walk in their fathers' shoes and worship other gods (1 Cor 10:14), their story will not end well either, for they "cannot drink the cup of the Lord and the cup of demons . . . cannot partake of the table of the Lord and the table of demons" (10:21). In other words, they cannot eat and drink both the Eucharist and foods offered to idols.

But why does Paul bring the Eucharist into discussion in the first place? What does he hope to achieve? To understand Paul's argument, we must first decipher what verse sixteen means: "The cup of blessing that we bless, is it not a sharing [*koinōnia*] in the blood of Christ? The bread that we break, is it not a sharing [*koinōnia*] in the body of Christ?" (1 Cor 10:16). The meaning of the Greek word *koinōnia*, translated above as "sharing," is debated. Does it refer to participation in Christ's blood and body or to fellowship with other believers, as some studies have concluded?[23] Paul's question is clearly rhetorical, which means that the Corinthians knew the answer. For us the key to interpreting Paul correctly lies in the sacrificial language Paul uses throughout chapters 8–10 and increasingly so in 1 Corinthians 10:14-22.[24]

As I have argued elsewhere, epigraphical and papyrological evidence from the Hellenistic period shows that *koinōn-* cognates were used in sacrificial contexts to denote the idea of participating in the sacrifice—a process that climaxed in the act of eating the sacrifices at the god's own table,[25] which

---

Kevin J. Vanhoozer, and Constantine R. Campbell, 87-102, WUNT 2/384 (Tübingen: Mohr Siebeck, 2014), 92, 93.

[22]Wayne A. Meeks, "'And Rose Up to Play': Midrash and Paraenesis in 1 Corinthians 10:1-22," *Journal for the Study of the New Testament* 16 (1982): 64-78.

[23]On the latter interpretation, see Norbert Baumert, "Koinōnia tou aimatos tou Christou (1 Kor 10,14-22)," in *The Corinthian Correspondence*, ed. Reimund Bieringer, 617-22, BETL 125 (Leuven: Leuven University Press, 1996); Harm W. Hollander, "The Idea of Fellowship in 1 Corinthians 10.14–22," *New Testament Studies* 55, no. 4 (2009): 456-70.

[24]The following expressions are found in chapters 8–10: *eidōlolatreia, eidōlothyton, eidōlon, eidōleion, daimonion, thysia, thyō, thysiastērion, katakeimai, esthiō, brōma, kreas, potērion, pinō, trapeza, metechō.*

[25]Wendell Willis has argued based on David Gill's work that the table in 1 Corinthians 10:21 is a special piece of cultic furniture (not to be likened to the altar) inside a pagan temple, on which a third of the offering was laid and eventually consumed by the devotees and cult officials. See David H. Gill, "Trapezomata: A Neglected Aspect of Greek Sacrifice," *Harvard Theological Review* 67, no. 2 (1974): 117-37; Wendell L. Willis, *Idol Meat in Corinth: The Pauline Argument in 1 Corinthians 8 and 10* (Eugene, OR: Wipf & Stock, 1985), 15-17.

created and maintained sacrificial bonds akin to a covenantal bond.[26] Moreover, since sacrifices were considered gifts from the deity's table in Judaism and Greco-Roman cults alike,[27] participation in sacrifices created not only human-human bonds but also human-divine bonds of reciprocity: the gift received from a god was also an obligation to worship that god.[28] In the words of a Finnish proverb: "Whose bread you eat, his songs you must sing."

When Paul mentions *koinōnia* in the blood and body of Christ in the context of his discussion about eating food offered to idols, he draws his language from the normal use of *koinōn-* cognates in sacrificial contexts. This means that Paul is asking the Corinthians whether they have not realized that their participation in the eucharistic meal has created a sacrificial bond both between them as well as between them and their God. At the same time, Paul considers this sacrificial bond to be special, since he clearly does not view it the same way as his Greek and Roman peers viewed sacrificial bonds. For them it was possible to eat at the table of Zeus in the morning and then spend the evening dining in honor of Dionysus.[29] For Paul, however, the sacrificial bond formed at the eucharistic meal is an exclusive covenantal bond: "You cannot drink the cup of the Lord and the cup of demons. You cannot partake of the table of the Lord and the table of demons" (10:21).

This means that Paul's argument continues along the same lines as in 1 Corinthians 10:1. The fathers broke their covenant with God and caused

---

[26]See Nikkanen, *Participation in Christ*, 166-77. Participation in the sacrifice is expressed with *koinōn-* cognates (with the genitive) and refers to participation in the whole sacrificial process, including eating. In some texts *metechō* and *koinōneō* are used interchangeably. See also John Young Campbell, "Κοινωνία and its Cognates in the New Testament," *Journal of Biblical Literature* 51, no. 4 (1932): 352-80; Heinrich Seesemann, *Der Begriff KOINΩNIA im Neuen Testament* (Giessen: Töpelmann, 1933); Norbert Baumert, *Koinonein und Metechein—synonym? Eine umfassende semantische Untersuchung* (Stuttgart: Katolishes Bibelwerk, 2003); Julien M. Ogereau, *Paul's Koinonia with the Philippians: A Socio-Historical Investigation of a Pauline Economic Partnership* (Tübingen: Mohr Siebeck, 2014); Julien M. Ogereau, "A Survey of Κοινωνία and Its Cognates in Documentary Sources," *Novum Testamentum* 57 (2015): 275-94. The sacrificial context of 1 Corinthians 10:16 was already noticed by Seesemann and Baumert, but they failed to recognize its importance for interpretation. Ogereau, however, recognizes its importance and suggests that scholars should consult documentary sources when interpreting 1 Corinthians 10:16.
[27]See especially Philo, *Spec. Laws* 1.221.
[28]See Arthur D. Nock, "The Cult of Heroes," *Harvard Theological Review* 37, no. 2 (1944): 141-74, 149; John M. G. Barclay, *Paul and the Gift* (Grand Rapids, MI: Eerdmans, 2015).
[29]See Larry W. Hurtado, *Destroyer of the Gods: Early Christian Distinctiveness in the Roman World* (Waco, TX: Baylor University Press, 2016), 38-44.

their own destruction when they ate, drank, and rose up to play before the golden calf. Now the Corinthian believers are heading down the same path. After all, the Eucharist testifies against them that they have formed a prior covenant with God!

The same kind of argumentation continues throughout 1 Corinthians 10:18-22, although translations often lose track of Paul's thought. In verse eighteen Paul talks literally about "Israel according to the flesh" (Gk. *Israēl kata sarka*) who are identical with "our fathers" in verse one. The fathers participated in whatever was put on the altar. This does not mean, however, that sacrificial food in itself contaminates the person. Rather, it is the idolatry that is dangerous, as Paul's next allusion to the Old Testament in verse twenty shows. Sadly, many Bible translations obscure Paul's allusion by following a textual variant most scholars consider to be a later addition: "No, I imply that what *pagans* sacrifice, they sacrifice to demons and not to God. I do not want you to be partners with demons" (1 Cor 10:20). Quite contrary to the translation above, Paul is not talking about the pagans and their sacrifices, for he did not write the word *pagans*, as textual critics have pointed out.[30] Rather, he has "our fathers" in mind, as his allusion to Deuteronomy 32:17 shows: "They sacrificed to demons, not God, to deities they had never known, to new ones recently arrived, whom your ancestors had not feared" (Deut 32:17).

Deuteronomy 32:17 talks about the Israelites provoking the Lord to anger by going after other gods their forefathers knew nothing about. At the same time, Paul's use of "present tense verbs . . . project[s] the action of the golden calf worshippers onto the screen of present experience," as Richard Hays has argued.[31] The Corinthians are walking in their Israelite fathers' footsteps and provoking the Lord to anger.

Paul's appeal to the Eucharist in verse sixteen shows that he regards the Eucharist as a covenant meal that demands exclusive allegiance to and worship of the one God. One cannot but notice here another similarity with

---

[30]On the text critical problem in 1 Corinthians 10:20, see Bruce M. Metzger, *A Textual Commentary on the New Testament* (Stuttgart: Deutsche Bibelgesellschaft, 1994), 494; David E. Garland, *1 Corinthians* (Grand Rapids, MI: Baker Academic, 2003), 484-85. While most scholars would agree with Garland that *ta ethnē* is a later gloss, many still think that it represents Paul's argument correctly.
[31]Hays, *Echoes of Scripture in the Letters of Paul*, 92.

the Passover meal: the exodus from Egypt was never considered an end in itself in the Torah. Rather, the purpose of the exodus was to free the Israelites so that they might go and worship God.[32] In fact, the book of Exodus does not climax in the exodus event, but in Israel's new vocation as God's covenant people, a kingdom of priests, among whom God dwells in the tabernacle (19:6; 24:1-8; 40:34-38). It is no wonder, then, that in the Second Temple period the Passover meal became central to Israel's understanding of its God-given vocation.[33] This is probably why tensions could easily build up into uprisings during Passover season, and why indecency and idolatry on the part of Romans were considered extremely offensive during this time.[34] For Paul, the Eucharist is the emblem of the vocation of God's people to worship the one God and the one Christ.

The idea of oneness—one God, one Christ, one people—is actually underscored earlier in 1 Corinthians 8:6 where Paul draws his language from the *Shema*—Israel's confession of faith in Deuteronomy 6:4:[35] "Hear, O Israel: The Lord is our God, the Lord alone [or: the Lord is one] (Deut 6:4)." Paul states, "Yet for us there is one God, the Father, from whom are all things and for whom we exist, and one Lord, Jesus Christ, through whom are all things and through whom we exist" (1 Cor 8:6).

Andrew Byers has shown that Paul's christological re-actualization of *Shema* has affected his use of the thrice repeated language of oneness in 1 Corinthians 10:17: "Because there is *one* bread, we who are many are *one* body, for we all partake of the *one* bread" (1 Cor 10:17, emphasis added).[36]

---

[32]Exodus 5:1, 3, 8, 17; 7:14; 8:1, 8, 20; 9:1, 13; 10:3, 7.

[33]Philo, *Moses* 2.22; *Spec. Laws* 2.148. See also Philo, *QE* 1.10; Josephus, *Ant.* 11.109.

[34]Josephus, *Ant.* 17.213-218; 20.105-112; *J.W.* 2.10-13, 223-28.

[35]Erik Waaler suggests that 1 Corinthians 8:4-6 is Paul's christological reading of Deuteronomy 6:4-5 and strongly linked to the idea of covenant. See Erik Waaler, *The Shema and the First Commandment in First Corinthians: An Intertextual Approach to Paul's Re-Reading of Deuteronomy* (Tübingen: Mohr Siebeck, 2008). See also James D. G. Dunn, *Christology in the Making: An Inquiry into the Origins of the Doctrine of the Incarnation* (London: SCM, 1980), 179-83; N. T. Wright, "Monotheism, Christology and Ethics: 1 Corinthians 8," in *The Climax of the Covenant: Christ and the Law in Pauline Theology,* ed. N. T. Wright, 120-36 (Edinburgh: T&T Clark, 1991), 129.

[36]Byers does not reject the idea that oneness language in 1 Corinthians 10:17 is also connected with Greco-Roman *homonoia* and *concordia* language. Nevertheless, he shows that Paul has Jewish parallels at hand, and that he uses them in 1 Corinthians 10:17. See Andrew Byers, "The One Body of the Shema in 1 Corinthians: An Ecclesiology of Christological Monotheism," *New Testament Studies* 62 (2016): 517-32. On *homonoia* and *concordia*, see Margaret M. Mitchell, *Paul and the Rhetoric of Reconciliation: An Exegetical Investigation of the Language and Composition of*

Consequently, the idea of exclusive allegiance to the *one* God is connected with the idea of being *one* people. This makes the connection between the Eucharist and the Jewish Passover meal even closer: just as the ancient Passover meal was a part of a sacrificial ritual through which participants claimed to be the one people of God, so the eucharistic meal is part of a sacrificial ritual through which the participants claim to be the one people of God whose worship of the one God and one Christ is exclusive. While Christ has given his life once and for all and cannot be re-sacrificed, the ritual meal keeps drawing the Christ-believers to partake of the bread that signifies "my body that is for you" and the cup that signifies "the new covenant in my blood" (1 Cor 11:24-25).

When we as Christ-believers partake of these signifiers, the covenantal bond binding us to God and other Christ-believers is reaffirmed: we have been united with Christ and with his people. Consequently, the believer is obliged to render exclusive worship to God and Christ and to consider others who have entered into the same covenantal relationship as her brothers and sisters: one bread, one body! At the same time the Eucharist stands as a hostile witness against those who partake of the signifiers but either fail to render exclusive worship to God or sow disunity among his people: they have entered into a covenantal relationship and yet they are breaking the covenant like their fathers did.

The Eucharist as embodied and transformative remembering in 1 Corinthians 11:17-34.[37] Paul addresses the Corinthians' inappropriate behavior at the eucharistic meal in 1 Corinthians 11:17-34: when the Christ-believers come together to eat, the community splits into groups, and while some carouse, others go hungry (1 Cor 11:21). Based on Paul's argument in 1 Corinthians 5 and 10, the idea of splitting into groups would have been appalling enough to Paul in itself, since this type of handling of the ritual creates separate Eucharists and draws lines of demarcation where there should be none: a separate Eucharist declares some Christ-believers as the people of God, while others are denied this identity. Based on 1 Corinthians 10, Paul would have been appalled at the Corinthians' treatment of the bread and the

---

1 *Corinthians* (Louisville, KY: Westminster John Knox, 1993), 90n140-41, 161-62; Dale B. Martin, *The Corinthian Body* (New Haven, CT: Yale University Press, 1995), 38-47, 92-96.

[37]On ritual and remembering see Johnson, *Knowledge by Ritual*, 39.

wine as well: at least some Corinthians had forgotten that the bread and the wine were signifiers of the Lord's sacrifice since they were careless enough to use the Lord's table for their own pleasure. Indeed, the arguments of both 1 Corinthians 5 and 10 are still present in 1 Corinthians 11:27-29 where Paul is not only interested in the community as the body of Christ but also in the way the signifiers of the Lord's sacrifice are handled in Corinth.[38] Paul has yet more to say about the Eucharist and the problems in Corinth, and he does this by citing a very early tradition:

> For I received from the Lord what I also handed on to you, that the Lord Jesus on the night when he was betrayed took a loaf of bread, and when he had given thanks, he broke it and said, "This is my body that is for you. Do this in remembrance of me." In the same way he took the cup also, after supper, saying, "This cup is the new covenant in my blood. Do this, as often as you drink it, in remembrance of me." (1 Cor 11:23-25)

The text is often read in the church without any regard to its original context and has become difficult for us to understand. Paul, however, clearly intends it as an explanation for why he does not see fit to commend the Corinthians on their eucharistic practice (cf. 11:20-22). To grasp the meaning of the text better, we must understand that Jesus and the people who wrote the tradition down were Second Temple Jews like Paul. Consequently, the imagery and ideas expressed in the tradition go back to Jewish texts and customs.

The tradition Paul cites has Jesus speaking about his body and blood in the context of a Passover meal.[39] This means that the Passover meal has to be included in the interpretive backdrop against which Jesus' words are understood regardless of whether or not the Last Supper was a proper Passover meal on Nisan 15. As we have seen in the previous subsections, Paul carries features of the Passover meal over to his interpretation of the eucharistic meal. There is, however, one feature we have not yet focused on: all paschal rituals were observed in order to remember the exodus from Egypt.

---

[38]See Anthony C. Thiselton, *The First Epistle to the Corinthians: A Commentary on the Greek Text* (Grand Rapids, MI: Eerdmans, 2000), 890.

[39]While the text never mentions "Passover" explicitly, a clear paschal picture emerges when all eucharistic texts in 1 Corinthians are viewed together. See Nikkanen, *Participation in Christ*, 214-15.

While modern Westerners often view remembering as a simple recollection of a past event, biblical remembering seeks to personalize the memory in such a way that it becomes relevant for the community and the person who remembers.[40] Often this is done through declarative prayer and worship: the person praises God for what he has done in the past for the people of God who live in the present, for the past action is directly relevant to the person and the community in the present (cf. Ps 71:15-17; 105:1, 5; 145:4, 6, 7).[41] This also seems to be Paul's intention in verse 26, where he talks about proclaiming the death of the Lord until he comes. Thus, remembering *in itself* is a transformative process.

At the Passover meal this transformative remembering reached a new height. According to Torah, the participants of the meal were supposed to engage in the same actions the exodus generation had done—they even dressed accordingly (see Ex 12:11)! Moreover, Exodus 13:8 commanded every father to tell his children on the day of the Passover meal that these ritual acts were done "because of what the LORD did for *me* when *I* came out of Egypt."[42] Here the remembering of exodus is strongly personalized, which means that no Israelite could stay detached from the events that had led to them becoming the covenant people of God. Instead, they were to identify with the exodus generation and participate in their story.

This means that the words Paul cites Jesus repeating twice at the Last Supper are crucial: "Do this in remembrance of *me*" (1 Cor 11:24, 25). Since these words were spoken in the context of Passover, they mean nothing less than a narrative takeover. In Paul's eyes, Jesus reinterprets the Passover meal, which was celebrated to remember the exodus from Egypt, as an occasion celebrated to remember him. Consequently, the exodus story is now transformed into Christ's story, but the manner in which this story is remembered stays the same. Now one must identify with Christ and participate in his story. And this is what we find elsewhere in Paul: "I have been crucified

---

[40]See Willy Schottroff, *'Gedenken' im Alten Orient und im Alten Testament: Die Wurzel* zākar *im semitischen Sprachkreis* (Neukirchen-Vluyn: Neukirchener Verlag, 1967), 316; Otfried Hofius, "The Lord's Supper and the Lord's Supper Tradition: Reflections on 1 Corinthians 11:23b-25," in *One Loaf, One Cup: Ecumenical Studies of 1 Cor 11 and Other Eucharistic Texts,* ed. Ben F. Meyer, 75-115, New Gospel Studies 6 (Macon, GA: Mercer University Press, 1993), 104.

[41]Hofius, "Lord's Supper," 105-7.

[42]Nikkanen, *Participation in Christ,* 34-36.

with Christ; and it is no longer I who live, but it is Christ who lives in me"
(Gal 2:19-20; cf. Rom 6:3-5; Col 2:11-13; 3:1-4; Eph 2:5-6).

This explains why Paul offers the citation as an explanation for why he
could not commend the Corinthians: to celebrate the Eucharist in the Lord's
honor is to remember him rightly, to identify with him, and to participate
in him. But while the Lord gave himself willingly for others, the Corinthians
have failed to do so! Instead, they are neglecting one another and using the
signifiers of the Lord's sacrifice for their own pleasure. They do not understand that the Eucharist is about becoming one with Christ in thought and
action. Indeed, 1 Corinthians 11:17-34 shows that the Eucharist is ultimately
about identity: at the table, the Holy Spirit seeks to transform our very core
through embodied remembering—to make everything outside Christ secondary to our identity and to place Christ's death and resurrection firmly at
the center of our being.

GLOBAL BENEFITS AND CONCLUSION

In this chapter we have explored Paul's understanding of the Eucharist as a
ritual that seeks to transform our perception of ourselves in relation to
Christ and to others in Christ. When we partake of the Eucharist, the ritual
act not only declares that we belong to the covenant people of God in
Christ but also challenges us to see others in the same way (1 Cor 5:1-13).
At the same time, the Eucharist serves as a place of reaffirming our union
with Christ. It demands that we render exclusive worship to our covenant
God and live as one with our covenant brothers and sisters in Christ
(1 Cor 10:14-22). Moreover, the Eucharist leads us to embodied and transformative remembering—to identify with Christ and participate in his
death and resurrection (1 Cor 11:17-34). In other words, our lives are centered on Christ as we partake of the bread and the wine. At the table we
remember who we are *in Christ*.

Much more could have been squeezed out of Paul's rich thought in
1 Corinthians 5:1-13, 10:14-22, and 11:17-34. For example, although almost
entirely absent from this chapter, it has not been my intention to say that
the Eucharist has nothing or very little to do with acknowledging the benefits the Christian has received through Christ's representative and substi-
tutionary death. I chose the topics I have discussed above because many

of them have been neglected and therefore have the most, in my mind, to offer in the global evangelical context. I want to conclude by stating what I mean by this.

First, viewing the Eucharist as a ritual that demarcates the covenant people of God (cf. 1 Cor 5:1-13) helps us to think about the topic of fencing the table. At least in Finland, the limits of communion with other Christians are often determined by denominational boundaries or one's willingness to adopt the same theological viewpoint on the Lord's presence at the table. In Paul's thought, the only thing that matters is whether the person is *in Christ*. In fact, the table is not the Corinthians' nor anyone else's. It is the *Lord's* table, and he decides who is welcome. If anything other than or in addition to faith in Christ (and baptism *into Christ*) is set as a prerequisite for participating in the Eucharist, it becomes *our* table instead of Christ's table. This truth of the table being the Lord's, in turn, helps us to view ourselves as part of God's global people, but also challenges us when we understand that not all God's people think and look like we do: "There is no longer Jew or Greek, there is no longer slave or free, there is no longer male and female; for all of you are one in Christ Jesus" (Gal 3:28).

Second, viewing the Eucharist as a ritual that affirms our covenantal union with God in Christ (cf. 1 Cor 10:14-22) helps us to rediscover our true purpose: to be a united and socially unique people of God who are totally devoted to him in exclusive worship. Our unwavering allegiance belongs to God alone, not to king or country, and to bring a national flag—even one as beautiful as the Finnish flag with its sky-blue cross—to the eucharistic table is an act of high treason. The Eucharist demands us to set our priorities right and to "not be conformed to this world, but be transformed by the renewing of your minds" (Rom 12:2).

Third, viewing the Eucharist as a ritual of embodied and transformative remembering (cf. 1 Cor 11:17-34) helps us to understand what participating in Christ means and entails when we come to the table without having to adopt a particular view on the Lord's presence. While participation in Christ is definitely a pneumatic phenomenon in Paul (cf. 1 Cor 6:15-20), it is also very closely connected with questions about who we are in relation to Christ's death and resurrection. Consequently, we can remember Christ at the table in his death and resurrection, identify with him, and participate in him by personalizing his narrative in such a way that we "consider [our-selves] dead to sin and alive to God *in Christ Jesus*" (Rom 6:11). This, in turn, can help us to redeem our lifeless eucharistic liturgies that are so often, at least, in the so-called "low church traditions" (like my own), done sloppily and with haste, when we should really be paying attention to what we are doing in order to remember ourselves rightly *in Christ*. After all, if the Eucharist is about being one with Christ and one with his people, this ritual is at the very center of our faith.

STUDY QUESTIONS

1. What is your most memorable eucharistic experience? Why?

2. How does your own theological tradition inform your eucharistic practice? What is emphasized? What is often overlooked? How does this chapter clarify, affirm, or challenge some of the ideas in your tradition and in your practice?

3. How has your eucharistic practice affected your spiritual formation in the past? How does this chapter enrich or explain your experiences?

4. What kind of changes could you make to your eucharistic practice in order to make it more spiritually formative?

CHAPTER SEVEN

SACRIFICE AND SURRENDER
AS SPIRITUAL FORMATION

JOHN FREDERICK
AND JONATHAN K. SHARPE

THIS CHAPTER WILL ARGUE THAT EPHESIANS presents the sacrifice
of Christ as the means and mechanism of the moral transformation of the
church. The sacrifice of Christ will be shown to be conceived of by Paul as a
twofold reality consisting of (1) the once-for-all event of Christ's sacrificial
death and resurrection by which redemption was achieved, and (2) an
ecclesial/ethical reality by which the church as the body of Christ perpetually participates in the death, resurrection, and eternal life of Christ by
performing grace-empowered acts of sacrificial love that result in individual
and ecclesial transformation. The theological significance of sacrifice and
surrender in Ephesians goes far beyond the merely behavioral function typically assigned to "works" in texts such as Ephesians 2:8-10 and 5:2-21. In
Ephesians, grace-empowered works of charity through ecclesial acts of surrender to Christ are instrumental—not merely evidential.[1]

Therefore, grace-empowered works do not simply demonstrate that one
has been saved; they allow one to actively and holistically participate in
the life of Christ and the transformative soteriological benefits of his sacrifice in the present. They are a channel, a means of grace by which the

---

[1]The view that works are evidential is not wrong. It is, however, incomplete. Christian works are
both evidential and instrumental to the appropriation of the soteriological benefits found solely
in the redemptive work of Jesus Christ.

church is conformed to the image of the God who is love through the en-actment and reception of cruciform love. Far from being antithetical to the gospel, the works that God has prepared in advance "that we might walk in them" are the God-ordained and Spirit-empowered means of progressive sanctification, spiritual formation, and participation in Christ; they are part of the very fabric of salvation itself. Christian belief, life, and worship should, therefore, be ordered according to Christ-ordained ecclesial acts of sur-render. Empowered by grace, this life of active embodied ecclesial charity brings individuals into the sweet harmony of life together in the eternal body of Christ thereby making them partakers in the divine nature (2 Pet 1:4).

What follows is a collaboration between two friends and colleagues across two continents—Australia and North America. Prior to one of us moving to Australia, we had planted and pastored an Anglican church together in Phoenix, Arizona, as a part of the Anglican Church in North America. Thus, this paper is situated within the global realignment, reformation, and worship of the Anglican Communion through a movement called GAFCON (Global Anglican Future Conference).[2] In addition, though an Anglican priest, one of the authors (John Frederick) lectures in New Testament at the theological college for the Uniting Church in Queensland, Australia. The Uniting Church is a mainline denomination that represents a diverse assortment of theological perspectives, including liberal, conservative, and evangelical approaches to theology and practice.[3]

In our current American and Australian contexts—in churches across denominations—any theology that insists on the absolute necessity of the church for sanctification and the fullness of salvation will, no doubt, be viewed as challenging and, in some cases, shocking to contemporary Chris-tians. Western Christianity, and the evangelical church in particular, has

---

[2] In North America, GAFCON includes the ACNA (Anglican Church in North American) and the ANiC (Anglican Network in Canada). Both networks were formed in response to a per-ceived pervasive theological liberalism in The Episcopal Church. The ACNA was formed and consecrated by the Bishops of the Global South who represent the vast majority of Anglicans across the globe. These provinces include: South Sudan, Nigeria, Uganda, Tanzania, Kenya, Congo, Rwanda, South America, Brazil, Myanmar, and Chile. Thus, while we write geographi-cally (in part) from a North American setting, we belong to a global Communion that is evangelical, charismatic, and catholic in faith, order, and practice. For more information, see www.gafcon.org.

[3] The Uniting Church in Australia would be most similar in ethos and theological diversity to the United Methodist Church. For more information, see https://assembly.uca.org.au/.

been wrestling with the force and pull of pervasive individualism both in-side and outside the church since the Enlightenment. Often—but not always—instead of providing a countercultural alternative, the church has simply capitulated to the dominant cultural ethos and recast itself as a consumeristic producer of religious goods and services. When it has not folded outward by openly embracing worldly individualism, it has tended to fold inward on itself by settling into the comfort of status-quo, twentieth-century "Churchianity" that focuses on things like church attendance and participating in programs without experiencing any real sense of commu-nity, vulnerability, sacrifice, or authentically transformational life together. When faced with the form of Christianity that is often consumeristic, secu-larized, and set within the framework of pseudospiritual pop psycho-logy, it is no wonder that many younger evangelicals have lamented: "I'll take Jesus, but not the church!" This chapter will affirm this lament, while rejecting both consumeristic Christianity and status-quo Churchianity. This is not merely a critique; it is a call. It is a call that is meant to be heard with urgency as a pastoral exhortation; a call to fully embrace, experience, and surrender to the perpetually efficacious sacrifice and sanctifying presence of Christ by participating in his life and person through his Spirit as his body, the church.

THE INSTRUMENTAL FUNCTION OF LOVE IN EPHESIANS

Instead of a prolonged exegesis of one passage, we will approach the text of Ephesians through the study of two key theological meta-themes, namely, love and works. Rather than working sequentially through the text, we will begin in Ephesians 5:1-2, where Paul's view of the connection between love and sacrifice is most clearly articulated. This will provide an interpretive lens through which to approach the other occurrences of love and works in the epistle.

In 5:1, Paul exhorts the church to become *mimētai tou theou*, "imitators of God." As is frequently noted, the theme of imitation in antiquity is commonly found in texts that speak about a child imitating their father.[4] It

---

[4]Cf. Margaret Y. MacDonald, *Colossians, Ephesians*, Sacra Pagina (Collegeville, MN: Liturgical, 2000), 310; St. Thomas Aquinas, *Commentary on Saint Paul's Epistle to the Ephesians*, trans. Mat-thew L. Lamb, O.C.S.O (Albany, NY: Magi, 1966). On the topic of imitation and filial adoption

makes sense, therefore, to situate the metaphor of imitation in a communal and familial setting in which the church is corporately designated as "beloved children." This familial imitation is carried out precisely by walking in the way of Christ's sacrificial love, which is described using Old Testament cultic phraseology as being "a fragrant offering and sacrifice to God." Sacrificial phraseology commonly takes on symbolic significance in Paul's epistles, and a similar usage of this phrase occurs in Philippians 4:18 in reference to a financial gift.[5]

Furthermore, Old Testament scholars have been aware for some time that the sacrificial texts of Leviticus, for example, exhibit varying degrees of symbolic, moral, and ethical significance. Recently, Leigh Trevaskis, in his monograph *Holiness, Ethics and Ritual in Leviticus* has demonstrated through the use of a cognitive linguistic approach that Leviticus contains, within its original literary form and intention, a symbolic ethical meaning in addition to its more literal ritual meaning.[6] These findings indicate that Ephesians employs its symbolic ethical approach to cultic terminology and concepts as a mechanism for moral formation in a way that is commensurate with the original canonical texts themselves. The theology of sacrifice as related to moral and ecclesial transformation is thus not an innovation of the New Testament but a coherent, covenantal theme observable across both testaments of the canon. Furthermore, New Testament scholars have long been aware of the ethical interpretation of ritual texts in Philo which—in line with the ethics of Middle Platonism—interpret sacrifice as a means of achieving moral and ethical likeness to God.[7]

Aquinas writes: "God . . . must be imitated insofar as it is possible for us to do so—a son must imitate his father. . . . He [God] says walk to signify 'you must always advance' as in Genesis 17 (1): 'Walk before me, and be blameless.' This should be in love since love is so good that man ought always to make further progress in it."

[5]In Philippians 4:18 the gift is "a fragrant offering, a sacrifice acceptable and pleasing to God" (cf. 2 Cor 2:15), and in Philippians 2:17 Paul refers to his own impending death as a drink offering being poured out upon the sacrificial offering of the churches' faith (cf. 2 Tim 4:6).

[6]Leigh Trevaskis, *Holiness, Ethics and Ritual in Leviticus*, Hebrew Bible Monographs 29 (Sheffield: Sheffield Phoenix Press, 2011), 21n34.

[7]For example, in *On the Decalogue* 20.97-98, Philo argues that on the basis of God's rest in creation he instituted the Sabbath as a means of assisting humans "to imitate God." Cf. John Dillon, *The Middle Platonists: A Study of Platonism 80 b.c. to a.d. 220* (London: Duckworth, 1977). Dillon demonstrates that for Plato, "likeness to God" was the central goal of ethics.

Taken on its own, Ephesians 5:1-2 functions to preface the section of para-nesis in verses 3-21, and the teaching on marriage that occurs in verses 22-33. The imperatival charge in verse 2, to walk in the way of the love of Christ, operates as a paradigm that informs the manner of the moral life of the church. Yet the theological significance of the church's active life of sacrificial love far exceeds the scope of the immediate context of Ephesians 5; it feeds the theology of moral and spiritual formation that is woven throughout the fabric of the entire epistle.

In Ephesians 1:4, for example, love is situated within another cultic met-aphor related to sacrifice. There we read: "he chose us in him before the foundation of the world, that we should be holy and blameless before him in love [*en agapē*]." The prepositional phrase *en agapē* is rendered by most in-terpreters as "in love." This translation, however, is too vague to be of any help. Given the instrumental function of love in 3:13-21, 4:11-16, and 5:25-33, it is more consistent to render *en agapē* as "by means of love" in Ephesians 1:4.

When the phrase *en agapē* is read instrumentally, love becomes the means by which the ritual and cultic designation "holy and blameless" is applied to believers. The holiness and blamelessness of Ephesians 1:4 is not meant to be a legal fiction or a status that is merely imputed to believers in virtue of their union with Christ; rather, as Chrysostom rightly recognized, the phrase is a reference to the holy transformation of the church that occurs through the enactment and reception of ecclesial and missional works of cruciform love.[8] Highlighting the corporate context of holiness in the Old Testament, Stephen Fowl has noted that Paul here situates those elected in Christ "within God's election of Israel." This election in Christ exists so that

---

[8]Chrysostom in his *Homily on Ephesians* 1.1.4 argues that while God "himself has made us saints," nevertheless "we are called to remain saints." For Chrysostom, a saint is a person who "lives in faith" and is "unblemished" leading "a blameless life." Thus, the phrase refers to sanctified, moral living in faith initiated and empowered by God rather than a merely external status extra nos. Cf. Andrew Lincoln, *Ephesians*, Word Biblical Commentary 42 (Dallas: Word, 1990), 24, who argues that the language of holiness and blamelessness in Ephesians 1:4 explicates the goal of election and redemption, namely, that believers should "exhibit a particular quality of life." Cf. Stephen Fowl, *Ephesians: A Commentary* (Louisville, KY: Westminster John Knox, 2012), 41. Fowl reads "in love" in Ephesians 1:4 "in the light of Phil 1:9 and 1 Thess 3:12-13." In those parallel Pauline texts a "superabundance of *agapē* in the lives of believers provides the wisdom and grace they will need to be holy and blameless before Christ." Notice that here, too, holiness and blame-lessness is not merely cultic and ritual, it is ethical and applied to the goal of believers' growth in holiness in Christ.

the church might grow in holiness which is "the communal end toward which God calls the church as a body."[9] Furthermore, when the same phrase occurs in 5:25-27, it is clear that the sacrificial love of Christ functions as the means or instrument by which the church is sanctified and presented as holy and blameless.

In the same way, in 3:14-21 love is portrayed as the means by which the church is filled with the fullness of God through the indwelling of Christ and the knowledge of his love. In 3:16 the telic function of *eis* is meant to communicate result or purpose rather than sphere or location. Thus, *eis ton esō anthrōpon* refers, as Markus Barth has argued, to growth "toward the inner man."[10] The indwelling Christ of verse 17 and the "inner man" of verse 16 are conceptually equivalent; both are references to Christ. This indwelling occurs through faith on the basis of believers' roots and foundation in love. All of this culminates in verse 19, in which the church is said to grow in the knowledge of Christ's love on the basis of his indwelling by means of their rootedness in love, in order that they might be filled with the fullness of God (*hina plērōthēte eis pan to plērōma tou theou*).

Of key importance here is that the fullness of Christ is experienced as the church. It is "with all the saints" (Eph 3:18) that we come to know the love of Christ (3:19). The fullness of God is not, therefore, a reference to individual and existential fullness but to ecclesial fullness experienced by the members of the body—collectively and individually—by means of the transformative presence of Christ in his body by the Spirit.[11] The fullness of God's

---

[9]Fowl, *Ephesians*, 40. Fowl draws on Aquinas here, who argues that holiness and blamelessness in Ephesians 1:4 refers to being "holy in virtues and unspotted by vices." We are thus dealing with concepts of moral formation (i.e., being made holy and blameless) not merely positional sanctification (i.e., being set apart as holy on the basis of Christ's holiness *extra nos*). Contra Best (Ernest Best, *Ephesians*, International Critical Commentary [Edinburgh: T&T Clark, 1998]), who acknowledges the cultic *and moral* usage of the terms "holy and blameless" in the Bible (and in Ephesians!) but then argues that, in Ephesians 1:4, the terms denote "a position before God" and are "primarily religious or cultic rather than moral terms" (121, 122-23).

[10]Barth, *Ephesians*, 369, 373.

[11]Consider the soteriological weightiness given to ecclesial works of love in the church in patristic exegetes. Jerome (Mark Edwards, ed., *Galatians, Ephesians, Philippians*, Ancient Christian Commentary on Scripture [Downers Grove, IL: InterVarsity Press, 1999], 169), for example, notes that the entire building up of the church as the body of Christ "increases cell by cell . . . through the mutual love of one for another." Likewise, Chrysostom (*Homily on Ephesians* 11.4.15-16) notes that being joined and knit together "requires the exercise of great care" because when "one thread is misplaced, the pattern is lost." He even argues that if we leave the body we "are not united and do not receive the Spirit."

love is never intended to be experienced alone, nor even only in a local
community of believers, but rather in communion with the fullness of the
eternal mystical body of Christ by means of participation in a local church.
Thomas Aquinas, in his commentary on Ephesians, argues in this manner:

> Since the Church was instituted on account of Christ, the Church is called the
> fullness of Christ. Everything which is virtually in Christ is, as it were, filled
> out in some way in the members of the Church. For all spiritual under-
> standing, gifts, and whatever can be present in the Church—all of which
> Christ possesses superabundantly—flow from him into the members of the
> Church, and they are perfected in them.[12]

Thus, just as in Ephesians 1:4, the grammatical and theological function
of love in 3:14-21 is instrumental and not merely evidential. Growth in
knowledge, the presence of Christ—and growth in love itself (3:19)—occurs
within believers when they receive Christ's love and respond by ecclesially
engaging in and enacting Christ's love together in the body (Eph 4:15-16;
Eph. 5:2-21). Sacrificial ecclesial love is not simply the ethical fruit of salvation. Rather, the fullness of salvation is the fruit of ecclesial love. It is the
way in which we "work out" (Phil 2:12) and appropriate the salvation accomplished through the life, death, and resurrection of Jesus Christ.[13] Yet,
the ecclesial work of love is unlike any other virtuous human habit. The habit
of cruciform love—charity—is the supernatural power, presence, and virtue
that transforms believers as it sifts and sanctifies them on a trajectory toward
their ultimate goal and created purpose, namely, a life of eternal communion
together with God, the beatific vision.[14]

---

[12]Aquinas, *Commentary on Saint Paul's Epistle to the Ephesians*. Cf. Lincoln, *Ephesians*, 343-44 on
the communal nature of God's love.

[13]Cf. Fowl, *Ephesians*, 290. Fowl clearly states that "God's action" has already accomplished redemption. Nevertheless, he rightly argues that "believers must appropriate this for themselves
by abandoning the old person, taking on the new and its activities, and allowing themselves to
be renewed." Emphasis mine.

[14]Aquinas, *Commentary on Saint Paul's Epistle to the Ephesians*: "The Apostle's intention is to
strengthen them in good . . . [and] habits, and spur them on to greater perfection." In the foot-
notes to verse 1, editor Mathew Lamb notes that regarding "love" as a "habit" requires knowledge
of Aquinas's differentiation between natural, cardinal virtues, available to all human beings, and
supernatural virtues, which are the gift of God accessed by the infusion of God's grace through
the sacraments. Lamb explains that, for Aquinas, "virtue, or '*bonus habitus*,' is a spiritually creative power which is the exact opposite of the mechanical repetition of acts associated with the
word 'habit.'" Furthermore: "The supernatural virtue of charity [love] is the 'effective form' of
all the other virtuous acts, and thus formally sanctifies us because it directs us to God as he is

In Ephesians 4:16 the sense of *en agapē* is once again clearly instrumental. It is by means of love that the body of Christ, the church, is held together and built up to perfection (Eph 4:13). As in 5:2, the "love" that perfects the body of Christ here is a reference not only to the church's reception of Christ's love but a description of the church's enactment and active embodiment of it. This theme of ecclesial perfection also occurs in Colossians where the goal of Paul's proclamation is to "present everyone mature in Christ" (Col 1:28) through a life of communal, others-focused, missional love, which "binds everything together in perfect harmony" (Col 3:14). Thus, in neither Colossians nor Ephesians does love function as a merely incidental paradigmatic basis for Christian ethical behavior. Rather, love is always functioning within a larger category of redemption in which it is a means, instrument, and channel of the appropriation of the soteriological and sanctifying benefits of the once-for-all—but perpetually efficacious—sacrifice of Jesus Christ for his body.

THE ECCLESIAL FUNCTION OF WORKS FOR SALVATION IN EPHESIANS

Given the emphasis on salvation by grace through faith apart from works in Ephesians 2:8-9, Ephesians has continually been at the crux of theological debate regarding the purpose of works in the economy of salvation. Typically, the works of Ephesians 2:10 "which God prepared beforehand to be our way of life" are viewed as good works that stem from salvation and typically play an evidential, authenticating role—but not an instrumental role in salvation. Yet, when the meta-theme of works is considered in relation to the instrumental role of love in Ephesians, it becomes clear that our fearful obsession with works-righteousness is not a worry or perspective shared by Paul. Thus, we will turn now to Paul's understanding of the instrumental role of love—through grace-empowered ecclesial works—in the nature of salvation.

As in the undisputed epistles of Paul, in Ephesians any activity, work, or effort undertaken by believers is preceded by, animated by, and empowered by the grace and agency of God (Phil 2:12-13). Thus, in Ephesians 1:11 God "works (*energountos*) all things according to his counsel and will." And, it

---

in himself. The acts of any other virtue are holy only insofar as they share in this Godward impulse of charity." My emphases.

is on the basis of the "working (*tēn energeian*) of [God's] great might" that Paul prays the church would come to know the power that God "worked (*enērgēsen*) in Christ when he raised him from the dead." Likewise, Paul was made a minister by the "working" (*energeian*) of God's power (Eph 1:19-20; 3:7).

The cause and source of salvation is the gracious work of God alone as opposed to the result of any human works or merit as Ephesians 2:9 makes abundantly clear. Yet, if "good works" in 2:10 are interpreted as general deeds of moral and ethical goodness that follow—but are inconsequential—to one's salvation, our exegesis jumps too soon into its comfortable Reformation clothing. It is crucial to correct course here. In arguing that salvation is *ouk ex ergōn, hina mē tis kauchēsētai* (literally, "not from/out of works, so that no one may boast"), Paul is pointing out that the origin and source of salvation is in the grace of God alone rather than human works of any kind.[15] When, in verse 10, Paul states that we are "God's workmanship created for good works which God prepared beforehand that we should walk in them" he is not contrasting the concept of "works-righteousness" with concept of "salvation by grace alone." Rather, he is speaking about the role of grace-empowered works in the working out of (cf. Phil 2:12) and appropriation of the salvation that is sourced in the once-for-all, yet perpetually efficacious redemptive work of Christ. There is, therefore, no reason to conjecture about the nature of good works in Ephesians.

When Paul speaks of believers' works in Ephesians, it is never a reference to Jewish ceremonial "works of Torah" (as in Galatians and Romans) such as circumcision, food laws, or sabbath. Neither is it a reference to the

---

[15]There are, of course, substantive differences between the vast array of Protestant theological systems and the magisterial teachings of the Roman Catholic Church. Yet, it is significant to note that it is also the case that for both Catholics and Protestants, the necessity and priority of the gift of God's grace for salvation does not imply total human passivity in the grace-empowered process of progressive sanctification. Thus, salvation by grace is not an exclusively Protestant or evangelical belief, even if the phrase *sola gratia*, in the historical and theological context of the Reformation, is typically associated with Protestantism. Nevertheless, the impossibility of salvation apart from God's grace is a theological concept that is shared by all major orthodox expressions of Christianity, including the Roman Catholic Church. Thomas Aquinas notes in his commentary on Ephesians that Paul rejects the idea that God gives us salvation on the basis of "the merit of our preceding actions." Aquinas also notes that the grace of salvation and justification is not given based on "previous works" and he affirms that whatever good works we accomplish "are [made possible] to us by God." See Aquinas, *Commentary on Saint Paul's Epistle to the Ephesians*.

Protestant boogeyman "works-righteousness" or even to random acts of Christian kindness. Rather, the works of Ephesians 2:8-10 refer to a very specific sort of activity—namely, the ecclesial work of sacrificial love that transforms believers by filling them with the fullness of God and the indwelling presence of Jesus Christ. Works are not the evidential proof of salvation but the participatory means of appropriating its benefits. It is crucial that faith be formed in love (Gal 5:6), not only to validate the authenticity of faith but to carry out its transformative purpose.

Faith at work through love transforms individuals and the church into the image of the God who is love. In articulating how this theology works in the thought of Thomas Aquinas, Daria Spezzano writes:

> While the Passion is an objectively satisfactory priestly act by Christ as the head of the body, it is also the cause and model of our own acts of satisfaction. Such satisfaction is offered in the exercise of the charity-infused virtue of religion . . . [and this] enables us to participate in and subjectively appropriate the benefits won for us by Christ's priestly satisfaction of the head of the mystical body.[16]

For evangelicals who are not accustomed or are even averse to thinking in a fully Thomistic system of "satisfaction," the theological principle articulated here is nevertheless entirely commensurate with Protestant theological systems. By replacing the Thomistic language of human "satisfaction" with the phrase "grace-empowered works of Christian love," the richness of Aquinas's theological point can be incorporated into more evangelical ways of thinking.[17] In fact, as J. Todd Billings has demonstrated, for John Calvin,

---

[16]Daria Spezzano, "'Be Imitators of God': Discipleship in the Letter to the Ephesians." *Nova et Vetera* 15, no. 2 (2017): 615-51 (619).

[17]Spezzano, "Be Imitators of God," 632-33 further explicates this idea within a Thomistic framework, but in ways that fit with commensurate evangelical emphases that likewise prioritize the work of Jesus Christ as the unique and sole source of salvation, apart from any prior human works. Spezzano articulates Aquinas's thought, saying: "While Christ's satisfaction is objectively superabundantly sufficient for human salvation, it seems that, for it to have full effect in us, we must imitate, and indeed participate in, Christ's charitable satisfaction as God's beloved children by our own filial sacrifice of Christ's loving obedience, which must involve the cross—that is, some temporal suffering for us—as a part of the journey to holiness." This "temporal suffering," in my view, is best understood as the ecclesial work of love which conforms the church into the image of God's suffering love as it embodies, enacts, and receives God's love as it supernaturally bears the burdens of one another and the world. Spezzano (640) finds this emphasis on "perfection in terms of a progressive participation in divinity by conformation to Christ" in *Summa Theologica* I, q. 12, a.5; q. 43, a.5; q. 93, a. 4; I-II, q. 112, a. 1; III, q. 23, a.3.

Christian acts of "love and almsgiving which are connected with the Lord's Supper are indispensable to participation in Christ in the heavenly places through the Spirit."[18]

The link between the meta-themes of work and love viewed as a transformative participation in Christ's sacrifice within the church can be observed most clearly in Ephesians 4:12 and 16. In these verses the work of ministry is carried out by the saints (thus situating it within an ecclesial context) resulting in the building up of the body of Christ. In 4:16, it is when each part of the body of Christ is "working properly" (*kat' energeian en metrō henos hekastou merous*) that the body grows and is built up to perfection (v. 13) "by means of love." A similar pattern of ecclesial growth in perfection through being "knit together by means of love" occurs in Colossians 1:28-29 and 2:2, 19.

Relatedly, it is worth noting that in Ephesians 5:2 Paul exhorts the church to "walk in love" (*peripateite en agapē*) and earlier, in 2:10, Paul uses the same Greek verb *peripateō* to argue that the church should "walk" in good works. Likewise, in 4:1-3, Paul again urges the church to walk (*peripateō*) in a manner worthy of their calling, and then immediately explicates this statement by defining its content as exercising humility, gentleness, patience, and the burden-bearing love of Christ.[19]

For Paul, then, the works prepared beforehand by God for the church are a reference to the ecclesial activity of the church at work in love. Rooted in the gift of divine love, Christ dwells within the hearts of believers as they are knit together in love, experiencing growth and unity as they are perfected through ecclesial works of love as one body in Christ. In offering our bodies as a singular living sacrifice (cf. Rom 12:1-2) as "one new man" (Eph 2:13; cf. 4:22) the church is actually "re-presenting" and

---

[18]J. Todd Billings, *Calvin, Participation, and the Gift: The Activity of Believers in Union with Christ* (Oxford: Oxford University Press, 2007), 137, emphasis mine. For Calvin, the ministry of alms and the diaconate extended into the broader society, including service in the public hospitals (176-77). The key, however, is that these works of charity and alms "are indispensable to participation in Christ" (137). For Calvin, Christian works of love were a mode of our union with and participation in the transformative life of Christ.

[19]Although the focus in this chapter is on the ecclesial and covenantal context of God's transformative love, it is clear in the New Testament that the election and blessing of the church is for the sake of the world not instead of the world. Divine, cruciform, ecclesial love transforms the church so that it can function as the body of Christ for the purpose of cruciforming the cosmos, that is, as God's instrument for the renewal of the world in the way and power of the cross.

"applying the fruit" of the one sacrifice of Christ in our midst.[20] The goal of this representation, application, and appropriation of Christ's sacrifice is to progressively conform our will and character to Christ so that we might experience everlasting communion with the living God as his adopted, beloved children.[21]

BENEFITS FOR GLOBAL EVANGELICALS

Christocentric cruciform community and practices. The work of the ministry of ecclesial love for others (Eph 4:12) is envisaged by the New Testament to be neither an entirely generic, abstract principle nor a limited and neatly defined set of practices. Yet while grace-empowered acts of love can take many forms, those who have been saved by Christ have access to and are called to share in several specific sacred Christian ecclesial practices that have been universally revealed to the church in the New Testament. From the beginning, believers were instructed to regularly gather together as one body, and to adhere to the sacred apostolic practices that exist to sanctify and unify the body in Christ. It was through faithful obedience to these practices that believers, together in the body of Christ, were enabled to tangibly and holistically participate in the body and become "partakers of the divine nature" (2 Pet 1:4).

Dietrich Bonhoeffer identified the core sacred practices provided to the church by Christ, via the apostles, for faithful participation in Christ as baptism, the confession of individual sin, Communion, marriage, and the preaching of the true word, unaltered, all in congruence with the apostolic teaching on these practices.[22] These sacred acts, instituted by Christ, provided specific, embodied ways for believers to have their hearts reoriented toward Christ, to habitually surrender to the sanctifying work of the Spirit,

---

[20]*Catechism of the Catholic Church* (Homebush: St Paul's, 1989), 334, CCC 1366.
[21]Spezzano, "Be Imitators of God," 618. I am influenced here by Spezzano's reading of Aquinas, which views his theology of satisfaction and penance within the larger category of deification. In this view, the grace-empowered work of Christians draws from the power and benefits of Christ's passion and applies them subjectively through works, which conform "God's adopted children" to Christ by means of the Holy Spirit. Though evangelicals would likely not think in terms of a Thomistic theology of penance, the concept of progressive holiness by grace is typically designated "sanctification" in Protestant thought.
[22]Dietrich Bonhoeffer, *Discipleship*, Dietrich Bonhoeffer Works 4 (Minneapolis: Fortress, 2003), 45-48; Dietrich Bonhoeffer, *Act and Being* (Minneapolis, Fortress, 2009), 130-32.

and to be enabled to personify Christ's love together in and with Christ, in his body, through the work of the Holy Spirit. Bonhoeffer called these essential acts of Christian life and worship the "arcane" practices of the faith, the divine mysteries that believers must actively participate in if they were to partake in Christ.[23] Bonhoeffer taught that believers were also called to engage in acts of charity toward others in the world. However, one could not ever offer genuine love to their neighbor in the world without being first transformed by Christ,[24] via surrender to Christ in faith in the particular sacred ways that he prescribed;[25] so that all genuine works of love were performed only in and through Christ himself, in his body, and not in the flesh.[26]

The grace-empowered work of confession. While space will not allow for a full exposition of all the sacred practices identified by Bonhoeffer, we will focus on one of the practices that is notably lacking in most evangelical churches today, namely confession. It is significant that, regarding the Christ-ordained acts that believers are called to follow in order to participate in Christ, Bonhoeffer stressed that the confession of individual sin before both God and others in the body must always come first because in this act alone can a person substantially enter into the actuality of being crucified with Christ (Gal 2:20), rather than allowing the death of a sinner to remain only an abstraction and never a present reality:

---

[23]Dietrich Bonhoeffer, *Life Together*, Dietrich Bonhoeffer Works 5 (Minneapolis: Fortress, 2005), 110-19; Dietrich Bonhoeffer, *Sanctorum Communio: A Theological Study of the Sociology of the Church* (Minneapolis: Fortress, 1998), 127. Bonhoeffer believed that all orthodoxy and orthopraxy must be centered in the living body of Christ, in reference to Christ who gives himself in revelation in the body.

[24]Dietrich Bonhoeffer, *Letters and Papers from Prison*, Dietrich Bonhoeffer Works 8 (Minneapolis: Fortress, 1997), 487; Bonhoeffer, *Act and Being*, 92.

[25]Irenaeus similarly argues that, in the fallen nature, persons are unable to act with virtue toward their neighbors, but in the act of faith directed only toward God, by the work of the Spirit they are conformed to the likeness of God and are then enabled to have, "righteous dealings with . . . neighbours." (Irenaeus, *Adversus Haereses* 5.6.1).

[26]Bonhoeffer, *Letters and Papers from Prison*, 127. Bonhoeffer claims: "Only through Christ does my neighbor meet me . . . in an absolute way. . . . Without Christ, even my neighbor is for me no more than a possibility of self-assertion." Also see Joel D. Lawrence, "Death Together: Thanatology and Sanctification in the Theology of Dietrich Bonhoeffer" (PhD diss., Cambridge University, 2006). Lawrence argues that in Bonhoeffer's soteriology, drawn from Martin Luther's, the primary problem for humanity was the "heart turned inward on itself." Thus, confession before God and others, and the reorienting of the heart, must precede all acts of love and justice for others in the world.

> In confessing actual sins the old self dies a painful, humiliating death before the eyes of another Christian. . . . And it is nothing else but our community with Jesus Christ that leads us to the disgraceful dying cross of Jesus Christ that shatters all pride. We cannot find the cross of Jesus if we are afraid of going to the place where Jesus can be found, to the public death of a sinner. . . . In confession occurs the breakthrough of the Cross . . . in the deep mental and physical pain of humiliation before a brother—which means, before God—we experience the Cross of Jesus as our rescue and salvation. The old man dies, but it is God who has conquered him. Now we share in the resurrection of Christ.[27]

Thus, in the confession of sin, we are provided with the first significant act by which a believer is called to respond to grace and tangibly participate with Christ in his death.[28] Then, too, in the act of confession before others, the Christian is given a means by which, after baptism, to continually participate in the reality of Christ's resurrection. Those who receive the confession of a brother or sister help their fellow believers to recognize the horrifying truth of their sin before God in the here and now in a way that no "psychological insight" can ever induce.[29] Furthermore, the certainty of both the eternal and present forgiveness of sins is made a present reality through both the hearing of a confession spoken aloud and the pronouncement of the reality of Christ's atonement for their sins.

Thus, in the act of confession, both parties reciprocally mediate the reality of Christ's forgiveness and sanctifying, sacrificial love to one another. Confession functions to apply the graces of Christ's once-for-all, yet perpetually efficacious sacrifice to believers here and now while binding the body of Christ together as one. Through the death of self that occurs in confession, the love of Christ is further generated and proliferated within believers as they experience the sanctifying power that comes through penitent, faithful obedience to Christ with and before one another in his body. The experience of embodying Christ's love afresh in the present through the sacramental power of confession and the consequent realization of absolution releases believers to act out of the freedom that comes through the

---

[27]Bonhoeffer, *Life Together*, 111-12.
[28]Bonhoeffer, *Discipleship*, 99.
[29]Bonhoeffer, *Life Together*, 115.

reality of divine, filial love. This love is not merely a warm feeling of human affection; rather the love of the sons and daughters of God is a participation in the very life of the Trinity.

Believers thus begin to bear a family resemblance to God—the Father, the Son, and the Holy Spirit—by participating in the divine DNA of faithful obedience, forgiveness, freedom, and love. The members of the church are, therefore, both eschatologically saved by the cross and progressively sanctified by the cross. Confession functions as one divinely revealed practice through which the sanctifying power of the cross and resurrection is experienced in the body eternally and in the present.[30] The basis of the transformative potential of confession, however, does not reside in something other than or in addition to the once-for-all sacrifice of Christ on the cross; confession is an application and appropriation of its perpetually efficacious power.

Extra ecclesiam nulla salus? *An evangelical assessment.* Some may wish to set aside essential acts given by Christ to the church, such as confession of individual sin, viewing them either as offensive or irrelevant to postmodern cultural mores or else as legalistic examples of "works-righteousness."[31] Yet the fullness of the resurrection life and divine love can only be experienced through communion with Christ in his body, the church, as it adheres to the apostolic faith and practice in its daily life. As the early church father Cyprian famously said, "Outside the church there is no salvation [*extra ecclesiam nulla salus*]."[32] This phrase, while often misinterpreted, and certainly in need of qualification and explanation, nevertheless provides a much-needed corrective to the common, individualistic ecclesiology practiced in many Protestant and evangelical churches.

---

[30]Bonhoeffer, *Life Together*, 111-12; Bonhoeffer, *Discipleship*, 99.

[31]See Jonathan K. Sharpe, "Faithful Reformation: The Importance of Apostolicity and Orthodox Consensus for Emerging Christian Expressions" (PhD diss., University of Pretoria, 2018). Sharpe conducted an historical, theological, and ethnographic study of emerging Christian expressions, placing them into conversation with St. Vincent of Lérins, Thomas Oden, and Dietrich Bonhoeffer around apostolicity and orthodoxy. His research revealed that many post-evangelical, post-Christian expressions still wished to identify as "creedal," or "orthodox," but had set aside core apostolic practices, such as confession of sin, by arguing that issues such as sexual preferences and acts, for instance, were matters of personal ethics, or current culture, unrelated to orthodoxy or creeds. Lérins and Bonhoeffer, however, saw a clear alignment of one's life and ethics with beliefs.

[32]Cyprian of Carthage, *Epistle* 73.21, as cited in the *Catechism of the Catholic Church*, 224, CCC 846.

By saying that "outside the church there is no salvation," we are not thereby making salvation contingent on one's active membership in a particular denomination or local congregation. Instead, the phrase serves as a reminder that God does not call us to exist as individualistic consumers or transmitters of religion but intends for us to become integrated co-communicants in Christ by baptism into his body. Thus, the *extra ecclesiam* is simply a recognition that to whomever salvation comes, it does so not through an individualistic appropriation of Christ's sacrifice but through the faithfulness of Christ, attested to by our faith in Christ and baptism into his body the church, which is the pillar and foundation of the truth (1 Tim 3:15).

Thus, the sanctification that God desires for the church is not achieved or applied in isolation or in the abstract. Grace-empowered acts of ecclesial love (such as confession) require the reciprocal and communal rehearsal of cruciform love—enacted and received together in the body in the present. Through these acts, the autonomous "I" of the individual self is redirected to Christ the center. And, revolving around that center are the Spirit-inspired apostolic acts that he ordained to hold believers together as one body, in one rhythm, in a bond that leads to perfection and peace. For instance, Bonhoeffer suggested that the act of holy matrimony—which is also provided in Ephesians as one means of enacting the self-sacrificial love of Christ—was not simply a symbol of two persons' love for each other but rather a sacred Christian rite that truly binds a man and woman together in God, not only bringing them into harmony with one another and God but upholding their love.[33] He explains: "It is marriage, and not merely your love for each other, that joins you together in the sight of God and man. . . . It is not your love that sustains the marriage, but from now on, the marriage that sustains your love."[34] Consequentially, just as love between two persons was now to be contained, lived out, and redirected from love of self to love of God and the other within the rite of marriage, so too all other Christian life, love, and work was to be lived within the body of Christ via obedience to the sacred rites provided to infuse and sustain the Christian life together.[35]

---

[33]See Ephesians 5; Bonhoeffer, *Letters and Papers from Prison*, 43.
[34]Bonhoeffer, *Letters and Papers from Prison*, 43.
[35]Bonhoeffer, *Life Together*. Here, Bonhoeffer describes how daily life in the body should be ordered.

For Bonhoeffer, the required Christ-ordained acts that believers were called to surrender to and perform also served as "marks" of the authentic church, since those practices had been followed by the true church from the apostles to the present age.[36] As Christians engage in these acts—these marks of the church—we are marked out as the church. And within the embrace of holy mother church, we are not only marked out by our practices; we are safeguarded by our doctrine so that we will be sanctified in truth (Jn 17:17). The point of doctrine is not merely to provide believers with correct facts about God but to renew them in the image of God and bring them into alignment with Christ and with his body. Doctrine, therefore, provides the penultimate framework of faithfulness that facilitates and generates a soteriological, sanctifying telos, namely, the transformative presence of Jesus Christ in the midst of his body, the church. In that sense, the act of doing theology could itself be considered a grace-empowered act of transformative ecclesial love.

Contemporary evangelical worship would, on the whole, benefit from an intensified focus on the formative practices of grace-empowered works of ecclesial love. It is only from a place of renewed ecclesial commitment to "the work of ministry" (Eph 4:12) as the body of Christ that we will represent Christ's sacrificial love to the world in witness, charity, and truth and thereby experience personal, ecclesial, and societal renewal in conformity to the image of God's Son.

CONCLUSION

Since the earliest days of the church, there have been significant streams of Christian theology that have believed that through the Eucharist, the benefits and power of the once-for-all sacrifice of Christ are re-presented and re-applied to the church.[37] This can be seen in most recent times in the theological approach of the Catechism of the Catholic Church, which argues that the memorial of the Eucharist is not simply a "recollection of past events" but a "mighty" proclamation that makes present that which it proclaims, namely

---

[36]Bonhoeffer, *Discipleship*, 45-48; Bonhoeffer, *Act and Being*, 130-32. Bonhoeffer claimed preaching of the word, confession, and administration of the sacraments, in congruence with apostolicity, as "marks" of the true church.

[37]*Catechism of the Catholic Church*, 344, CCC 1366.

the sanctifying, saving power of the cross of Jesus Christ. The event of the cross and its effect becomes "present and real" and sacramentally assists believers in conforming their lives to the way of the cross by the power of the Spirit.[38] In a similar way the transformative power of the event of Christ's sacrifice that definitively and exclusively accomplished salvation once for all in the life, death, and resurrection of Jesus is continually experienced anew in the active life of lived charity in the church through other grace-empowered acts of ecclesial love. As the love of Christ is embodied, enacted, received, and re-presented, the church is formed into the image of the God who is love through the perpetual sacrifice of the ecclesial Christ. When the church engages in the transformative work of ecclesial love, this is more than a result of the gospel; it is a primary goal of the gospel. It is more than a result of salvation; it is the very outworking of salvation and one of its constituent parts.

STUDY QUESTIONS

1. Do you currently practice confession? If so, how does it contribute to your spiritual life and formation? If not, are you averse to incorporating it into your ecclesial life? Why or why not?

2. In the chapter we focused on the general disposition of a life characterized by grace-empowered works of ecclesial love and the specific biblical practice of confession as one example of these works. What other specific biblical practices or patterns can you think of that would help make the concept of grace-empowered acts of ecclesial love more tangible?

3. This chapter drew from Scripture, the early church fathers, and both Catholic and Protestant theologians throughout all ages of the history of the church. How might such a broad approach to theological engagement contribute to a healthy, spiritually formative approach to doing theology? What might we lose by reading from within only one theological stream or era of the church?

4. The gospel calls us to surrender ourselves fully, not only to Christ but to his body, the church. Given our often low views of the church over

---

[38]*Catechism of the Catholic Church*, 343, CCC 1363.

against our own individual personal relationships with Jesus, this can strike contemporary Christians as being a radical claim. What parts of your own life have you tried to hold on to, cover up, or avoid instead of surrendering them to Christ and his church?

5. How might a theology of sanctification through grace-empowered acts of ecclesial love contribute to refreshing and recalibrating local church liturgies (i.e., orders of service) so that the worship service operates as a "work of ministry" (Eph 4:12) contributing to the transformational building up of the body of Christ?

CHAPTER EIGHT

THE BEATIFIC VISION
AS SPIRITUAL FORMATION

An Augustinian Ressourcement

RYAN A. BRANDT

BELOVED, WE ARE GOD'S CHILDREN NOW; what we will be has not
yet been revealed. What we do know is this: when he is revealed, we will be
like him, for we will see him as he is" (1 Jn 3:2 NRSV). The close connection
between the beatific vision ("seeing God") and spiritual formation has lin-
gered strongly in the Christian tradition. Indeed, the beatific vision and
spiritual formation go hand in hand as the anticipation, hope, and experience of the vision plays an essential part in spiritual formation. While a
recovery of the beatific vision is well underway in Protestant theology and
has been deeply rooted in Roman Catholic and Eastern Orthodox theology,
a discussion of the benefits of the beatific vision toward spiritual formation
is underdeveloped in the evangelical tradition. Hans Boersma has recently
written an "unapologetic ressourcement" connecting spirituality and the
beatific vision using the writings of Gregory of Nyssa; he also wrote a book
exploring the vision in the Christian tradition, though the theme of spiritual
formation is less pronounced throughout.[1] This chapter intends to continue
this program, but it focuses the discussion as a global invitation to the
importance and value of the beatific vision for the purposes of a healthy

---

[1]Hans Boersma, "Becoming Human in the Face of God: Gregory of Nyssa's Unending Search for
the Beatific Vision," *International Journal of Systematic Theology* 17, no. 2 (2015): 131-51; and
Boersma, *Seeing God: The Beatific Vision in Christian Tradition* (Grand Rapids, MI: Eerdmans, 2018).

account of spiritual formation, using my own tradition in Reformed theology as a background.

This chapter will flesh out the idea that a robustly developed understanding of the beatific vision (as the end of theology and life) is a necessary linchpin for healthy spiritual formation. The chapter first introduces the beatific vision and, using tools from Augustinian thought, shows its connection to spiritual formation. It then addresses the central emphasis of the beatific vision as looking upon God in the face of Jesus Christ by the Spirit, a vision that is located fundamentally in the triune God and is extended to those in Christ as they partake in his vision. This is the necessary background to spiritual formation and the spiritual disciplines. Finally, the chapter briefly explores how this perspective might benefit other global Christian theologies, as a retrieval of the vision fosters a powerful and dynamic account of spiritual formation.

A Definition of the Beatific Vision

While this chapter will address the meaning of the beatific vision as it continues, it is beneficial to begin by defining it briefly. The beatific vision is traditionally understood to be the end of humans in which they gaze upon God. What this gazing upon looks like, what its precise object is, and when exactly it occurs have been debated throughout the history of Christianity. Suffice it to say that the vision is typically construed as the person's immediate vision of God, a vision that beatifies and leads to perfect happiness.[2] This vision—or at least elements of this vision—is often construed as taking place now in some proleptic way, but the language of the beatific vision itself is usually reserved for the intermediate state (after bodily death) or the final, resurrected state. Some Christians, notably from Reformed and Puritan thought, emphasize that the beatific vision is not only a soulish, immaterial, and intellectual experience but also a bodily or ocular experience of gazing upon God's glory, even essence, through the person of Jesus Christ.[3] This

---

[2]For relatively comprehensive theological treatments, see Kenneth E. Kirk, *The Vision of God: The Christian Doctrine of the Summum Bonum, The Bampton Lectures for 1928* (London: Longmans, Green, 1932); Vladimir Lossky, *The Vision of God*, trans. Asheleigh Moorhouse, 2nd ed., Library of Orthodox Theology 2 (Leighton Buzzard, UK: Faith, 1973); and Boersma, *Seeing God.*

[3]This statement should not entail that only the Reformed tradition upholds the christocentric nature of the vision. For example, Simon Francis Gaine, in reply to Hans Boersma and

event, therefore, takes place in the final, resurrected state, and through the event the human being is able to gaze upon God in the face of the God-man, Jesus. Since it is beatific, it is the completion of the human capacities as they are transformed through the gaze upon Christ's person: "when he is revealed, we will be like him, for we will see him as he is" (1 Jn 3:2).

I will assume throughout this chapter that the beatific vision, at least minimally, is the knowledge, love, and sight of God through Jesus Christ.[4] Following Jonathan Edwards, I also prefer the view that the vision occurs progressively: presently in the new covenant (through a mirror dimly by faith), and then to a more direct vision upon bodily death (wherein the soul gazes upon God through the eyes of the mind), and finally is full and complete in the glorified state in the new heavens and earth. The more precise nature of this will be further developed later.[5]

Augustine's Distinctions in Relation to the Beatific Vision

This chapter begins with resources drawn from Augustine. He developed two intuitive distinctions that show how the vision and spiritual formation are connected: signs/things and use/enjoyment.[6] Things, strictly speaking, do not "signify something" but rather they simply are. God is of course the most ultimate "Thing." Signs are used to signify something else. Thus, "things are learned about through signs."[7] From this distinction Augustine employs another distinction between use and enjoyment. Enjoyment "consists in clinging to something lovingly for its own sake"; use consists of

---

Suzanne McDonald, argues that Thomas's understanding of the beatific vision is in fact thoroughly christological as it upholds Christ's human nature as the cause of our own beatific visions, not only to acquire the vision initially but also to continue in the vision for eternity (Simon Francis Gaine, "The Beatific Vision and the Heavenly Mediation of Christ," *TheoLogica* [2018]: 116-28).

[4]It is helpful to take the language of vision as a metaphorical imagery and tie this language with other imagery of knowing and loving God in Scripture, such as hearing, love, fellowship, and truth.

[5]How it is that the vision is intellectual and/or ocular (physical and/or nonphysical), and how these work together, are open questions that will not be answered in this chapter. Suffice it to say that, whether or not the vision is immaterial/intellectual and/or physical/ocular does not substantially change the following discussion of the beatific vision and its significance toward spiritual formation.

[6]Augustine, *Teaching Christianity: De Doctrina Christiana*, ed. John E. Rotelle, trans. Edmund Hill (Hyde Park, NY: New City, 1996), 1.2.2.

[7]Augustine, *Teaching Christianity* 1.2.2.

employing something lesser to "what your love aims at obtaining."[8] Whereas
things can be enjoyed in themselves, signs cannot be enjoyed in themselves
as they signify something else.[9] Stated another way, things make us happy;
signs are means to be used "on our way to happiness, providing us, so to say,
with crutches and props for reaching the things that will make us happy."[10]
This does not entail that higher-order signs—say, a human person—ought
to be used by another person: "Augustine does not call us to any old use of
the finite creature," Susannah Ticciati comments, "but to its use as a means
to the end of the contemplation of God. The creature is to be treated as sign,
not of me, but of God."[11] All signs are meant to denote the higher reality of
things, which is God himself. Take the example of this chapter in particular
and this book as a whole. My chapter contains words that form ideas and
arguments that express meaning. The words themselves are not the purpose
for which the chapter was written. The words are signs that point toward the
chapter's meaning and purpose, which in this case is spiritual formation for
the global church. Augustine would conclude ultimately, moreover, that the
thing this book signifies—or at least I hope it signifies!—is God himself, or
the contemplation of God himself.

These distinctions present a particular conundrum for the Christian, as
Augustine notes: Christians in this world can choose to enjoy signs or things,
and they can make the improper choice. If we choose to enjoy signs, we are
"impeding from our progress" and "deflected from our course," since we are
"blocked by our love for inferior things."[12] Signs point to a greater meaning
in God, but if they terminate in themselves, love is misplaced. They cannot
be loved for their own sakes. Augustine uses this analogy: a Christian is like
an exile in a foreign land; to return home, he or she must use land-based
vehicles or seagoing vessels to arrive at the destination. In this process, she

---

[8]Augustine, *Teaching Christianity* 1.4.4.

[9]In Rowan Williams's view, we must "use" and not "enjoy" the created world, since it prevents
people in the world from treating people "as the end of desire, conceiving my meaning in terms
of them and theirs in terms of me" (Rowan Williams, "Language, Reality and Desire in
Augustine's *De doctrina*," *Journal of Literature and Theology* 3, no. 2 [July 1989]: 140; see also Peter
Lombard, *Sentences*, vol. 1, *The Mystery of the Trinity*, trans. Giulio Silano [Toronto: Pontifical
Institute of Mediaeval Studies, 2007], 6 [1.2.5]).

[10]Augustine, *Teaching Christianity* 1.3.3.

[11]Susannah Ticciati, "The Castration of Signs: Conversing with Augustine on Creation, Language
and Truth," *Modern Theology* 23, no. 2 (April 2007): 167; cf. 169, 176-77.

[12]Augustine, *Teaching Christianity* 1.3.3.

must be careful lest the scenery, quaintness, and adventure of the journey are enjoyed, or else she will never complete the trek home. The person who begins to enjoy the journey for its own sake steers in such a way to make the journey longer. The exile here has "lost interest in [his or her] own country." In the same way, "If we wish to return to our home country, where alone we can be truly happy, we have to make use [of] this world, not enjoy it."[13]

Augustine's distinctions illustrate two related points, which conclude this initial discussion: in some sense, all created existence helps us know or see God, and yet only God himself is the final means and end of our knowledge.[14] On the one hand, the distinctions serve as helpful reminders that all created existence is a signpost pointing to God.[15] If created reality is so utilized, it is used well; if it is enjoyed for its own sake, then it is not used well. John Calvin summarizes, "Let this be our principle: that the use of God's gifts is not wrongly directed when it is referred to that end to which the Author himself created and destined them for us, since he created them for our good, not for our ruin."[16] Creation ought to be a sign on our way of knowing and loving God and enjoying him for his own sake—that is, the beatific vision, where complete and full enjoyment in God occurs. Consequently, on the other hand, only God, the true "thing" to be "enjoyed," is the one who ought to be the termination of our knowledge, will, and delight. Augustine's distinctions might seem to be merely instrumental on the surface, but they ultimately serve to guard and remind the Christian against any kind of idolatry, whether in theology or practice. His words point us to the longing and hope for the beatific vision, which is for Augustine and traditional Christianity the ultimate aim of the Christian. It is our end in which we see God and are transformed. It is the highest goal, since

---

[13] Augustine, *Teaching Christianity* 1.4.4.

[14] For the purposes of this chapter, the discussion here was brief. For more elaboration on the two distinctions, see the illuminating interpretation by Williams, "Language, Reality and Desire in Augustine's *De doctrina*," 138-50; see also Ticciati, "The Castration of Signs," 161-79; and Susannah Ticciati, "The Human Being as Sign in Augustine's *De doctrina Christiana*," *Neue Zeitschrift für systematische Theologie und Religionsphilosophie* 55, no. 2 (2013): 20-32.

[15] Hans Boersma similarly argues in his understanding of vision as pedagogy. Instead of using the language of Augustine's distinctions, he uses the language of creation as sacramental and thus pointing inextricably to God himself as Creator and sustainer of all (Boersma, *Seeing God*, 387-429; cf. Boersma, *Heavenly Participation: The Weaving of a Sacramental Tapestry* [Grand Rapids, MI: Eerdmans, 2011]).

[16] John Calvin, *Institutes of the Christian Religion*, ed. John T. McNeill, trans. Ford Lewis Battles (Louisville, KY: Westminster John Knox, 2006), 3.10.2.

God is our ultimate destination and the only proper Thing to be enjoyed. In sum, it is only through God and to God that change is possible.

THE BEATIFIC VISION FOR THE PURPOSES OF SPIRITUAL FORMATION

Augustine's distinctions serve as resources for thinking about the beatific vision and its relation to the rest of life, especially spiritual formation. The created world—and all that is in it—points to God himself and is therefore a reminder of the beatific vision. The discussion of the beatific vision and spiritual formation begins and ends by looking upon God in Jesus Christ by the Spirit. It is our vision of God that changes us, and this change allows us to perceive the inexorable connection between sign and thing, use and enjoyment. These two ideas are elaborated in order.

First, it is through gazing upon Jesus that spiritual formation occurs.[17] Speaking about the new covenant in Christ by the power of the Spirit, Paul says, "And all of us, with unveiled faces, seeing the glory of the Lord as though reflected in a mirror, are being transformed into the same image from one degree of glory to another" (2 Cor 3:18). Paul understands the new covenant as a vision taking place now wherein "the veil is removed" (v. 16), a veil that obstructs the person's understanding and appreciation of God; thus, believers in the new covenant are seeing God "with unveiled face" (v. 18), that is, more clearly and directly than in the old covenant. Through this gaze we are transformed into the image of Jesus Christ. John Calvin comments, "He presents himself to us at present, so as to be seen by us, and openly beheld, in so far as is for our advantage, and in so far as our capacity admits of."[18] This active, transformational vision is presently imperfect, "for now we see in a mirror, dimly, but then we will see face to face" (1 Cor 13:12).[19]

---

[17]Of course, "gazing upon" here as elsewhere is a visual metaphor that stands in for knowing, understanding, and being raptly attentive to Jesus Christ (see Boersma, *Seeing God*, 1-5; cf. Augustine, *Teaching Christianity* 1.12-15).

[18]John Calvin, *Epistles of Paul the Apostle to the Corinthians*, trans. John Pringle (Grand Rapids, MI: Baker, 2009), 188. Thomas Aquinas notes, "For since all knowledge involves the knower's being assimilated to the thing known, it is necessary that those who see be in some way transformed into God" (St. Thomas Aquinas, *Commentary on the Letters of Saint Paul to the Corinthians*, ed. J. Mortensen and E. Alarcon, trans. F. R. Larcher, B. Mortensen, and D. Keating [Lander, WY: The Aquinas Institute for the Study of Sacred Scripture, 2012], 3.3.114).

[19]John Calvin comments on this: "The knowledge that we have of God for the present is obscure and slender, in comparison with the glorious view that we shall have on occasion of Christ's last coming" (*Epistles of Paul the Apostle to the Corinthians*, 187).

The present gaze through the new covenant is fulfilled in the final, beatific vision upon our death and bodily resurrection. Paul here clarifies that seeing Christ is the foundation of being changed like him. The new covenant entails a gaze upon God in Christ through the power of the Spirit, a gaze that changes us presently as we gaze upon Christ through Scripture (and creation) and ultimately in the beatific gaze as we directly gaze upon God himself in Christ.

Situating this discussion more broadly, the beatific vision is located fundamentally in the Trinity. In other words, the vision is ultimately something God does of himself, and he brings us into it as we are united to Christ. To use the language of Jonathan Edwards, God was "happy from the days of eternity in himself, in the beholding of his own infinite beauty."[20] The new covenantal vision of God is thus derivative of the eternal triune vision. Kyle Strobel summarizes Edwards: the Father gazes upon the Son, "and the Son gazes back, spirating perfect happiness (Holy Spirit)"; thus, as believers are in Christ, Christ "mediates, almost like a lens," those in him, so that they can see in a beatified manner.[21] The vision is not so much one of gazing upon God's essence (whatever that would mean) as it is of himself as the triune God. Edwards elaborates: those "in Christ shall partake of the love of God the Father to Christ. And as the Son knows the Father, so they shall partake with him in his sight of God, as being as it were parts of him. As he is in the bosom of the Father, so are they in the bosom of the Father."[22] Edwards suggests that those in Christ are brought up with Christ, the eternal Son, into God's triune love. Consequently, as sons and daughters, "They shall see that he is their Father, and that they are his children. . . . Therefore they shall see God, even their own God; when they behold this transcendent glory of God."[23]

---

[20]Jonathan Edwards, "Nothing upon Earth Can Represent the Glories of Heaven," in *Sermons and Discourses, 1723–1729*, vol. 14, ed. Kenneth P. Minkema (New Haven, CT: Yale University Press, 1997), 153; cf. Jonathan Edwards, "Charity and Its Fruits," in *Ethical Writings*, vol. 8, ed. Paul Ramsey (New Haven, CT: Yale University Press, 1989), 373.

[21]Kyle C. Strobel, *Jonathan Edwards's Theology: A Reinterpretation*, ed. John Webster, Ian A. McFarland, and Ivor Davidson (London: Bloomsbury, 2013), 27, 118.

[22]Jonathan Edwards, *The Works of President Edwards: With a Memoir of His Life*, vol. 8 (New York: S. Converse, 1830), 267-68 (quotation edited for clarity). These comments as well as the following comments from Edwards are from his Romans 2:10 sermon.

[23]Edwards, *The Works of President Edwards*, 267.

The Father is gazing upon them in Christ (and vice versa) with a glad result that the human soul partakes in God's triune gaze. God is the active agent in this gaze and, through his initiative and activity, souls are nurtured and empowered, and respond back to God: "God will communicate, and as it were pour forth himself into the soul" like "the flowers open before the sun."[24] Edwards here describes that the soul will be blessedly caught—"inflamed with love"—in the triune gaze: "The soul shall not be an inactive spectator, but shall be most active, and in the most ardent exercise of love towards the object seen."[25] Edwards uses vibrant language to suggest that, in the act of seeing God, the soul will be perfected (or beatified) as far as creaturely possible: "it shall be as full as it can hold" including the "understanding," "will," and "pleasure."[26] The soul (in Christ by the power of the Spirit) is thus brought into the trinitarian gaze of delight. This trinitarian gaze begins in the new covenant and is completed in glory.

As the believer is beatified through the triune gaze in Christ, spiritual formation takes place. The "new self" is conformed "according to the image of its creator" (Col 3:10), which entails the putting away of the old self and its vices and putting on the new self and its virtues.[27] Believers in Christ are given a new ability to relate to God, notably including a spiritual power to see and act, relational abilities that come from the triune God and disperse throughout the whole person, changing the way they act and see the world.[28] Peter, picking up on this idea, says that in Christ, we become "partakers of the divine nature," as we increasingly escape from the "corruption" of the

---

[24]Edwards, *The Works of President Edwards*, 269.

[25]Edwards, *The Works of President Edwards*, 268.

[26]Edwards, *The Works of President Edwards*, 268. He elsewhere says it will be a perfect sight "according to men's capacity" (266).

[27]While Paul has in mind chiefly the Christian virtues (Col 3:5-8, 12-15), his understanding of spiritual formation here necessarily implicates a different way to do life and perceive the world as a new self, for he is thinking about "all wisdom" and "whatever you do, in word or deed" (vv. 16-17). Elsewhere, Paul also contrasts the old life/self and new life/self, mentioning that the former is characterized by "futility of their minds" (Eph 4:17) and being "darkened in their understanding" (v. 18) and he thus calls these "to be renewed in the spirit of your minds" (v. 23). Paul is thus more broadly referring to the whole capacity as a Christian, and not simply to a new ethic.

[28]In other words, God restores the inward "spiritual senses" (that internal capacity to see God) so that the believer may discern God in and through the world and may discern justice, beauty, and truth. For a helpful survey of the spiritual senses in the Christian tradition, see Paul L. Gavrilyuk and Sarah Coakley, eds., *The Spiritual Senses: Perceiving God in Western Christianity* (Cambridge: Cambridge University Press, 2012).

world and share in the divine virtues ("everything needed for life and godliness," 2 Pet 1:3). Partaking in the divine nature echoes the reality that human beings united to Christ participate in him so that, among other things, his righteousness becomes theirs, his immortality theirs, his incorruptibility theirs, and his virtues theirs. Paul reflects this idea in his teaching on justification by faith, as righteousness is not a human work but from God (Rom 10:3-4) and is reckoned to the believer in Christ by faith (4:22; 5:17-18), so that they are now "slaves to righteousness" in Christ as the Spirit dwells in them (6:18-19; cf. 8:9-10). He also affirms this idea in his understanding that our bodies will take on the incorruptibility and immortality of the Son's glorified body (1 Cor 15:53-54; cf. Rom 8:11). Paul summarizes this well elsewhere: "He is the source of your life in Christ Jesus, who became for us wisdom from God, and righteousness and sanctification and redemption" (1 Cor 1:30). Again, this all happens as believers participate in the triune gaze, that is, as they are united to Christ and receive his benefits by the power and bonding of the Spirit. Gazing upon Jesus changes you, imperfectly now but perfectly in the future.

Second, in this context spiritual formation becomes meaningful to believers' lives as they, among other things, are enabled to perceive the inexorable connection between sign and thing, use and enjoyment. As the triune God orders us so that we can correctly perceive God through creation, we are able to enjoy God in the world. Hans Boersma aptly summarizes, "The purpose of all of matter . . . is to lead us into God's heavenly presence, to bring about communion with God, participation in the divine life."[29] For example, when we gaze upon a beautiful sunset, we do not gaze to enjoy the sunset itself so much as the sign to which it points. Sunsets, and all created beauty, are signifiers of Beauty itself. They are reminders of the glorious beatific vision of God himself. As such, the sunset is a vehicle of knowledge of God, a distinct pointer to the power and beauty of God, as well as a preparation for the surpassing glory of gazing upon God himself. When we taste a well-crafted deep-dish pizza (a particularly American example), or any other food or drink, the pizza is meant to remind us of the glorious and

---

[29]Boersma, *Heavenly Participation*, 9. He continues, "The entire cosmos is meant to serve as a sacrament: a material gift from God in and through which we enter into the joy of his heavenly presence."

everlasting goodness and sublimity of God himself as epitomized in the eternal wedding banquet in the new heaven and new earth. It is a vehicle or vessel to help us traverse our exiled land and know the surpassing nature of God. The uses of these signs are not improper or obsequious; rather, they are divinely intended to bring us to enjoyment in God. In fact, all of creation is created by God as a collection of signs intending our proper worship and enjoyment of God.[30] Therefore, a proper theology of the vision clarifies exactly how we go about Paul's near-formulaic command: "So, whether you eat or drink, or whatever you do, do everything for the glory of God" (1 Cor 10:31). In response, the created world is composed of signs or pointers to the triune God, a helpful image of the final reality of the beatific gaze.

As we are transformed within by God, we are enabled to practice the spiritual disciplines in a way that points us to God. The disciplines are means of becoming what we truly are. We fast from foods because the attending hunger reminds us that we are not God—we are contingent creatures who find their meaning in God alone. Our weakened bodies ache in anticipation of the coming completion of the new heavens and earth. We seek solitude because the attending loneliness reminds us that our truest relationship and—might I say—truest friendship is God in Christ, reminding us of who we really are. We contemplate God in all things as a reminder that all things are really God's and God is the most beautiful thing—even Beauty itself—that we can enjoy.[31] Spiritual formation thereby takes on its meaning in this trinitarian, christocentric context, a context that illuminates the rest of life as we are conformed and transformed into the image of the Son as a reminder and preparation for the eternal bliss which is ours in the Son—the beatific vision.

---

[30]Therefore, it is important not to dichotomize too starkly the relationship between signs and things, use and enjoyment. Augustine, for example, was not an ascetic who despised being happy on account of good food, drink, or conversation. As the translator Edmund Hill notes, "In telling us to use the world and not to enjoy it, he is telling us not to make enjoyment of it our goal, our one aim in life" (Augustine, *Teaching Christianity*, 111n4). So, the distinction ought to be considered a technical one, whereby Augustine implores Christians to use this world for its ultimate purpose of knowing and loving God. Food, for example, is not ultimately about pleasure in this world but rather about a greater and lasting pleasure found only in God.

[31]My goal here is not to describe and rehash the spiritual disciplines in detail. For helpful and holistic takes on the spiritual disciplines, see Richard J. Foster, *Celebration of Discipline: The Path to Spiritual Growth* (New York: HarperCollins, 1978); Donald S. Whitney, *Spiritual Disciplines for the Christian Life* (Colorado Springs: NavPress, 1991); and Evan B. Howard, *A Guide to Christian Spiritual Formation: How Scripture, Spirit, Community, and Mission Shape Our Souls* (Grand Rapids, MI: Baker Academic, 2018).

In summary, the beatific vision, and its attending consequences in spiritual formation, begins and ends by looking upon God in Jesus Christ by the Spirit. Our vision of God changes us, and this change allows us to perceive the inexorable connection between sign and thing, use and enjoyment. Spiritual formation, and the spiritual disciplines in particular, are theologically grounded in the beatific vision.

GLOBAL BENEFITS OF THE BEATIFIC VISION FOR SPIRITUAL FORMATION

The kind of approach suggested in this chapter provides several benefits for global evangelical theologies and ministries. I will mention four of the most pertinent ways that this connection between the beatific vision and spiritual formation is helpful to the global church.

First, the view as discussed in this chapter is an organic means to achieving a theocentric and christocentric view of theology and life. The vision reminds us that all created existence is about the triune God (who we have access to in Christ). All things come from God, and thus all things point back and return to God.[32] Moreover, the second person of the Trinity, the Son, Christ, is the one who provides access to knowing and loving God. The Son is the means by which we partake in the beatific vision (as we are brought up into the triune God through him), and thus he is also the means by which we are changed (as we are conformed into his pattern, the image of God, through the power of the Spirit). The distinctions, sign/thing and use/enjoyment, thus serve to guard the Christian against any kind of idolatry, whether in theology or practice, as they remind us of a theocentric and christocentric view of theology and life.[33]

Second, and closely related, spiritual formation happens, and only happens, when we are transformed into the image of God in Christ. There is thus a close connection between the vision and purity. As Jesus declared, "Blessed are the pure in heart, for they will see God" (Mt 5:8). This process of transformation moves slowly, as Augustine reminds us, as "a kind of walk,

---

[32]For a classic expression of this, see Thomas Aquinas, *Summa Theologiae*, Ia, q. 44. In fact, emanation and return summarizes the structure of his *Summa* as a whole.

[33]For a helpful and illuminating perspective here, see Michael Allen, *Grounded in Heaven: Recentering Christian Hope and Life on God* (Grand Rapids, MI: Eerdmans, 2018), 89-132.

a kind of voyage toward our home country," that is, God.[34] We receive the instructions, the guide so to speak, in Wisdom himself, who became human and adapted to the fallenness of the world, giving us an "example of how to live."[35] Christ, Wisdom incarnate, is thus the explanatory means by which to understand what purity is (through his life) and how we receive it (through faith in him by the power of the Spirit). Therefore, the longing for the beatific vision, the blessed sight, is also a reminder that we are not there yet. We are still sinful, in need of redemption, and thus still on our journey. This is a humble reminder that we, as we are bound to Christ, will one day receive our inheritance in full. He took on what was ours and made it his own, redeeming humanness as he did. To echo Augustine once more, he who is our home has also made himself into the way home for us.[36]

Third, a retrieval of the beatific vision in theology is an organic means to synthesize theology and spiritual formation. The vision and spiritual formation go hand in hand. One might understand the vision to be the means by which spiritual formation takes place, since we become what we behold. One might also see the vision as the end to which spiritual formation proceeds; namely, spiritual formation reminds us that things in this world are mere signs that remind us of our true and final destination. Spiritual formation is a slow process, frustrating at times, but the beatific vision reminds us that the destination is ahead, and it is even available to those pilgrims now by faith though not yet by sight. Augustine shows a particularly promising path for both Western and Eastern evangelicals to reconsider as a way forward of uniting theology and spiritual formation, two elements of Christianity that are often dichotomized or at least not properly integrated.

Fourth, and somewhat combining the former two points, the view discussed in this chapter helps to foster a more contemplative mindset in the practices of theology and life. By contemplation, I refer to the rapt attention to God in all things, an ecstatic enjoyment of the one who made all things.[37] Recovering focus on the beatific vision, which is the terminus of this

---

[34] Augustine, *Teaching Christianity* 1.10.10.

[35] Augustine, *Teaching Christianity* 1.11.11.

[36] Augustine, *Teaching Christianity* 1.11.11.

[37] See my chapter, "Gospel-Centered Contemplation? A Proposal," in *Embracing Contemplation: Reclaiming a Christian Spiritual Practice*, ed. John H. Coe and Kyle C. Strobel (Downers Grove, IL: IVP Academic, 2019), 185-202.

enjoyment, helps to foster a way to see the triune God in all things, as the terminus of all things, and the meaning behind and in front of all things.[38] The triune God renews the mind of a believer in such a way that she is able to see and enjoy the hand of God even in this life, even in the material things that God has made. Edwards explains that God "sometimes is pleased to remove the veil, to draw the curtain, and to give the saints sweet visions. Sometimes there is, as it were, a window opened in heaven, and Christ shows himself through the lattice."[39] The whole world becomes a lattice of signs that point believers back to the power and beauty of Christ. Indeed, sometimes God himself "manifest[s] himself to them."[40] In either case, Edwards notes that the result of this clearer vision in this world is a sweet repose, a rest in Christ, and a transformation into the image of him. There is certainly great advantage to developing a more contemplative mindset in theology and life.

Conclusion

Augustine begins and ends his theology with a dynamic desire to know God, to see him, and to be made like him. His constant reminder is, in the words of the author of Hebrews, without holiness "no one will see the Lord" (Heb 12:14).

This chapter has sought to constructively deploy some of his resources into order to show that the beatific vision is a necessary linchpin for spiritual formation. Augustine's distinctions, sign/thing and use/enjoyment, helpfully frame the spiritual life as a pilgrimage toward the vision, whereby one perceives the teleological connection of all of creation to God (and a perfected vision of God) as well as the means, form, and end of him who changes us—Father, Son, and Holy Spirit. The vision changes us relationally as we are in Christ and thus empowered by the Spirit; we are thereby able to perceive and appreciate the "thing" behind the "signs," that is, God in the midst of creation. This is the context of spiritual formation generally and the spiritual disciplines specifically. Therefore, a theology of the beatific vision

---

[38]For a helpful account along these lines, see Boersma, *Heavenly Participation* and Martin Bucer, *Instruction in Christian Love*, trans. Paul Traugott Fuhrmann (Eugene, OR: Wipf and Stock, 2008), 28.

[39]Edwards, *The Works of President Edwards*, 232.

[40]Edwards, *The Works of President Edwards*, 232.

helpfully integrates various strands of spiritual formation. The chapter then explored how this perspective benefits other global Christian theologies, as a retrieval of the vision fosters a powerful and dynamic account of spiritual formation that organically integrates theology and life.

The Christian life is about doing everything for God's glory; it is about using signs to enjoy God himself. The vision reminds us that all of life is a progression toward this vision, even as we experience the vision now. It is thus a reminder that, in our journeys now, while we use and experience signs in this world, and while we experience temporary and fleeting visions of beauty and power now, we remember that they signify God and anticipate the day when there will be perfect vision and enjoyment.

Study Questions

1. Using the definition in this chapter as a starting point, how do you personally imagine the beatific vision?

2. What particular things or activities are you drawn to in your life? What enraptures or captivates you? What do you find most beautiful on this side of heaven? (creation, art, stories, etc.)? What does this tell you about your spiritual longings?

3. How might you start to identify the work of the triune God through these things and/or activities? In what ways do they help you understand God or help you point back to Christ?

4. How does the anticipation of seeing God—one day perfectly and completely according to our capacities—affect how you think about and live your life now? In what ways does this perspective convict you? In what ways does it encourage you?

PART THREE

CHRIST, CONTEMPORARY CULTURE, and SPIRITUAL FORMATION

CHAPTER NINE

OLD TESTAMENT ETHICS AND SPIRITUAL FORMATION

S. MIN CHUN

THE TITLE OF THIS CHAPTER, "Old Testament Ethics and Spiritual Formation," includes a seemingly unusual combination that needs justification. First, how much, if at all, does the Old Testament contribute to spiritual formation? It is obvious to most people that the New Testament plays a critical role in Christian spiritual formation, with its focus on the person and character of Jesus Christ and its apostolic teachings on the transformative reality of the indwelling Holy Spirit. Many wonder, however, whether the Old Testament is relevant to Christian spiritual formation. This point can be illustrated, for example, by the fact that only a handful of references to the Old Testament are listed in the index of *Life in the Spirit: Spiritual Formation in Theological Perspective*, a book dedicated to the topic of spiritual formation.[1] An even more comprehensive work, the *Dictionary of Christian Spirituality*, contains only one chapter on the Old Testament.[2] Therefore, it is fair to say that in recent literature on the topic of spiritual formation, the Old Testament is undervalued.[3] Second, is it necessary to

---

[1]Jeffrey P. Greenman and George Kalantzis, ed., *Life in the Spirit: Spiritual Formation in Theological Perspective* (Downers Grove, IL: IVP Academic, 2010). I am particularly stunned by the fact that there is no reference to the creation account of Genesis in the index.

[2]Mark J. Boda, "Old Testament Foundations of Christian Spirituality," in *Dictionary of Christian Spirituality*, ed. James D. Smith III, Glen G. Scorgie, Simon Chan, and Gordon T. Smith (Grand Rapids, MI: Zondervan, 2011), 40-45.

[3]Christo Lombaard, a South African scholar, delineates ten possible reasons for a "diminutive role" of the Old Testament "in the practice and study of spirituality." See Christo Lombaard, "The

ask how Old Testament ethics is related to spiritual formation in the Old Testament? Is emphasizing ethics not a sort of legalism that works against the sanctifying power of the Spirit? Can we really talk about ethics in relation to spiritual formation?

In this chapter I will first try to clear the ground for discussing Old Testament ethics and spiritual formation by demonstrating the relationship between the Old Testament, ethics, and spiritual formation. Then, I will expound Leviticus 19, a biblical text that showcases the integration of ethics and spiritual formation in the Old Testament. Finally, I will propose that the spirituality of creation, everyday life, and the public sphere constitutes the crux of Old Testament spirituality that needs to be emphasized in contemporary Korean contexts and in the various cultural settings of global Christianity.

THE OLD TESTAMENT, ETHICS, AND SPIRITUAL FORMATION

The Old Testament and spiritual formation. Jeffrey Greenman defines spiritual formation theologically as "our continuing response to the reality of God's grace shaping us into the likeness of Jesus Christ, through the work of the Holy Spirit, in the community of faith, for the sake of the world."[4] As I ponder over this definition as an Old Testament scholar, I notice that it describes spiritual formation by using concepts that are primarily derived from the New Testament. The Old Testament, for example, does not have a direct witness to the incarnated Jesus Christ. Thus, if spiritual formation is about being shaped into the likeness of Jesus Christ, it could be argued that it is anachronistic to link it to the Old Testament.

Yet the simple observation that the New Testament cites and alludes to the Old Testament to construct its understanding of spiritual formation indicates the integral nature and the fundamental relevance of the Old Testament for a Christian theology of spiritual formation. For example, being "holy" is probably one of the most critical elements of Christian spiritual

---

Old Testament in Christian Spirituality: Perspectives on the Undervaluation of the Old Testament in Christian Spirituality," *Hervormde Teologiese Studies* 59 (2003): 433-50. See also Christo Lombaard, *The Old Testament and Christian Spirituality: Theoretical and Practical Essays from a South African Perspective*, International Voices in Biblical Studies 2 (Atlanta: Society of Biblical Literature, 2012).

[4]Jeffrey P. Greenman, "Spiritual Formation in Theological Perspective," in *Life in the Spirit*, 24.

formation. In order to lay a foundation for his exhortation for Christians to "be holy," the apostle Peter appeals to the Old Testament: "as he who called you is holy, be holy yourselves in all your conduct; for it is written, 'You shall be holy, for I am holy'" (1 Pet 1:15-16; cf. Lev 19:2). Furthermore, according to the author of Hebrews, Christ is "the exact imprint of God's very being" (Heb 1:3). Thus, being shaped into the likeness of Jesus Christ is theologically analogical to the more general concept of "imitating God."[5] For all its inherent limitations (humans are not God, after all, and there are certain divine actions that are not appropriate for humans to replicate)[6] the concept of *imitatio Dei* is a key feature that defines the lives of God's people (Gen 18:19; Deut 10:12-19).[7] From the perspective of biblical theology, therefore, knowing Jesus is knowing God, which is a core component of Old Testament spirituality.

What does it mean, however, to pursue Christlikeness through the Old Testament? Christopher Wright is helpful here. He argues that "we seek to be 'Christlike' by reflecting what we know to have been true of Jesus in the choices, actions and responses we have to make in our own lives."[8] As a Jew, the choices, actions, and responses of Jesus were based on his own understanding of and obedience to the teachings of the Old Testament. Wright explains:

> [The Old Testament words] are the words [Jesus] read. These were the stories he knew. These were the songs he sang. These were the depths of wisdom and revelation and prophecy that shaped his whole view of "life, the universe and everything." This is where he found his insights into the mind of his Father God. . . . In short, the deeper you go into understanding the Old Testament, the closer you come to the heart of Jesus.[9]

---

[5]Christopher J. H. Wright, *Old Testament Ethics for the People of God* (Leicester, UK: Inter-Varsity Press, 2004), 37-38.

[6]John Barton (*Ethics in Ancient Israel* [Oxford: Oxford University Press, 2014], 263-72) is one of many who suggest the possibility of *imitatio Dei* being one of the bases of Old Testament ethics. Cyril Rodd (*Glimpses of a Strange Land* [London: T&T Clark, 2001], 65-76) criticizes the concept of "imitation" as being anachronistic and too strong to fairly describe what is found in the Old Testament.

[7]Wright, *Old Testament Ethics*, 40; Christopher J. H. Wright, *The Mission of God: Unlocking the Bible's Grand Narrative* (Downers Grove, IL: IVP Academic, 2006), 362-65.

[8]Wright, *Old Testament Ethics*, 38, emphasis original.

[9]Christopher J. H. Wright, *Knowing Jesus Through the Old Testament* (Downers Grove, IL: IVP Academic, 1992), ix; cf. 182.

The spiritual life of Jesus, therefore, was formed as he read the Hebrew Scriptures and lived out their values (Lk 2:41-52). Thus, it is through both the Old and New Testaments that we pursue spiritual formation in the way of Jesus Christ.

Old Testament ethics and spiritual formation. Ethics and spiritual formation are analogous in that both are responses to God's gracious action. The moral teaching of the Old Testament starts from the fact that "God acts first and calls people to respond" and "ethics, then, becomes a matter of response and gratitude within a personal relationship."[10] This resonates with Greenman's theology of spiritual formation that is, in part, "our continuing response to the reality of God's grace."[11]

This ethical dimension of spirituality is, of course, clear in the New Testament. It is especially evident in texts that focus on believers' love of God and neighbor, such as, for example, 1 John 4:20-21 and Matthew 22:37-40 (cf. Mk 12:29-31; Lk 10:27). Here it cannot be overemphasized that the double love command of the New Testament is originally from the Old Testament. The command to love God is from Deuteronomy 6:5 and the command to love neighbors is from Leviticus 19:18. In addition to these, the ethical dimension of spirituality is clearly presented in Old Testament texts that focus on the transformational reality of "knowing God." Passages such as Jeremiah 9:24 (23)[12], 22:13-17, and Hosea 6:6 form the basis of the Old Testament testimony to this concept. Jeremiah 22:16 says, "He [Josiah] judged the cause of the poor and needy; then it was well. Is not this to know me [God] (Hb. *da'at 'oti*)?" Jeremiah criticizes the injustice done by Jehoiakim and contrasts him with Josiah, his father. Unlike Jehoiakim, Josiah reigned with a concern for the poor and the needy, and this concern was evidence that he knew God.

Knowing God is a component of authentic Old Testament spirituality, and judging the cause of the poor and needy is a particularly salient component to authentic Old Testament ethics. Ethical actions, therefore, are the evidence of authentic spirituality. In the Old Testament, God himself "act[s] with steadfast love, justice, and righteousness in the earth," and he

---

[10]Wright, *Old Testament Ethics*, 25.
[11]Greenman, "Spiritual Formation in Theological Perspective," 24.
[12]The verse in the parentheses is that of the MT.

delights in these things. Furthermore, the knowledge of this kind of God—namely, a loving, just, and righteous God—is the basis of Israel's boast (Jer 9:24[23]). Furthermore, Hosea 6:6 claims that God desires the "knowledge of God"—true spirituality—and not mere burnt offerings or acts of empty religious observance. What makes this verse critical to the study of Old Testament spirituality is the meaning implied by the parallelism observed in the text.

> For I desire steadfast love (Hb. *ḥesed*) and not sacrifice,
> the knowledge of God (Hb. *da'at 'elohim*) rather than burnt offerings
> (Hos 6:6).

Here "steadfast love" (Hb. *ḥesed*) is paralleled with "the knowledge of God" and "sacrifice" with "burnt offerings." The pairing of "sacrifice" with "burnt offerings" is usual, but that of "steadfast love" with "the knowledge of God" invites careful reading. The Hebrew term *ḥesed* has broad semantic meanings in terms of its beneficiary. It can be directed from believers toward God and also toward other human beings. When *ḥesed* is used of other human beings, it refers to "faithfulness in human relationships" or to "humane duty/responsibility/obligation applied to the relationships between the spouses, between parents and children, between relatives, between friends, between guest and host, between senior and junior."[13] In short, *ḥesed* is an ethical virtue. Thus, we can see here, again, the strong link between ethics ("steadfast love," *ḥesed*) and spirituality ("knowledge of God," *da'at 'elohim*). Spirituality without ethics is delusional; spiritual formation without ethical formation is void (cf. Is 1:3, 10-17).

Having clarified the relationship between Old Testament ethics and spiritual formation, now I will expound Leviticus 19, the text from which the New Testament command to love one's neighbor and the exhortation to "be holy" are derived. If the love of neighbor signifies the horizontal aspect of the Christian life, the call to holiness signifies its vertical aspect. According to Leviticus 19—in both its own Old Testament context and in its New Testament reception—the vertical and horizontal aspects need to be integrated in order to achieve an authentically biblical account of spiritual formation.

---

[13]Jun Hee Cha, *The Spirituality of the Twelve Prophets* (Seoul: Holy Wave Plus, 2014), 20-21. My translation of the Korean original.

Leviticus 19 provides a comprehensive picture of transformative holistic holiness in which spirituality is integrated with ethics.

HOLINESS AS THE INTEGRATION OF SPIRITUALITY
AND ETHICS IN LEVITICUS 19

Holiness is one of the most commonly misunderstood themes in relation to spiritual formation. The most common misunderstanding is to think of it as "being extra specifically religious."[14] In Leviticus 19, however, holiness is not simply being religious but rather refers to an ethical life lived out with one's neighbors. Holiness is the key virtue of spiritual formation, and it is easy to lose sight of this in the middle of the rather detailed exposition below. Therefore, as we unpack this theme, the reader should always keep in mind that this entire discussion is framed around the topic of holiness as it relates to spiritual formation.[15]

An invitation to holistic holiness. In verses 1-2a, we see the speaker and the addressee of the passage: the LORD and the whole Israelite community. The range of the addressees demonstrates that holiness matters not only to the priestly class but also to the entire community. Holiness is holistic in terms of the range of people to which it applies and the way it integrates ethics and spirituality. Furthermore, the holistic nature of holiness can be seen in the fact that it includes theological, social, and economic aspects in Leviticus 19.

Verses 3-4 display the multiple aspects of holiness. In verse 3a, holiness governs the relationship to one's parents, that is, the *social aspect* of holiness, while sabbath keeping relates to the *economic aspect* of holiness in verse 3b.[16] The sabbath can be considered economic because it concerns such topics as land, human and animal labor, and the relationship between work and rest (Ex 20:10; 34:21). A further aspect of holiness, namely the *theological aspect*, is noted in the prohibition of idolatry (v. 4a). These three aspects of

---

[14]Christopher J. H. Wright, *Knowing Jesus Through the Old Testament*, 200.

[15]The earlier versions of this section are found in S. Min Chun, *Worldview Preaching* (Seoul: Scripture Union Korea, 2018) and "Down-to-Earth Holiness: An Ethical Interpretation of Leviticus 19," *Gospel and Context* 111 (March 2001): 90-104. See also Keunjoo Kim, *Public Nature of the Gospel* (Paju: Viator, 2017) on "Holy Life," 200-229. All works in this note are in Korean.

[16]Sabbath keeping also has a theological aspect, since it relates to creation and redemption (Ex 20:11; Deut 5:15).

holiness—the social, economic, and theological aspects—are packed into two verses (Lev 19:3-4).

Each command, however, demonstrates more than one layer or aspect of holiness. Sabbath keeping is a notable example. While the keeping of the sabbath is itself an economic matter, the rationale behind the observance of this command is theological. Furthermore, the social aspect of holiness, namely, revering one's parents, has theological tenor. The Hebrew verb translated as "revere," *yr'*, appears four times in Leviticus 19 (vv. 3, 14, 30, and 32). The verb used in the Decalogue, however, is *kbd*. Given the fact that the other three appearances of the verb *yr'* in Leviticus 19 are related to fearing God or revering his sanctuary, one might wonder whether the choice of the verb *yr'* rather than *kbd* in Leviticus 19 is deliberate in order to put theological weight on the act of revering parents.[17] Idolatry, which is the next vice mentioned in Leviticus 19:4, likewise has economic as well as theological and social aspects. At the surface level, the motivation for idolatry is economic on many occasions. The import of the Baal cult for agricultural affluence is a typical example of this phenomenon. Yet the sin of idolatry clearly has deep theological and social implications as well.

Moreover, the order of the commands in verses 3-4 is worth noting. The three commands in Leviticus 19:3-4—revering parents, observing the sabbath, and avoiding idolatry—are respectively the fifth, fourth, and second commandments of the Decalogue. The order of their appearance is reversed in Leviticus 19.[18] This flipped order may indicate that every aspect of holiness carries the same theological weight and significance. The economic and social aspects of these commandments—the aspects that relate to everyday life—are just as important as the theological aspects.

Thus, the pursuit of holiness in Leviticus is never a purely religious or individual affair. The pursuit of holiness has a holistic impact, moving beyond the individualistic pursuit of personal character formation to result in a more comprehensive and integrated communal, social, and economic effect. It is this multivalent reality, I propose, that provides the framework

---

[17]This is the only occasion the verb *yr'* takes human beings as its object. A. Marx, *Lévitique 17-27* (Genève: Labor et Fides, 2011), 82, recited from Sun-Jong Kim, *Theology and Ethics of the Holiness Code in Leviticus* (Seoul: Christian Literature Center, 2018), 217, in Korean.

[18]This numbering follows the Reformed tradition.

for New Testament thinking about spiritual formation. Without under-standing the Old Testament framework for holistic holiness, however, we run the risk of overindividualizing spiritual formation into a series of sanc-tification solo projects devoid of its intended social and communal impact. The Old Testament, therefore, and Leviticus in particular, provides a "norming norm" to the often New Testament–centric definitions of Christian spirituality thereby providing us with a *fully biblical* understanding of spiritual formation.

Each verse in this section is sealed by the phrase, "I the LORD your God am holy" (v. 2) or "I am the LORD your God" (vv. 3, 4b). Wherever these phrases appear afterwards, they function to remind the reader of the holistic nature of holiness in Leviticus 19. Now we will examine three aspects of holiness respectively: namely, the theological, social, and economic aspects of holiness.

Theological aspects of holiness. The theological aspects of holiness can be perceived from the law about fellowship offerings (vv. 5-8), the prohi-bition of inappropriate uses of God's name (v. 12), the exhortation to fear God (vv. 14b, 32b), and the admonition to keep the sabbath and revere the sanctuary (v. 30). It is helpful to begin with the admonition of sabbath keeping because this admonition is also found in the opening paragraph of Leviticus 19. Furthermore, it is grounded on two key foundational ele-ments of Old Testament theology and ethics, namely creation and re-demption. By keeping the sabbath, Israelites were to remember God's creation and redemption. This is a key ethical thrust in many exhortations in the Old Testament.[19]

While the primary reasons for sabbath keeping are theological, at the same time it is a confession of God's economic lordship. It is a confession that God—not human labor—is the source of economic well-being (cf. e.g., the manna story in Ex 16:13-30). The literary context of sabbath keeping in verses 29-30 is likewise economic. Relatedly, the prohibition

---

[19]The theme of the creation of humanity in the image of God functions as the foundation for the equal treatment of all human beings. This feature is especially salient in the Wisdom literature. For example, we read in Proverbs 14:31, "Those who oppress the poor insult their Maker, but those who are kind to the needy honor him" (cf. Prov 22:2). Likewise, in his final defense Job appeals to God, basing his entreaty on the fact that he has respected his slaves as fellow human beings whom God created (Job 31:13-15).

against making one's daughter a "prostitute" (v. 29) has economic as well as social and theological facets. This is particularly evident when it is understood that the term *prostitute* refers specifically to cultic prostitutes for fertility. Thus, a paraphrase of verses 29-30 could be the following: "Do not conspire to gain economic fertility in an apostate way following your surrounding culture; rather, keep it in your mind that I, the LORD, am your true economic provider." The command to keep the sabbath, therefore, demonstrates the multifaceted holistic nature of holiness in the Old Testament.

In like manner, while the regulation for the "sacrifice of well-being" in verses 5-8 is theological, its connection to other aspects of holiness can also be demonstrated. Most notably, the literary structure of verses 5-8 and 9-10 confirms the relationship between the theological and economic elements at play in regard to the sacrifice. While these two sets of verses may seem to deal with different matters, with verses 5-8 focusing on cultic matter and verses 9-10 focusing on economic matters, they are actually a part of the same singular literary unit. There is no "paragraph division mark" after verse 8.[20] Christopher Wright explains this connection between the two regulations in terms of the common theme of generous sharing.[21]

The theological aspect of holiness in Leviticus 19 never stands alone.[22] It always relates to other aspects of holiness. This holistic nature of holiness explains the dynamics between cultic rituals and everyday life. Cultic rituals enable people to live out the economic and social realities of their everyday life in ways that accord with and cultivate authentic transformative holiness. The theological aspect of holiness begins through a relationship with God and is then embodied in the practical, social, and economic behaviors which characterize that relationship, leading naturally to loving engagement with one's neighbors.

Social aspects of holiness. The social aspects of holiness can be observed in the exhortations to respect and care for the weak (vv. 14a, 32-24) and to be a good neighbor (vv. 15-18), the prohibition against mixed breeding

---

[20]Walter C. Kaiser Jr., *Toward Old Testament Ethics* (Grand Rapids, MI: Zondervan Academic, 1983), 119. See also Gordon J. Wenham, *The Book of Leviticus*, NICOT (Grand Rapids, MI: Eerdmans, 1979), 263.

[21]Christopher J. H. Wright, *Leviticus*, NBC (Downers Grove, IL: InterVarsity, 1994), 147.

[22]Janzen explains that the prophets criticized the self-existing tendency of the cultic sphere. Waldemar Janzen, *Old Testament Ethics* (Louisville, KY: Westminster John Knox, 1993), 160-63.

(v. 19), the law dealing with the case of sexual assault to the betrothed slave girl (vv. 20-22), and the prohibition against pagan customs (vv. 26-31).

The key organizing idea to the social aspects of holiness is sanctification in the sense of "being different" from one's surroundings. In articulating this idea, it is helpful to begin with the exposition of the prohibition against mixed breeding in Leviticus 19:19. Along with the dietary laws on clean and unclean animals, this prohibition reflected the distinctiveness of Israel in its ordinary life from the surrounding culture. As Israelites preserved the differences in the created world that defined them as a people and contributed to their holy identity, they were reminded that they also had to preserve this distinctiveness.[23] The various prohibitions in verses 26-31 function to keep Israel from assimilating to the surrounding cultures.[24] The command of sabbath keeping is placed along with these prohibitions (v. 30). The theological rationale for sabbath keeping, rooted as it is in God's creation and redemption, may explain this placement. Redemption makes Israel "different," and such a difference is remembered in a transformative way by upholding and preserving the distinctions that God created and commanded for Israel. In this way, the theological rationale of creation and redemption works behind the social aspect of the prohibitions as well.

The law regarding sexual assault to a betrothed slave girl (v. 19) is enacted on the principle of qualified tolerance.[25] This law tolerates slavery, but it is qualified: the law protects the slave girl from being condemned for adulterous acts that occur as a result of forced and exploitative sexual assaults. Qualified tolerance leads to a transition from *preservation/separation* (passive holiness, as it were) to *transformation* (active holiness). While slavery existed in Israel, its institution was different from other nations in that it was qualified by a concern for neighbors as equal human beings made in the image of God.

In addition to people with disabilities and the elderly, Israel was exhorted to care for and respect another group who needed protection (v. 14 and v. 32),

---

[23]Gordon J. Wenham, "The Theology of Unclean Food," *Evangelical Quarterly* 53 (1981): 6-15; cf. Chun, *Worldview Preaching*.

[24]Baruch A. Levine, *Leviticus* (New York: Jewish Publication Society, 1989), 132; Wenham, *Leviticus*, 272.

[25]Wright, *Old Testament Ethics*, 329-37.

namely the aliens (*ger*) who did not possess land (vv. 33-34). Their living circumstances mostly depended on how the indigenous people of the land treated them (cf. Ex 1:8). Thus, Israelites, knowing what it means to be aliens (Deut 23:9), were exhorted to love sojourners and resident aliens as themselves, treating them equally as natives of Israel. In doing so, Israel reflected God's gracious attitude toward the alien, of which they themselves had been beneficiaries (Deut 10:18). Other laws in the Torah illustrate how to love the alien and treat them as the native-born. For example, aliens were supposed to benefit from the sacrificial system (Num 15:15-16, 26) and from the annual festivals (Deut 16:11, 14). They were also not to be mistreated in the economic sphere (Deut 24:14-15) or in judicial procedures (Deut 24:17; 27:19). These regulations in other Old Testament texts are the combination of the exhortations in Leviticus 19 (mainly vv. 13, 15, and 34).[26]

The love command in verse 34 ("you shall love *the alien* as yourself") expands the scope of the love command in verse 18 ("you shall love *your neighbor* as yourself"), which is the climax of an exposition on what it means to be a good neighbor (vv. 11-18).[27] Being a good neighbor includes being honest (vv. 11-12), not exploiting of the weak (vv. 13-14), doing justice in court (vv. 15-16), and loving others (vv. 17-18).[28] In this context, the love command in verse 18 can be understood in social terms. While the Old Testament is concerned for the heart as well as actions (v. 17; cf. Deut 10:16), love toward one's neighbor in verse 18 is not "a matter of private feeling or inter-personal generosity only, but of practical social ethics in the public sphere, including the legal process."[29] Loving one's neighbor is no less than active holiness in the social sphere. Such socially active expressions of love are found not only in the social aspects of holiness but also in the economic aspects of holiness.

Economic aspects of holiness. The economic facet of holiness can be perceived in the laws on gleaning (vv. 9-10), the admonition about stealing and lying (vv. 11-12), the exhortation on timely payment of wages (v. 13), the regulation on managing an orchard (vv. 23-25), the prohibition against

---

[26]The combination of v. 13 and v. 34 results in Deuteronomy 24:14-15; v. 15 and v. 34 results in Deuteronomy 24:17; 27:19.

[27]Wenham, *Leviticus*, 267.

[28]Wenham, *Leviticus*, 267-69.

[29]Wright, *Leviticus*, 148.

making one's own daughter a "prostitute" (v. 29), and the command for commercial integrity (vv. 35-36).

The regulation on how to manage an orchard in verses 23-25 can be a good starting point for examining the economic dimensions of holiness. This regulation is God's claim on the ownership of the land and its produce.[30] A similar law can be found in the Law of Hammurabi 60, which seems to be about the share of produce to the landlord.[31] In the Law of Hammurabi, the gardener cannot take fruits for himself until the fifth year since the field was given from a seignior. In the fifth year, he can share the produce with the owner of the field. The reason that the gardener cannot take the fruit until the fifth year is that he is not the owner of the field. The law in Leviticus 19 claims the same principle: God is the owner. As mentioned earlier, the term "prostitute" in verse 29 likely refers to a fertility cult functionary through whom economic affluence could be invoked.[32] If that is the case, this prohibition is grounded on the fact that God is the only source of wealth. The admonition of keeping the sabbath (v. 30) and the promise of a produce increase (v. 25) also emphasizes the same principle: God is the only true economic provider. By giving up some produce, which is apparently the outcome of one's labor, Israel can live according to the economic aspect of holiness.

True worship is not just a matter of sacrifice in form. Deep acknowledgment of God's true ownership calls for stewardship accompanied by a sincere spirit of sharing. Legislation on gleaning in verses 9-10 immediately follows the regulation for the "sacrifice of well-being" in verses 5-8 without any literary division marker. This legislation was one of the programs to help the poor in Israel.[33] It implies that showing personal charity is not sufficient. The societal dimension should also be considered. Norbert Lohfink suggests that verse 13 was a part of the "poverty prevention system" of Israel.[34] Deuteronomy 24:14-15 embodies the same spirit as Leviticus 19:13. It provides the reason for the immediate pay of wages to laborers: "they are poor and

[30]Wenham, *Leviticus,* 271.
[31]James Bennett Pritchard, *The Ancient Near Eastern Texts* (Princeton, NJ: Princeton University Press, 1969), 169.
[32]Beatrice A. Brooks, "Fertility Cult Functionaries in the Old Testament," *Journal of Biblical Literature* 60 (1941): 227-53, esp. 236-39.
[33]John D. Mason, "Biblical Teaching and Assisting the Poor," *Transformation* 4, no. 2 (1987): 1-14.
[34]Norbert Lohfink, SJ, "Poverty in the Laws of the Ancient Near East and of the Bible," *Theological Studies* 52 (1991): 34-50. Lohfink quotes Deuteronomy 24:14-15 instead of Leviticus 19:13.

their livelihood depends on them." If the laborers are not given their daily wages, they have nothing with which to support their families that day. If one acknowledges the stewardship of what is given by God, he or she should prevent such a miserable state from coming upon a laborer. This is another economic implication and aspect of holistic holiness.

Likewise, the commercial integrity commanded in verses 35-36 must also be regarded as an example of economic holiness. Two Hebrew terms in these verses illuminate the importance of commercial and economic integrity for a theology of holiness and spiritual formation, namely *ṣedeq* (righteousness) and *toʻebah* (abomination). The latter, in particular, is used to refer to sexual perversion and idolatry. The measures used for Israel's commerce are to be "righteous," and thus dishonest trade is thought to be just as evil as idolatry; it is an "abomination" to God (Deut 25:13-16). This principle can be seen elsewhere in the Old Testament, such as when the prophet Micah criticizes corrupt meddling with measures in commercial transactions (Mic 6:10-11; cf. Amos 8:5).

Summary. Leviticus 19 presents a view of down-to-earth holiness that is related to all areas of everyday life, whether personal or public. It is important to understand that all of the elements covered in Leviticus 19—no matter how secular they may seem—are focused on expounding the Old Testament approach to holiness. One also must notice that the laws in Leviticus 19 require much more than mere *personal charity*. They attempt to establish a *public structure of holiness* in which the weak of society are protected. Thus, if one regards holiness as a key component of spiritual formation, then spiritual formation that is faithful to Leviticus 19 and to the Old Testament must include social and economic—as well as personal— transformation. Holiness, as it is presented in Leviticus 19, involves the integration of spirituality and ethics in the Christian life; holiness is holistic.

THE SPIRITUALITY OF CREATION, EVERYDAY LIFE, AND THE PUBLIC SPHERE IN A KOREAN CONTEXT

Now, I propose that spiritual formation that is integrated with Old Testament ethics should emphasize a spirituality of creation, everyday life, and the public sphere. I make this proposal with a Korean context especially in mind, but I trust that it can be meaningfully applied in other global evangelical contexts.

Spirituality of creation. A spirituality of creation affirms the goodness of
the created world (including the physical realm) because God created the
whole world and pronounced it to be "very good" (Gen 1:31). This is the
starting point of Old Testament spirituality and the foundation for the spirituality of everyday life.[35] The spirituality of creation acknowledges that all
human beings are created equally in the image of God. Thus, human dignity
should be sincerely appreciated and firmly protected regardless of a person's
background without any discrimination.

While the idea that creation is the foundation of Old Testament spirituality might seem to be obvious, the popular perception of Old Testament
spirituality suggests that this might not be the case. The themes of creation-
fall-redemption are often suggested as shorthand for the biblical drama.
Among the three themes, many Korean Christians give the greatest emphasis to the fall (and, subsequently, to redemption as its antidote) as the key
concept that provides the foundation for their understanding of Christian
spirituality. When I question Korean Christians about human nature, the
most common response—if not the only response—I receive focuses on
sinfulness of all human beings. While this is surely a biblical response, it
should be secondary to the fact that human beings are created in the image
of God and remain in God's image even after the fall. It is worth noting, for
example, that in Genesis 9:6, a postfall passage, the reality of the nature of
humanity created in the image of God is still intact. In the New Testament,
James 3:9 is a good indication that fallen humans remain in the image of
God.[36] As to a healthy, biblical dynamic between creation and the fall,
Timothy Keller's comment is poignant: "The doctrine of sin means that as
believers we are never as good as our right worldview should make us. At
the same time, the doctrine of our creation in the image of God, and an
understanding of common grace, remind us that nonbelievers are never as
flawed as their false worldview should make them."[37]

---

[35]Cf. Dennis P. Hollinger, "Creation: The Starting Point of an Ecclesial Ethic," in *Ecclesia and Ethics:
Moral Formation and the Church*, ed. E. Allen Johns III et al. (London: Bloomsbury, 2016), 3.

[36]As to the view that the divine image is not damaged even after the fall, see John F. Kilner, "Humanity in God's Image: Is the Image Really Damaged?" *Journal of the Evangelical Theological
Society* 53, no. 3 (2010): 601-17.

[37]Timothy Keller, *Center Church: Doing Balanced, Gospel-Centered Ministry in Your City* (Grand
Rapids, MI: Zondervan, 2012), 109.

Despite Keller's warning, a preoccupation with the fall that leads to an emphasis on the fallen state of the world and humanity has shaped the spirituality of Korean Christianity to a large extent. As a result, Korean Christians can easily default to a condemning, if not demonizing, attitude toward nonbelievers. In this context, spiritual formation anchored in creation spirituality should be able to provide a necessary theological corrective to assist Christians in developing a humble and gentle attitude toward nonbelievers who are also created in God's image (cf. 1 Pet 3:16).

An overly negative perspective on the world, however, creates and reinforces various types of sub-biblical dichotomies such as the dichotomies between the following: the sacred and the secular, the church and the world, the clergy and the laity, ministry and work, and Sunday and the other six days. A spirituality of everyday life is the remedy for such theologically unsound and biblically deficient dichotomies.

Spirituality of everyday life. The spirituality of creation expands to the spirituality of everyday life. Every area of life is relevant to Christian spirituality because all of creation is, figuratively speaking, touched by the good hands of the Creator God. We have already seen the importance of the spirituality of everyday life from Leviticus 19. The contexts of everyday life in which holiness was applied included the agricultural field (vv. 9-10), the labor market (v. 13), the judicial court (v. 15), animal breeding and textile work (v. 19), sexual relations (v. 20-22), orchards (vv. 23-25), and the marketplace (vv. 35-36).[38] According to the Old Testament, there is no area of life that is inconsequential to the radical pursuit of holistic holiness.

In opposition to this spirituality of everyday life is "the spirituality of Sunday." For many, the clergyperson who ministers on Sunday at church is regarded as spiritually superior to the laity who works in the world during the other six days. Against this backdrop, the spirituality of everyday life can be particularly encouraging to believers who may feel that they are only second-tier Christians because their vocations and career fields are not related to the ministries that take place on "Sunday."

The spirituality of everyday life is based on creation, but it is also illuminated by the eschatological visions of the prophets. In Ezekiel 48, a paradigm

---

[38]Kim, *Public Nature of the Gospel,* 206.

shift occurs in which the phrase signifying the divine presence, "The LORD is there" (*'adonay šammah*, 48:35), no longer refers to the temple (the usual place where one expects the divine presence) but to the city. The city is the nonreligious dwelling place of the workers who cultivate certain parts of the portion that is set apart (48:8). One can easily misconceive that the religious arena represented by the temple is the only area for the divine presence. Ezekiel, however, proclaims that the city, located in a place for the "ordinary use" (48:15), is the place that deserves the name "The LORD is there."[39] This is in line with Zechariah's vision in 14:20-21, which proclaims, "On that day there shall be inscribed on the bells of the horses, 'Holy to the Lord' . . . and every cooking pot in Jerusalem and Judah shall be sacred to the Lord of hosts." At the eschaton that the prophets announced, the border between "the sacred" and "the secular/ordinary" will vanish, and Christians are proleptically fore-living that eschatological reality here and now by the power of the Spirit.

Spirituality of the public sphere. The last aspect of Old Testament spirituality that is particularly relevant to current Korean Christianity is the spirituality of public sphere. Holiness is, for example, required in the contexts of the judicial court and the marketplace, and Leviticus 19 makes a notable case for this proposition (v. 15 and vv. 35-36). The spirituality of the public sphere is interested in seeking the common good of society where both believers and nonbelievers live together.[40] Appreciating the common humanity shared by the members of society is a key foundation for this aspect of Christian spirituality and spiritual formation. In this respect, the spirituality of creation is the foundation of the spirituality of the public sphere.

Having said that, one might wonder whether the common good can be pursued with nonbelievers given the catastrophic results of the fall. As to this question, Albert Wolters's explanation on the continuing power of creation is worth pondering:

> Outside of redemption . . . the devastating effects of sin in creation are also restrained and counteracted. . . . [God] maintains his creation in the face of all the forces of destruction. . . . Creation is like a leash that keeps a vicious dog in check. . . . It is because of the leash that fallen man [sic] is still man [sic],

---

[39]For a full exposition of Ezekiel 47-48, see Chun, *Worldview Preaching*, 217-26.
[40]SukWhan Sung, *Public Theology and Korean Society: Religious Discourse and Public Role of Church in a Post-Secular Society* (Seoul: New Wave Plus, 2019), 8, in Korean.

that crooked business is still business, that atheistic culture is still culture, and that humanistic insights are still genuine insights.[41]

Although nonbelievers may not experience the salvific blessing of the redemptive work of Christ, "the leash of creation" maintains them, although fallen, as still human. They are still the bearers of the divine image and they benefit from the common grace bestowed by the Spirit. Thus, the pursuit of the common good is possible.

The Wisdom literature in the Old Testament also implies that seeking the common good with nonbelievers is possible. As Christopher Wright explains,

> The wise in Israel found it possible to affirm many values and teachings that they found in noncovenant nations. . . . One reason for this must be the strong creational assumption that Israel made about the whole world and all humanity. The wisdom of the Creator is to be found in all the earth, and all human beings are made in his image. . . . Israel had no monopoly on all things wise and good and true. Neither, of course, have Christians.[42]

The spirituality of the public sphere is particularly relevant to contemporary Korean Christianity. For years, the Korean church has been known for its colossal growth. Over recent decades, however, the church has experienced a crisis that still continues today. Outwardly, the number of Christians has been dropping and the declining number of churchgoing teens is significant.[43] More important, the loss of the social credibility of the Korean church among nonbelievers has been drastic.[44] This is a result of the church operating within its own otherworldly mindset that tends to ignore common sense. This phenomenon is, perhaps, most clearly evident in the church's attempts to excuse itself for its egregious moral failures, including various sexual scandals and instances of financial corruption which are unacceptable—even unimaginable—in eyes of nonbelievers.[45] One critical reason for this phenomenon is the near absence of the spirituality of public sphere in Korean approaches to Christian spirituality and spiritual

---

[41] Albert Wolters, *Creation Regained: Biblical Basics for a Reformational Worldview*, 2nd ed. (Grand Rapids, MI: Eerdmans, 2005), 60.

[42] Wright, *The Mission of God*, 445-46.

[43] Sung-Bihn Yim, *Public Theology for Korean Church and Society* (Seoul: PUTS Press, 2017), 113-15, in Korean.

[44] Yim, *Public Theology*, 119.

[45] Jongwon Choi, *From Text to Context* (Paju: Viator, 2019), 83, in Korean.

formation. Korean Christians have learned too little about the public nature of their faith to be good citizens in society. Given this situation, spiritual formation that takes seriously the public nature of the Christian faith is required in order for the Korean church to recover its vocation to work for the shalom of others (cf. Jer 29:4-7).[46]

CONCLUSION

How is ethics related to spiritual formation in the Old Testament? First, the Old Testament is the channel, as it were, through which we come to learn Jesus' values and thus become Christlike. The better our understanding of the Old Testament, the more closely to Jesus' heart and mind we come. Second, Old Testament ethics is the grateful response of believers to the prevenient acts of God's grace. And, this is analogous to the definition of spiritual formation. Leviticus 19 is a critical chapter that showcases that holiness is not achieved by pursuing a life of individualistic, otherworldly religious activity but by cultivating a down-to-earth spirituality that is integrated with biblical ethics. The "knowing God" passages in the Old Testament (such as Jer 22:13-17) proclaim that authentic spirituality must be integrated with ethics.

I proposed that the spirituality of creation, everyday life, and the public sphere are particularly urgent and relevant to contemporary Korean Christianity. The spirituality of creation affirms: (1) the goodness of the whole creation, and (2) the common dignity of all human beings. This good creation is the basis for the spirituality of everyday life. There is no spiritual hierarchy between the sacred and the secular. Members of the clergy who minister on Sundays at church are not spiritually superior to the laity who work in the world during the other six days. "The LORD is There" (Ezek 48:35) is not the name of the temple but the name of the city where the "ordinary" workers dwell. This signifies that the divine presence dwells with ordinary people amid the seemingly ordinary affairs of everyday life, and that it is *precisely there* that spiritual formation occurs. The common dignity of human beings as made in the image of God is still maintained by "the leash of creation" that is stronger than the effects of the fall. This makes it possible

---

[46]Richard J. Mouw, *Uncommon Decency: Christian Civility in an Uncivil World*, 2nd ed. (Downers Grove, IL: InterVarsity, 2010), 70.

for believers to pursue the common good with nonbelievers in society. This is the spirituality of public sphere. The Wisdom literature of the Old Testament likewise testifies to the fact that nations other than Israel have wisdom to contribute to the common good. In this respect, developing the virtue of convicted civility should be an important aspect of spiritual formation. This is the direction that spiritual formation inspired by the Old Testament must take, especially given the current issues being experienced by Korean Christians and likely across the global Christian church in some form or other.

To conclude, when we take the Old Testament seriously, the horizon of spiritual formation is rightly broadened. Spirituality is about the whole creation. The arena of spiritual formation is not only the church on Sunday, nor merely in our personal quest for spiritual health and growth within the confines of our own hearts, but also in the world on the weekdays. The world is a public sphere where Christians live with their non-Christian neighbors pursuing the common good together. Old Testament ethics uniquely elucidates the importance of these features for a fully integrated and holistic approach to spiritual formation.

STUDY QUESTIONS

1. What role do you see for the Old Testament in informing Christian ethics and spiritual formation? Can you make connections between them? If so, how? If not, why not?

2. In Jeremiah 22:13-17, the Scriptures attest that knowing God is directly related to caring for the weak in society. Why do you think that is the case? Is this a part of your own experience of God and spiritual formation?

3. What is your understanding of holiness? How is it similar to or different from the holistic holiness that Leviticus 19 presents?

4. Which aspect of spirituality among the spiritualities of creation, everyday life, and public sphere, is most relevant or urgent in your context? Why?

5. Can you think of some concrete actions or virtues that embody the three spiritualities mentioned above?

CHAPTER TEN

SECOND PETER, POSTMODERNITY, AND SPIRITUAL FORMATION

LE CHIH HSIEH

WHAT IS SPIRITUAL FORMATION?

In Taiwan, where I live, when Christians talk about spiritual formation, they
think of reading Scripture, going to church, fasting, and praying. Spiritual
formation refers to what happens behind closed doors and in the darkness
(Mt 4:6). It has to do with the intimate and intense relationship between God
and the individual human being, distanced from other relationships and
mundane concerns. However, is this what the Bible and the Christian tradition teach about spiritual formation?

If spiritual formation were indeed what I have just described, then Jesus
during his earthly ministry would have done a better job isolating himself
in remote deserts, hiding in caves, or climbing up towers in order to
concentrate day and night on prayer and Scripture reading. Though Jesus
did occasionally seclude himself in remote places for prayer, hiding behind
doors was not primarily what he did during his stay in the land of Israel. So,
again, the question is: what is spiritual formation?

We can begin by asking what "spirit" means when we speak of spiritual
formation. In the history of Christianity, Christians have often been lured
by the sirens of Gnosticism and have tended to be attracted to the doctrines
of dualism, deprecating the body as filthy and honoring the soul, or whatever
is left remaining after the body decays, as heavenly, pure, and glorious.[1]

---

[1]E. R. Dodds, *Pagan and Christian in an Age of Anxiety: Some Aspects of Religious Experience
from Marcus Aurelius to Constantine* (Cambridge: Cambridge University Press, 1965).

However, the Bible suggests a different point of view. At both the beginning and the end of this world the Bible speaks of the body. In Genesis, God breathes into the clay, and the clay becomes human.[2] Also, the redeemed human being is not without a body (1 Cor 15).

For this reason, spiritual formation is not to be restricted to the training or the development of the soul but involves the body, and the world that nourishes the body. Spiritual formation refers to a way of life that forms and transforms the person as a whole, embracing the various dimensions of human life, including a person's relationship with God, with the world, with others, and with themselves. Spiritual formation is, in essence, the process of becoming a human being—becoming what God intended us to become. Spiritual formation is, in essence, the process of becoming what God intended us to become.

Spiritual formation defined as human flourishing connects the biblical view of spiritual formation with the eudemonistic ethics of the classical world.[3] By the classical world, I refer not only to the Western world but also to the Eastern and Chinese philosophical traditions. Between the Bible and eudaimonic ethics, there are many similarities. Both are deeply concerned with the full development of the human being. Yet to the questions of what constitutes a human being and how one may achieve and embody the ideal human being, the Bible and the *eudaimonists* give different and sometimes opposing answers.

In the Western tradition, Aristotle's idea of *eudaimonia* plays an important role. Aristotle said that to achieve *eudaimonia* one must obtain both internal and external goods.[4] External goods include good birth, good looks, health, and so on. Internal goods refer to the excellent performance of one's

---

However, Williams notes that Gnostics also had some positive things to say about the body. Nevertheless, he does not overturn the conclusion that the material body is viewed as negative by the Gnostics, only that Gnostics have a broader understanding of the word "body" and that in some cases the body does have a positive meaning. See Michael A. Williams, *Rethinking "Gnosticism": An Argument for Dismantling a Dubious Category* (Princeton, NJ: Princeton University Press, 1996).

[2] Steven R. Guthrie, *Creator Spirit: The Holy Spirit and the Art of Becoming Human* (Grand Rapids, MI: Baker Academic, 2011).

[3] Julia Annas, *The Morality of Happiness* (New York: Oxford University Press, 1993) and Pierre Hadot, *Philosophy as a Way of Life: Spiritual Exercises from Socrates to Foucault* (Malden, MA: Blackwell, 1995).

[4] Aristotle, *Eth. nic* 1.8.15.

characteristic function (*ergon*).[5] The characteristic function of the human being, according to Aristotle, is reason, including both intellectual reason and moral reason. To achieve *eudaimonia*, one must know how to put the faculty of reason to use—not only to use it, but to use it *perfectly* in order to perfect it. Only *perfect* practice makes perfect. Moreover, virtue (perfection) requires that one must enter into the social and political realm, for only in politics can the social virtues, such as justice, be developed. Human beings are political animals. Therefore, the fullness of *eudaimonia* can be achieved only by including participation in the realm of politics as a part of the virtuous life.

In Chinese culture, Confucianism holds a status similar to Aristotelianism in the West. Confucianism also regards both internal and external goods as necessary for *eudaimonia*, including goods such as longevity, wealth, peace, virtue, and peaceful death.[6] Also, in agreement with Aristotle, Confucianism acknowledges that human beings find their full development only in the realm of politics. Human virtue progresses through different stages, from the inner heart radiating out to one's behavior, and further to one's family, society, country, and up toward the renewal of the world.[7]

This brief summary of both Aristotle's and Confucius's idea of *eudaimonia* shows that both Western and Eastern cultures are attracted to the idea of *eudaimonism*, and both agree that *eudaimonia* requires external and internal goods. It does not require that one be born rich, but it does require that one's daily basic needs are met. These examples also show that classical cultures emphasize the relational character of the human being. The human being can thrive only when he or she dwells in a social and political system and contributes to that system.

The classical culture and the cultural traditions of both the West and the East are today under incessant attack. In many places, the idea of human flourishing has been redefined, and it no longer has the full development of human capacities in view. Happiness today is often coarsely defined as having one's wishes come true. In Taiwan, this new form of happiness is

---

[5] Aristotle, *Eth. nic.* 1.7.10.

[6] James Legge, trans., "The Sacred Books of China: The Texts of Confucianism," in *The Sacred Books of the East*, ed. F. Max Mueller (Oxford: Clarendon, 1879–1910), 3:149.

[7] James Legge, trans., *The Chinese Classics* (Hong Kong: Hong Kong University Press, 1960), 357-59.

called "little happiness," referring to the pursuit of culinary delicacies, overseas travel, good movies, and a cozy place to stay. A more sophisticated version would define the happy life as the search for "authenticity": to be who you are, to live out your true self, or to be faithful to your own feelings. The paradox is that the true self that the modern people are in search of often turns out to be the self that is unconsciously determined by the consumer culture—the image that is created by the large corporations and the cultural industry. The truth is that there is no "self" that exists in isolation or independence from the social-historical world. The unique self that modern human beings are in search of is really not that unique after all but is rather the self that is formulated by the modern narrative, the self that is in pursuit of the "little happiness."

Authenticity has indeed become the ethics of the modern era. No longer do we speak of imitating others. Also, rarely do we speak of contributing to our society or our country, or of honoring our parents or our family. What is the cause behind this radical shift from a soul that is oriented beyond itself to a soul that looks introspectively inward?

To answer this question, I would like to examine some of the social-historical reasons why moderns seek not full *eudaimonia* but the truncated version of the "little happiness." I will use Taiwan, my home country, as an example. Next, I ask how the Bible might help to counteract this truncated version of happiness. My strategy is to reread the book of 2 Peter, for scholars have argued that 2 Peter is a polemic against Epicureanism, and that Epicureanism is the philosophical worldview underpinning the modern idea of happiness. Through a rereading of 2 Peter, I hope we can find a way of doing spiritual formation that will truly make us *spiritual*, becoming the people that God intends us to be for the greater glory of God. I also examine the obstacles in modern society that thwart the full development of human beings, using Taiwan as an example. However, I believe other modern societies face similar challenges. Therefore, in the last section of this paper, I ask how these insights might contribute to the global church.

TAIWAN: HUMAN FLOURISHING IN CONTEXT

Taiwan is a country sitting on a small island off the coast of China. It is situated at a critical location on major North-South and East-West trade routes.

Therefore, it has been preyed upon by many great political powers—the Dutch, the Portuguese, the Qing dynasty, Japan, and the Republic of China. The island and its inhabitants experienced a series of rapid changes during the twentieth century.

Politically, Taiwan at the end of the nineteenth century was under the rule of the Qing dynasty. They were defeated by Japan in the First Sino-Japanese War (1894–1895), and as a result, Taiwan was ceded to Japan as part of the peace treaty. Japan was defeated in the Second World War in 1945. Due to this, Taiwan was handed over to the Republic of China. Later, war broke out in China between the Chinese Communist Party and the Republic of China. The latter was forced to retreat to Taiwan and began thirty-eight years of martial rule in Taiwan. In 1987, Taiwan ended martial law. From then on Taiwan became a democratic country with the right to free speech and general elections. In other words, Taiwan in the twentieth century experienced monarchy, colonialism, martial rule, and democracy.

Economically, Taiwan began the twentieth century as an agriculturally based economy. It underwent rapid industrialization in the 1960s. In the 1980s, Taiwan forged a strong semiconductor industry. Between the years 1960 and 1999, Taiwan maintained an economic growth of approximately 6 percent annually, second only to South Korea. Beginning in the 1990s, the service industry began to replace agriculture and manufacturing as the largest sector of Taiwan's economy.

Socially, at the beginning of the twentieth century, Taiwan was a place where traditional local communal communities thrived. Taiwan was, at that time, divided into various different ethnic groups: Minnan, Hakka, and various different indigenous tribes. Each had its own language, its own social structure, and its own culture and mores. With the coming of industrialization and urbanization, radical uproot took place. Local communities began to decay rapidly, replaced by urban life and culture, professional roles, and economic classes.

In sum, Taiwan underwent various stages of changes in the twentieth century; it went from a traditional society to a postmodern society. The living condition of its citizens have improved greatly. However, the citizens of Taiwan during this process have become more and more atomized. First, affluent modern society has created self-sufficient, autonomous individuals.

We no longer depend on family or friends for our daily needs. Second, urbanization has pulled citizens out of their traditional social and cultural environments and has made them into independent individuals. Parallel to this atomizing process is the construction of ever-more expansive and complex social structures. Politics is moving in the direction of becoming oligarchical politics, and the economy has become a globalized economy. These social structures have become impersonal and are no longer under the influence of the individuals within the society. Individuals feel a sense of powerlessness under these superstructures. Both the atomization of the individual and the reification of the superstructures caused the individual to turn away from the external world and toward the internal.

However, there is not only a push away from the external, but there is also a pull that drags us toward the internal. The pull comes from the ideology and the worldview that underpins and supports postmodern society. This ideology is the philosophy of Epicureanism. Epicurean philosophy and the postmodern social condition are like water and fish meshing together perfectly. Epicureanism believes that everything in the world is made up of atoms colliding with one another accidentally and that the world has no purpose. According to Epicureanism, the only thing that an individual can do and should do in this world is to live in the present and pursue happiness. This is a philosophy of life that is fully integrated with the postmodern world. How are we to talk about spiritual formation in a postmodern context? I suggest that we must first reform our thoughts and our hearts. Only by freeing ourselves from Epicureanism can we move on to change the social and political structures of the world in the process of becoming whole people.

SECOND PETER, EPICUREANISM, AND THE POSTMODERN CONDITION

In his commentary on 2 Peter, Jerome H. Neyrey pointed out that the opponents in the book of 2 Peter are the Epicureans.[8] Epicureans deny the judgments of God (2 Pet 3:9; 2:3-9; 3:7, 9-13), the afterlife (3:7, 10-13), and postmortem retribution (2:4, 9, 17; 3:7, 10). Thus, we see in 2 Peter 2:3 that the author, while refuting his opponents and reminding his readers of the truth of

---

[8]Jerome H. Neyrey, *2 Peter, Jude: A New Translation with Introduction and Commentary*, AB (New York: Doubleday, 1993), 122. See also Jerome H. Neyrey, "The Form and Background of the Polemic in 2 Peter," *Journal of Biblical Literature* 99 (1980): 407-31.

the gospel, emphasizes that there will be postmortem retribution. 2 Peter 3:9 further explains the reason why God has delayed this judgment: not because there will be no judgment, but because of God's mercy awaiting repentance.

For the Epicureans, the existence of postmortem judgment is not only an issue for metaphysical debate but also an issue that determines whether or not human beings can find happiness in life. The Epicureans believe that the greatest obstacle that obstructs the human being from finding happiness is fear: the fear of God, the fear of judgment after death, and the fear of falling into eternal damnation. For the Epicureans, the only way human beings can find freedom and liberation is to understand that there is no God and that there is no judgment after death.

Underlying this concept of freedom is the Epicureans' most basic and most important moral and ethical principle: that is, to avoid pain and seek pleasure.[9] The whole of Epicurean thought is based on this simple principle.[10] In response, we see in 2 Peter the author refuting not only the Epicureans' denial of postmortem judgment but also their underlying moral principle, and various other teachings based on this very same principle, including their views on friendship and politics.

Of course, we must emphasize that the teachings we find in the book of 2 Peter are not the exact ones that are taught by the Epicureans themselves. Rather, we read in 2 Peter a description and evaluation of Epicureanism presented to us from the Christian perspective. Although these descriptions may not reflect the true and precise teachings of the Epicureans, they do reflect the impressions that the Epicureans have on those who encounter them and interact with them.

First, Epicureans teach the moral principle of avoiding pain and pursuing happiness. The happiness that the Epicureans talk about is not a kind of vulgar and primitive hedonism. Epicureans emphasize that people must use good practical reason to distinguish between true and false happiness.[11] Happiness in the present moment may not be true happiness, for the present happiness may cause pain in the future; likewise, short-term pain may not necessarily be bad or need to be avoided, for short-term pain may result in

---

[9]Epicurus, *Diogenes Laertius* (abbreviated as DL), 10.137; cf. 10.128-29.
[10]Tim O'Keefe, *Epicureanism* (Berkeley: University of California Press, 2010), 111-15.
[11]Epicurus, *DL*, 10.132.

long-term blessings. For example, exercise may be painful, but it may bring us health and happiness in the long run. Therefore, to find true happiness one needs to make good use of practical wisdom. However, the problem is: who can know what the future will be? Therefore, it is easy for the Epicureans to fall into hedonism in practice. This explains why, in 2 Peter, we see the author frequently chastising his opponents for indulging themselves in desires (2 Pet 1:4; 2:10, 18; 3:3) and greed (2:3, 14; cf. 2:3, 16). Lust and greed corrupt both their speech and their deeds. 2 Peter often talks about their way of speaking: they malign the truth (2:3), use deceptive words (2:4), slander the glorious ones (2:10-11), and speak bombastic nonsense (2:18). Their behavior is licentious (2:2, 7, 18), corrupt (1:4; 2:12, 19), and blemished (2:13; cf. 3:14).

In addition to emphasizing the importance of seeking pleasure, the Epicureans also emphasize the importance of friendship; but for the Epicureans, the purpose of friendship is not friendship itself, but the benefits that it provides.[12] Friendship is like a safety net. It provides help when help is needed. In providing security, friendship appeases anxiety and brings peace to the mind, which for the Epicureans is one of the greatest pleasures in life. Therefore, the Epicureans highly value friendship, not because friendship is good in and of itself but because it brings pleasure to life. In other words, their friendship is based on the benefits it brings and is ultimately based on self-interest. In the eyes of the author of 2 Peter, Epicurean friendship easily deteriorates and becomes merely a means of achieving pleasure.

As for politics, Epicureans believe it is best avoided.[13] Friendship is good because friends will help one another and give peace to the mind. But those who are not of the same mind might act foolishly and harm others for reasons that are irrational, for example, to please the gods. Therefore, Epicureans find friendship, but not politics, comforting. Politics is to be avoided if possible. However, in rejecting conventional politics, the Epicureans did not reject the possibility of building a countercultural *polis* that is based on friendship and on the principle of mutual nonaggression: "natural justice is a token of advantage, to prevent one human being from harming or being

---

[12]Epicurus, *Principal Doctrines*, 27; *Vatican Sayings*, 52, 78.
[13]Epicurus, *Principal Doctrines*, 14; *DL*, 10.119; *Vatican Sayings*, 58; Plutarch *Lat. viv.*, 1128a-1129b; *Adv. Col.*, 1126e-1127c.

harmed by another."[14] This idea of political justice is derived directly from the basic moral principle of avoiding pain and pursuing pleasure.

However, in the eyes of the author of 2 Peter, Epicurean politics results in injustice and slavery. First, avoiding conventional politics leaves politics in the hands of the powerful, resulting in domination and injustice. Second, if avoiding pain becomes the guiding principle of justice, there is no reason why we must not harm others, especially when harming others may help to protect ourselves. Thus, 2 Peter often speaks of the injustices of the surrounding world, including the unjust world at the time of Noah (2 Pet 2:5), the unjust cities of Sodom and Gomorrah at the time of Lot (2:6), and the unjust economy of the world (2:13, 16).

In sum, we see in 2 Peter that the Epicureans are practical atheists. They claim that death is the end of life and that there is no future life after death. In this world without a future, the only thing that is left to pursue is the maximizing of one's own interests and the enjoyment of the present moment of life. The Epicureans depicted in 2 Peter reflect the postmodern way of thinking and the postmodern way of life.[15] In today's world, few people talk about life after death or postmortem judgment. The present moment is all that there is; as a result, the pursuit of self-interest has become the most basic ethical principle of life. Everything is evaluated from this point of view, including family life and societal life. If we find no benefit in the family or in the social community, we can always change our identity and join some other group or other community. Similarly, citizens in the postmodern world care less and less about politics and public issues. When they do get

---

[14]Epicurus, *Principal Doctrines*, 31.

[15]The study of the relationship between modernity and Epicureanism has recently seen a renaissance in the scholarly world. See, for example, Catherine Wilson, *Epicureanism at the Origins of Modernity* (Oxford: Oxford University Press, 2008); Catherine Wilson, "Epicureanism in Early Modern Philosophy," in *The Cambridge Companion to Epicureanism*, ed. J. Warren, 266-286 (Cambridge: Cambridge University Press, 2009); Catherine Wilson, "The Presence of Lucretius in Eighteenth Century French and German Philosophy," in *Lucretius and Modernity: Epicurean Encounters Across Time and Disciplines*, ed. Jacques Blake Lezra, 71-88 (New York: Palgrave Macmillan, 2016); Gerard Passannante, *The Lucretian Renaissance Philology and the Afterlife of Tradition* (Chicago: University of Chicago Press, 2011). The topic has also received a more popular treatment in Stephen Greenblatt's 2011 book *The Swerve: How the World Became Modern* (London: W. W. Norton, 2011). The book tells the story of how Poggio Bracciolini (1380–1459) found the book *De rerum natura* (DRN; *On the Nature of Things*), a book that was written by the first century Epicurean Lucretius, and how the book became the source and inspiration for modernity.

involved, it is usually for reasons of self-preservation. With pleasure as their highest aim, people tend to cling together in groups of like-minded people. They gather into groups where they feel secure and safe, whether it be among people of the same household, clan, party, race, or gender. We are unable to think beyond our borders and think publicly. Politics is, for this reason, reduced to the minimum of social contract theory. Politics is the result of fear. We are bound together because of our common fear of one another and of death. Beyond the justice of avoiding harm, we find it hard to accept any other substantial notions of justice.

SECOND PETER, SPIRITUAL FORMATION, AND THE GLOBAL CONTEXT

The world that the author of 2 Peter presents is different. First, human beings not only have a present life; they are on a journey moving toward the goal that God has destined for humankind. Death is not the end of life. There is life after death. Our final goal is to enter into the kingdom of God and to attain the glory of God. If indeed the kingdom of God is our goal, then the Epicurean ideal of avoiding pain and pursuing pleasure can no longer be the guiding principles of our life. We should instead pursue holiness and godliness, and we should prepare ourselves for the kingdom of God.

On our journey, we also must learn to love our brothers and sisters (2 Pet 1:7), that is, we need friendship between brothers and sisters. This friendship is not the kind of friendship advocated by the Epicureans—not a friendship centered on self-interest—but a friendship centered on love. Love is not self-seeking (1 Cor 13). In other words, friendship requires that we no longer look to our own interests but to the interests of others (Phil 2:4).

The author of 2 Peter demonstrates what he means by friendship through his letter writing. He calls his readers his "beloved," that is, they are his friends in Christ (2 Pet 3:1, 8, 14, 17). Of course, the word *beloved* means—first and above all—that the brothers and sisters are loved by God, but this word also expresses the love that the author has for his readers (3:15). Following the word *beloved*, the author constantly shows his concern for his readers, teaching them and exhorting them with the Word of God. To love someone is to encourage them with the Word of God so that they may walk steadfastly in the way of the Lord. The best gift that we can give one another is the Word of God. Friendship exists not for our own interests but for the interests of others.

Finally, we must learn not only to love our brothers and sisters (*philadelphia*) but also to *love* (*agapē*) all others (2 Pet 1:7). This love is expressed in our pursuit of fairness and justice (2:5, 7-9, 13, 15, 21). In classical Greco-Roman philosophical tradition, justice is the highest virtue. The Bible also constantly emphasizes the importance of justice. God's purpose in calling Israel is for Israel to maintain justice (Gen 18:19; Mic 6:8; Is 56:1). Sadly, Israel did not achieve this but instead became a source of injustice. For this reason, God sent his beloved Son into the world to reveal his justice (cf. Rom 1:16-17; 3:21-26).[16]

The book of 2 Peter also puts great emphasis on justice. The concept of justice is mentioned in the beginning and at the end of the book. In the beginning, the author characterizes God as the God of justice (2 Pet 1:1); toward the end, the author says that there will be justice in the new heavens and the new earth (3:13). Justice is the character of both God and his kingdom. The world, on the contrary, is characterized by injustice (2:5, 6, 13, 16). Since justice is the character of God and his kingdom, those who want to establish justice must live according to the principles of God. Thus, we often see the author of 2 Peter contrasting justice with ungodliness and godliness with injustice (2:5, 6, 9).

So how exactly do we establish justice in this world? First, we must learn to mourn whenever and wherever we see injustice (2 Pet 2:7-8). We should never hide our faces; we must learn to see and to mourn.[17] Sadness means that we know that certain things are wrong. Sadness means that we feel the pain of injustice. Sadness means that we are not willing to sit and watch. Second, we must declare the message of righteousness to the unjust world (2:5). We must point out the injustices of the world according to the truth. What secular justice advocates is noninterference: I don't interfere with you; you don't interfere with me. This is a politics of isolation and of indifference. The faith instead calls for a *prophetic voice*. God calls us to be tearful prophets who are willing to reveal the injustices of this world through the Word of God, especially for those who are oppressed.

[16]N. T. Wright, *Evil and the Justice of God* (Downers Grove, IL: InterVarsity, 2006), 43-74.
[17]Walter Brueggemann, *The Prophetic Imagination*, 2nd ed. (Minneapolis: Fortress, 2001), 39-58.

So how do you practice spirituality in this generation? If human beings are indeed (as is taught by the Epicureans) the result of swerving atoms colliding with one another, then avoiding pain and pursuing pleasure, shunning politics, and finding comfort in friendship communities would be the correct way of doing spiritual formation. How we do spiritual formation depends on how we understand ourselves and our world. Therefore, to speak of spiritual formation we must first understand that we are not a conglomeration of free, wandering atoms seeking to protect our own existence. On the contrary, we are Christ-followers, participating in a journey toward the final eschaton, the kingdom of God.

The first step in spiritual formation is to reclaim ourselves as participants in the story of God. The story that 2 Peter tells is precisely such a story about God, of how he has created (2 Pet 3:4-5), cares for, sustains (3:7), and renews the world (3:13). We find ourselves within this grand narrative: we have escaped from sin (1:9) and are now on a journey (1:10) on our way toward the kingdom of God (1:11). Only within this story can a countercultural spiritual formation be sustained.

Second, we must build virtue within ourselves. Virtue requires wisdom, discipline, and patience. Virtue also requires the idea of a telos and the knowledge that we are to stay on that path with persistence, day in and day out. Rather than licentiousness, corruption, and blemished behavior, 2 Peter emphasizes holiness (3:11) and godliness (1:3, 6, 7; 3:11). Whatever belongs to God is holy (1:18, 21; 2:21; 3:2). To be holy is to belong to God and to hear and obey his words.

Third, we must learn to establish friendships with brothers and sisters in Christ. Friendship is not easy. The establishment of friendship takes time. It requires the opening up of oneself to the other; it requires sacrifice and the cultivation of all the virtues mentioned earlier. However, the most important step in developing genuine friendships is to learn how to support, remind, and encourage one another through the Word of God. Moreover, gleaning from Markus Nikkanen's chapter in this volume, friendship also involves being coparticipants in the act of breaking bread together in the Eucharist.

Finally, spiritual formation requires that we become people who care for justice, for God is just and his kingdom is just. We do not huddle together in isolated faith communities merely to find warmth in each other. We must walk out to our neighbors and into the world, criticize unrighteousness, and bring hope.

Spiritual formation involves the self, the community of faith, and the world of our neighbors. Only by building up our characters, engaging in friendship and in the affairs of the world, can we elevate our spiritual lives and continue to grow, mature, and reflect the glory of God in the world in which God has called us to participate.

Spirituality is not something that is airy and abstract; spirituality should always be concrete and embodied in real life. Spirituality is the life of virtue. Spirituality is the friendship of love. And spirituality is the politics of justice. Christians become *spiritual* by pouring out our love for God, for friends, and for neighbors, just as God constantly pours out his love for us. Spirituality is not an escape from this world or a dwelling high above the world, but it is to be lived out in our lives, our friendships, and our world.

STUDY QUESTIONS

1. If the goal of spiritual formation is human flourishing, we need first to understand what the human being is. What does it mean to be a fully human being? Or, what is the *telos* of the human being?

2. In the place where you live, are there any social or political factors obstructing the full development of human beings? How might we respond to these obstructions as the church?

3. What biblical passage or book helps overcome the obstacles that thwart the development of the full human being? What kind of spiritual formation do we need to flourish as human beings?

CHAPTER ELEVEN

THE HOLY SPIRIT, SUPERNATURAL INTERVENTIONISM, AND SPIRITUAL FORMATION

J. KWABENA ASAMOAH-GYADU

IN THIS CHAPTER, I EXAMINE SPIRITUAL FORMATION from an African perspective using the spirituality of the Pentecostal/charismatic movement to interrogate the issues. Pentecostalism is used here to refer to a specific expression of Christian spirituality in which the experience of the Spirit is valued, affirmed, and consciously promoted as part of normal Christian life. In other words, any church or movement may profess belief in the Spirit or may even claim to experience the Holy Spirit, but in Pentecostal/charismatic Christianity (henceforth, simply Pentecostal), these pneumatic experiences have been mainstreamed, and that is what gives them their ecclesial identity.

Pentecostalism could be said—to some reasonable extent—to now constitute the representative face of Christianity in Africa. One of the main contributions that Pentecostals have made for global Christianity is the critical attention that they place on the Holy Spirit in formation and in the life of the church. Through its worldwide growth and impact, Harvey Cox predicted, Pentecostals were set to transform the face of religion in this century.[1] Pentecostalism is a movement of the Holy Spirit,

---

[1]Harvey Cox, *Fire from Heaven: The Rise of Pentecostal Spirituality and the Reshaping of Religion in the Twenty-first Century* (Reading, MA: Addison-Wesley, 1995).

who, as Pentecostal New Testament theologian Gordon D. Fee titles one of his books, is "God's empowering presence" among his people.[2] An illustration of the empowering presence occurs in John 20:21-22, where the resurrected Christ appears to the disciples, saying to them, "As the Father has sent me, I am sending you." With those words, he then "breathed on them" and said, "Receive the Holy Spirit."[3] In other words, the "sending forth" and the empowerment, that is, breathing the Spirit on them, occurred at the same time.

PENTECOSTAL SPIRITUALITY

In Pentecostal theology and spirituality, it is believed that the Spirit of God transforms, sanctifies, and empowers believers for greater works in Christ. Among the works of the Spirit, we shall focus on the way in which he empowers people for the interventionist ministries that relate to healing from sickness and deliverance from evil.

These ministries take place within the context of what Pentecostal Christians call spiritual warfare. The Holy Spirit progressively builds up God's people into temples fit for his dwelling. It is therefore not surprising that the Pauline metaphor of the Christian's body and the body of Christ as temples of the Holy Spirit is one of the most cherished in Pentecostal thought. In the following quotation, Frank D. Macchia draws out the implications of the global rise of Pentecostalism for its non-Western versions such as those of Africa:

> [There] is globally, a shift occurring today toward a "new Christendom" that has its greatest . . . strength in the southern hemisphere and that tends to encourage charismatic, widely participatory, and mission-minded congregations. Multiple and extraordinary gifts among ordinary Christians such as prophecy, exorcism, and divine healing are emerging as far more relevant to the vibrancy of the missionary church globally than North American and European theologians laboring under the challenges of the Enlightenment could have imagined. . . . This renewal tends toward an energized laity active

---

[2] Gordon D. Fee, *God's Empowering Presence: The Holy Spirit in the Letters of Paul* (Peabody, MA: Hendrickson, 1994).

[3] Biblical references in this chapter are from the NIV (*The Holy Bible*, New International Version [Grand Rapids, MI: Zondervan, 2011]).

in the realm of the Spirit in diverse and unique ways to build the body of Christ and to function as witnesses for Christ to the world.[4]

The issues of spiritual formation that Macchia refers to here in the Pentecostal expression of Christianity are based on the experience of the Holy Spirit. In this experience, theological sophistication and priestly successions are not necessarily considered to be the prime indicators of genuine spirituality. Rather, it is the ability of the Holy Spirit to fill ordinary people and endow them with some gifts of grace with which to serve the church. It is revealing that in his epistle to the Ephesians, Paul talks about the fact that the gifts of the Spirit are granted "to equip [God's people] for works of service, so that the body of Christ may be built up until we all reach unity in the faith and in the knowledge of the Son of God and become mature, attaining to the whole measure of the fullness of Christ" (Eph 4:12-13). The reference to becoming "mature" and the attainment of "the whole measure of the fullness of Christ" are important because these are the ends to which spiritual formation ought to be directed.

For Pentecostals, this pneumatological approach to formation grants to the church an interventionist ministry, an approach that often lies marginalized in historic Christendom, partly because of its Enlightenment heritage. The underlying assumption of the creedal confession in the third article of faith, "I believe in the Holy Spirit," is that any church, if it is to be called Christian, must be one that does not merely give creedal assent to the existence of the Spirit. Confession of belief in the Spirit is important but, for Pentecostals and their historically younger progenies, the charismatics, the mere confession of belief in the Spirit as an article of faith is not enough. Our confession of belief, Pentecostals say, must always move in tandem with the experience of the Spirit. In other words, in Pentecostal spiritual formation, belief, and *experience* are expected to be held inseparably together when it comes to matters of the Spirit. Theological education and formation that is overly cerebral and academic is, for example, presumed to be deficient because it does not empower people to engage in ministries that are backed by the power of the Spirit. Thus, Pentecostals often talk about people with a

---

[4]Frank D. Macchia, *Baptized in the Spirit: A Global Pentecostal Theology* (Grand Rapids, MI: Zondervan Academic, 2006), 158.

"proven ministry," which would usually mean that they are persons whose pastoral activities are followed by manifestations of the Spirit such as the grace to pray for the restoration of health from sickness and deliverance from spiritual afflictions in particular.

THE HOLY SPIRIT AND INTERVENTIONISM

We find the interventionist ministry—which defines Pentecostal formation and spirituality—in the manifestation of the power of the Holy Spirit. In this discussion, we look at the intersection between the Holy Spirit and super-natural interventionism as a critical part of Pentecostal spiritual formation in the African context.

Consider, for example, two of the most popular interventionist ministries in Pentecostalism: healing and deliverance. The expressions are usually conjoined to describe situations where demonic powers are believed to have taken over the executive faculties of the individual. Here the invocatory words "in the name of Jesus" and "in the power of the Holy Ghost" are just two of the most common expressions that one hears as charismatic persons try to free such victims from the hold of the devil. The ministries of healing, exorcism, and deliverance from the demonic constitute what I refer to as the interventionist strategies associated with certain streams of Christianity whose spirituality centers on the power of God in action. The power of God in action by the Spirit is what some refer to as the "anointing." This power is often invoked to heal diseases, incapacitate demonic forces, release those who may be spiritually bound by Satan, or even curse the spirit of poverty and delay in life.

These interventionist ministries make sense in the African context be-cause indigenous Africans still function in a universe that is alive with pow-erful spiritual entities. What I have referred to as worldviews, Andrew F. Walls casts as "maps of the universe."[5] In an Enlightenment universe with its orientation toward rationality and science, spirit possession, for example, was seen as a form of insanity like most irrational behavior. In the African Christian context, such situations of affliction are read in terms of the same phenomena that Jesus dealt with in his ministry: possession and oppression

---

[5]Andrew F. Walls, *Crossing Cultural Frontiers: Studies in the History of World Christianity* (Maryknoll, NY: Orbis, 2017).

by negative spirits. This is how Andrew Walls captures these thoughts as he explains the tensions between the Enlightenment universe and African religiocultural realities:

> For one thing, when [African] Christians find themselves in difficulty for which they can see no help in the Christian system, they may make some recognition of the divinities, not permanently, not putting them back into their old places on the map, but as a one of occasional resort. This fact probably reinforces a tendency, very evident within the charismatic movement in Africa, to see the divinities as demons. . . . In this case the divinities do not drop off the map altogether: they take a new place on it but as demonic forces—a category clearly to be seen in the Bible, but absent from the operational maps of many "modern" post-Enlightenment Christians.[6]

The objective of Pentecostal interventionist ministries is twofold: the release of persons from affliction and their empowerment for prosperity and flourishing.

In the African Christian context, Pentecostalism has acquired much significance, with its emphasis on the power of Jesus to heal and bring deliverance to troubled persons and places such as haunted physical spaces. Pentecostal spirituality is open to the possibility of supernatural interventions and miraculous events to occur in signs and wonders. This resonates with the African religious orientation of mystical causality. Etiology and diagnosis in Africa often ask the following basic question: "Which spiritual entity is responsible for this or that misfortune or calamity in my life?" Thus, the African religious context, we could say, is one in which religion is not a system of theological ideas but a source of power for dealing with life's issues and situations for which Western Christianity may not have answers.

What I am describing here as supernatural interventionism consists in the deployment of the power of the Holy Spirit as a means of spiritual formation and pastoral care. How does supernatural interventionism inform spiritual formation in contexts like Africa, where matters of the Spirit are taken seriously in religious expression? Generally, in the approach to mission that Christian traditions of the West brought to Africa in the early nineteenth century, matters relating to the experience of the Spirit were treated

---

[6]Walls, *Crossing Cultural Frontiers*, 46.

as marginal to, or even aberrations of, the Christian faith. Worship was very liturgically ordered, and prayers came from European collects that were used within contemporary African situations whether they fit our circumstances or not. African Christians were disenchanted by the inability of the historic denominational approach to mission to respond adequately to their deep-seated spiritual concerns; thus, they left to join one of the many independent churches that had started forming from the second decade of the twentieth century. A number of other charismatic lay leaders were also excluded from the fellowship of these mainline churches on account of the spiritual experiences in which they claimed to be able to heal by prayer, to prophesy, and to interpret dreams and revelations.

In one particular case occurring in the early 1920s and recounted by Christian G. Baëta in *Prophetism in Ghana,* a Methodist lay catechist was dismissed by his superiors because his Holy Spirit experiences—speaking in tongues, healing, extemporaneous praying, and exorcistic activities— were castigated as belonging to the "occult." "The Methodists were not like that," he was told. Having been dismissed from the Methodist Church in Ghana in 1923, William Egyanka Appiah, the catechist in question, proceeded to form the Musama Disco Christo Church (MDCC), also known as the Church of the Army of the Cross of Christ.[7] It became one of the most popular and dynamic independent churches in Ghana and known for its prophetic and healing ministries. The MDCC belongs to the family of independent spiritual churches that came to be collectively referred to as the African independent/instituted/initiated churches. They are credited to be the first group of churches to integrate charismatic renewal phenomena into Christianity in Africa, and, to that end, they made their mark on the religious terrain as the precursors of the Pentecostal movement in Africa.

THE HOLY SPIRIT AND PENTECOSTAL HERMENEUTICAL KEYS

I propose that a way to understand the work of the Holy Spirit in spiritual formation is to look at the biblical material through the three hermeneutical keys of *promise, fulfillment,* and *experience* as they relate to Pentecostal

---

[7]Christian G. Baëta, *Prophetism in Ghana: A Study of Some Spiritual Churches* (London: SCM, 1963), 35.

spirituality. The coming of the Holy Spirit, biblically speaking, was the fulfillment of a promise made by God and subsequently repeated in other parts of the Bible, including by John the Baptist, Jesus Christ, and Peter on the day of Pentecost. Pentecostals, then, usually start their story with reference to the prophetic promise of God in the book of Joel:

> And afterward, I will pour out my Spirit on all people. Your sons and daughters will prophesy, your old men will dream dreams, your young men will see visions. Even on my servants, both men and women, I will pour out my Spirit in those days. I will show wonders in the heavens and on the earth, blood and fire and billows of smoke. The sun will be turned to darkness and the moon to blood before the coming of the great and dreadful day of the LORD. And everyone who calls on the name of the LORD will be saved; for on Mount Zion and in Jerusalem there will be deliverance. (Joel 2:28-32 NIV)

In the New Testament, Jesus also promises to send the Holy Spirit upon his disciples: "And see, I am sending you what my Father promised; so stay here in the city until you have been clothed with power from on high" (Lk 24:49). This promise is repeated in Acts 1:4-5 and 8 (NIV), where it reads:

> On one occasion, while he was eating with them, he gave them this command: "Do not leave Jerusalem, but wait for the gift my Father promised, which you have heard me speak about. For John baptized with water, but in a few days you will be baptized with the Holy Spirit. . . . But you will receive power when the Holy Spirit comes on you; and you will be my witnesses in Jerusalem, and in all Judea and Samaria, and to the ends of the earth."

When the *promise* was eventually *fulfilled* on the day of Pentecost, Peter, in an inspired sermon, makes direct connections between the prophetic declaration in Joel and what a bewildered crowd was "seeing" and "hearing" concerning the mighty acts of God in Christ. In the end, convicted by the message, they asked the apostles, "What shall we do?" Peter's response was that the promise of the outpouring of the Holy Spirit could be experienced by present and future generations: "Peter replied, 'Repent and be baptized, every one of you, in the name of Jesus Christ for the forgiveness of your sins. And you will receive the gift of the Holy Spirit. The promise is for you and your children and for all who are far off—for all whom the Lord our God will call'" (Acts 2:38-39).

These and other Bible passages—which inform the legitimacy of Pentecostalism as a movement of the Holy Spirit—could be grouped under one of these interrelated triadic themes. They are passages that relate to promises concerning, first, the coming of the Holy Spirit; second, how the promise of the coming of the Spirit was fulfilled in the Scriptures; and third, how these promises are supposed to be experienced by believers today. If the rise of Holy Spirit movements around the world has anything to teach the church of Jesus Christ about formation, then it is the fact that God has been faithful in fulfilling his promise to pour out the Holy Spirit on all flesh.

The Pentecostal hermeneutical triad of *promise*, *fulfillment*, and *experience* helps to define certain aspects of renewal ecclesiology and also to understand their approaches to spiritual formation. In the traditional episcopal churches, for example, apostolic succession usually refers to inheriting particular church traditions in terms of power, governance, and authority. Pentecostals look at things differently. At Pentecost, as Frank Macchia argues, the Spirit descended on all the faithful and therefore "the historic claim to apostolic succession cannot be used to anchor the marks of the church as centrally subsisting in one communion only, since these marks are polycentric, belonging to all communities who come to Christ to drink from the Spirit and to find help in time of need."[8] The outpouring of the Spirit on all flesh democratizes access to graces, which also decentralizes spiritual formation. When we talk about apostolic succession within the Pentecostal/charismatic renewal traditions, it means something different from its meaning in, say, Catholicism, because in Pentecostal communities the promise of the Father that was fulfilled in the ministries of the disciples at Pentecost is believed to be the same one which is now experienced by all in the contemporary church without ethnic, gender, and social boundaries. That is how Pentecostals would understand the expression: "The promise is for you and your children and for all who are far off—for all whom the Lord our God will call" (Acts 2:39). God calls the church of today, the Pentecostals would argue, to claim that same promise of the Spirit and do "greater works" in the name of Jesus Christ as Lord.

---

[8]Macchia, *Baptized in the Spirit*, 206.

We are therefore successors to the apostles not simply in terms of authority, power, and governance but, most important, in terms of the fact that the ministry of the Spirit continues in the life of the church today. The question is: What did the experience of the Holy Spirit help the early church, especially the apostles, to do? When we consider this in the African context, we find a particular emphasis on the acts of power that accompanied the ministry of those who experienced the Spirit in the biblical material. Luke begins the prophecies relating to the ministries of John the Baptist by noting that "his father Zechariah was filled with the Holy Spirit and prophesied" (Lk 1:67). A Holy Spirit-inspired prophecy suggests that the declarations being made, or the information being released, is coming from God and was previously unknown to the prophet. What did the Holy Spirit inspire Zechariah to declare?

> Praise be to the Lord, the God of Israel,
>> because he has come to his people and redeemed them.
> He has raised up a horn of salvation for us
>> in the house of his servant David
>> (as he said through his holy prophets of long ago),
> salvation from our enemies
>> and from the hand of all who hate us—
> to show mercy to our ancestors
>> and to remember his holy covenant,
>> the oath he swore to our father Abraham:
> to rescue us from the hand of our enemies,
>> and to enable us to serve him without fear
>> in holiness and righteousness before him all our days. (Lk 1:68-75)

It is clear that the Holy Spirit inspired Zechariah to establish the relationship between the ministry of John the Baptist and that of Jesus Christ as the Messiah on the one hand, and the Old Testament promises on the other. In Luke 1:72, the prophetic utterance explains all that was going to happen as part of God's covenant promise to Abraham and his descendants. The Zechariah prophecy we have been considering made reference to "salvation from our enemies and from the hand of all who hate us," which means that God was going to intervene in accord with his desire to deliver abundant life to those who love him. From an African perspective, one way in which the ministry of intervention is seen is through what Pentecostal Christians call spiritual warfare.

SPIRITUAL WARFARE: AFRICAN PERSPECTIVES
ON A GLOBAL PHENOMENON

Although spiritual warfare and the activities related to it are not uniquely African, I explore the phenomenon from an African perspective. This is because the frustrations of Pentecostals with the older forms of missionary Christianity lies in the fact that the latter does not seem to take account of the encounter with evil in spiritual formation. In contrast, Pentecostal Christianity, especially its African versions, takes supernatural elements of the faith seriously.

This is particularly evident in the belief that the Spirit, in empowering people, enables them to exercise certain graces such as dealing with the evils of witchcraft, which is an important African sociocultural and religious concern. The reference to "principalities and powers" in spiritual warfare discourse brings to mind Paul's thoughts on the reality of evil powers and how to deal with them as articulated in Ephesians 6:10-12 (KJV). The hypothesis, as articulated by believers and practitioners, is that not only does Christian discipleship involve spiritual warfare, but also that the believer must exercise his or her authority in Christ to proactively battle evil spirits and other powers that are inimical to our well-being. The successful subjugation of the supernatural influences of evil paves the way for human well-being and prosperity. This subjugation is also a tool for evangelism, discipleship, and spiritual formation. In other words, the ability of Pentecostal Christianity to bridge the two worlds of biblical and African cosmologies—especially as it relates to supernatural evil and how to deal with it—has made the movement attractive within the African public sphere.

Pentecostal spiritual warfare imagery consciously deploys the references that Paul makes in Ephesians and links them to the fact that, in this world, Christians do not only wrestle against flesh and blood but also against principalities and powers in high places. In the historical-critical hermeneutical approach to the Bible, the passage in Ephesians 6 has, for example, often been applied to the difficult relationship that the Christian community had with imperial powers of the time. The powers in "high places" in the overly academic hermeneutics of theology would therefore refer to those who exercise authority. Spiritual warfare hermeneutics is, however, adamant that it can refer only to the fact that there are powers in high places, that is, evil supernatural powers in the universe. The Christian, based on the experience of the Spirit, therefore ought to be fully armed with the whole armor of God in order to be able to do war or battle these forces of supernatural evil. Apostle Professor Opoku Onyinah, a Pentecostal theologian and former head of Ghana's largest classical Pentecostal denomination (the Church of Pentecost), follows this understanding in his book *Spiritual Warfare*. Commenting on Paul's submission, Onyinah notes that the use of the expression "the devil's schemes" in some translations of the Ephesians passage shows that "the devil uses strategies and tricks to work out his plan," and Christians must have confidence that they are empowered by God to stand against those schemes or strategies.[9]

On this particular point regarding the works of the devil, Peter's words to Christians in the diaspora is frequently cited by Pentecostals in support of the position that evil spirits actively work or scheme against God's people: "Discipline yourselves, keep alert. Like a roaring lion your adversary the devil prowls around, looking for someone to devour. Resist him, steadfast in your faith, for you know that your brothers and sisters in all the world are undergoing the same kinds of suffering" (1 Pet 5:8-9 NRSV). The Bible speaks about demons and evil spirits. The general understanding of demonology is that the reference to the devil "prowling around like a roaring lion" includes his activity through evil spirits to bring Christians down in their walk with God. It is important to establish that supernatural interventionism—in the form of the casting out of demons, exorcising spirits, and healing the sick and disabled—were all part of the ministry of Jesus. The disciples picked this ministry up, especially in the post-Pentecost period; wherever the message of the gospel was preached, these supernatural activities of interventionism were integrally related to it. Thus, African Pentecostal spiritual warfare hermeneutics sees in this ministry a sort of "apostolic succession" not in terms of occupying episcopal offices but in terms of continuing ministry in the same power that was observed in the

---

[9]Opoku Onyinah, *Spiritual Warfare: A Centre for Pentecostal Theology Short Introduction* (Cleveland, TN: CPT, 2012), 24.

post-Pentecost era. This included preaching the Word and engaging in spiritual warfare activities.

DEMONIC DOORWAYS

In typical Pentecostal contexts sources of affliction, demonic doorways, or demonic entry points, may be revealed through dreams, visions, revelations, or even through some prophetic utterance. Spiritual warfare is supposed to culminate in the deliverance of people from whatever holds them in bondage.

There are thousands of Africans who visit Pentecostal/charismatic churches and healing camps in search of deliverance. Deliverance from the demonic and other forms of oppression in life, it is believed, only occurs through spiritual warfare. Many pastors and Christian leaders specialize in this form of ministry. To understand how it works in the African context, it is important to understand what we are referring to as demonic doorways. There is a range of these demonic doorways, but the basic one is sin. When people lead morally sinful lives, the idea is that they give the enemy access into their lives. Thus, spiritual formation from this perspective begins with a life sanctified for holy living. In healing and deliverance hermeneutics, a woman who engages in adulterous sex could have the devil turn that sin into sexual promiscuousness. In most cases, it is the type of affliction that determines the source of the trouble. The orifices of the body could also constitute demonic doorways, so what a person listens to, eats, smells, sees, or who one has sexual relations with could all serve as "entry points" for demonic affliction.

Spiritual warfare activity has been institutionalized in African Christianity. Spiritual warfare has to do with supernatural interventionism as a form of Christian resistance against the influence of the powers of evil. In Ghana, for example, as in other African contexts, it is not uncommon for one to encounter specially established healing camps where people may even be quarantined for help for as long as their problems persist. Custodians of healing camps and other healing and deliverance exponents often design extensive "deliverance questionnaires" that enable them to determine where afflictions had originated from.[10] In a context like Africa, family ties

---

[10]Opoku Onyinah, *Pentecostal Exorcism: Witchcraft and Demonology in Ghana* (Dorset, UK: Deo, 2012).

can always be cited as a major demonic doorway, for many believe that envious family members could bring them to ruin spiritually through evil medicines and curses. Moreover, African traditional religious and cultural practices are considered to be serious demonic doorways. If people have been taken through or participated in any rite of passage—birth, puberty, marriage—or even traditional fetish dances, or have any ancestral roots in traditional chiefship, their later problems in life could be explained in terms of these things. In other words, one of the frontiers that African Christian spiritual warfare takes place is the intersection between traditional religion and Christianity.

In many Pentecostal/charismatic communities in Africa, it is not uncommon for people's Christian testimony to be built around the fact that they came to Christ or joined a particular church because they were in some form of spiritual affliction and now experienced deliverance, deciding to join the ministry of the particular pastor through whom the Lord helped them. The thought that spiritual warfare constitutes a means of pastoral care, human flourishing, or well-being is based on the understanding of the words of Jesus in John 10:10: "The thief comes only to steal and kill and destroy. I came that they may have life and have it abundantly" (NRSV).

Pastoral care has to do with the deployment of and reliance on biblical, physical, and spiritual resources for the restoration of troubled persons to proper functioning order. With the strong belief in supernatural evil, spiritual formation within the African Pentecostal context involves building personal and communal capacities to ensure that such spiritual resources as prayer and exorcism—which are required for dealing with situations of affliction—are harnessed for restoring and reconciling the troubled person to God. In the African context, witchcraft—the ability of human beings to possess supernatural powers of evil and use it to harm others—is the single most important target of warfare prayers.

The general understanding of the proponents of spiritual warfare theology is that Christians are authorized and empowered by the Spirit of God to wage war against agents of the devil. In African Pentecostal spiritual hermeneutics, for example, the belief is that sometimes the devil can hold whole nations captive through the work of territorial demons. At other times, demons may hold individuals and families captive in diverse ways. This includes influencing their lives and activities negatively. In such situations, it is believed that "power evangelism"—which means engaging in warfare activities to break the hold of the enemy so that they may receive the gospel—remains an important option for the Christian church. In world Christianity, the Pentecostal/charismatic churches and movements seem to have integrated these ministries of supernatural interventionism into the forms of spirituality better than the historic mission churches, and this is understandable, since the latter have historical links with Western European Christianity. In many African churches the "prayer warriors' ministry" is an established part of the ministerial structure. This is usually made up of individuals known to be "filled with the Holy Spirit" who are also prayerful. Their ministry is to constantly engage in prayer to break the bonds of affliction in order to free people from demonic bondage or to obtain effective results for evangelism activities.

SPIRITUAL WARFARE: GLOBAL AND LOCAL

The theology of spiritual warfare, as we noted at the beginning, is not necessarily a uniquely African Christian concern. Except for a few Westerners, such as Peter Wagner and Klaus Koch, most Western theologians have taken an intellectualist, secularist, and mythological view of spiritual warfare devoid of real cosmic battles between the supernatural and natural realms of the universe.[11] Indeed, John Wimber and his followers were deeply convinced that the contemporary church was powerless because of its intellectual approach to Christianity.[12] The Western intellectualist tone suggests that discourses on supernatural evil only serve to encourage belief in nonexistent "mythological monsters."[13] The general Western approach argues on the assumption that when Paul spoke of principalities, authorities, powers, world rulers, and elemental spirits, he was using mythological language to describe spiritual realities of the time.

In recent years, Walter Wink has tweaked this approach by arguing for an "integral worldview" in which he redefines the "principalities and powers"

---

[11]See for example, G. B. Caird, *Principalities and Powers: A Study in Pauline Theology* (Oxford: Oxford University Press, 1956).

[12]Martyn Percy, *Words, Wonders and Power* (London: SPCK, 1996), 33.

[13]James K. Beilby and Paul Rhodes, eds., *Understanding Spiritual Warfare* (Grand Rapids, MI: Baker Academic, 2012), 3.

as "inner and outer aspects of any given manifestation of power."[14] When any particular individual or institutional power becomes "idolatrous," by positioning itself in contradiction or as a challenge to the purposes of God for the common good, then, Wink notes, that power becomes demonic. Evil is a fact of human existence, Wink's ideas suggest, but they are perpetuated not by actual spirit realities but by the misuse of institutional power and authority against human good and progress:

> Commonly, Western academics dismiss contemporary belief in angels and demons as an unfortunate idiosyncrasy with such questionable belief systems as the New Age movement or religious "fundamentalism." Some, while retaining a place for the linguistic categories of "Satan" and/or the "demonic," do so only in a thoroughly reinterpreted form, reducing them without remainder to metaphors for purely naturalistic forces.[15]

In contrast, the whole theology of spiritual warfare as understood within African Christianity generally, but Pentecostalism in particular, takes the existence of supernatural forces and fallen angels seriously. Ghanaian practical theologian Esther Acolatse has discussed the polarized positions of the West and Africa in her book *Powers, Principalities and the Spirit: Biblical Realism in Africa and the West*. She points out that the biblical world was conscious of the existence of supernatural evil. Acolatse states that the Ephesians "believed in a world teeming with personal spiritual forces accounted for by the language Paul used in his admonition and encouragement to the church," pointing out that "an invitation for alertness, and a strategy for ensuring victory in the war against the devil are what stand out most in these verses."[16] In other words, there is a coherence between the biblical and African worlds when it comes to the reality of supernatural evil.

SPIRITUAL WARFARE AND HUMAN FLOURISHING

Human flourishing is synonymous with Jesus' idea of "abundant life" or "fullness of life" in John 10:10. Human flourishing is related to spiritual

---

[14]Walter Wink, *Naming the Powers: The Language of Power in the New Testament* (Minneapolis: Fortress, 1984), 5.

[15]Beilby and Rhodes, *Spiritual Warfare*, 17.

[16]Esther Acolatse, *Powers, Principalities, and the Spirit: Biblical Realism in Africa and the West* (Grand Rapids, MI: Eerdmans, 2018), 164.

warfare in the sense that Jesus refers to the "devil" as one who comes to "steal, kill and destroy" in contrast to himself as the Good Shepherd, who comes that we might have life and have it to the full.

We have noted that the contemporary Pentecostal view of the reality of the demonic is based on the understanding of Paul's text in Ephesians about our own spiritual reality, which wrestles not against flesh and blood but rather against principalities and powers in high places. When Peter cautions Christians to be wary of the wiles of the devil because he "prowls around like a roaring lion looking for someone to devour" (1 Pet 5:8), it is understood in terms of Satan working through negative spirits that oppose the work of God. Pentecostalism is the stream of Christianity that speaks that language the loudest.

This is where the prosperity gospel relates to spiritual warfare. The ministry of spiritual warfare often takes care of the shortfalls associated with the prosperity message. The prosperity gospel declares physical and spiritual well-being on the believer, but things do not always work out as expected. In spite of the fact people fulfill the requirements of prosperity such as naming and claiming what they desire and fulfilling their tithing obligations, afflictions still occur. The usual explanation for why the promises of prosperity do not materialize is the work of witches and demons. The way to handle these obstacles to human flourishing is spiritual warfare.

Therefore, my thesis is that when people are not flourishing or enjoying abundant life, there may be supernatural evil at work that is impeding their prosperity. The general understanding of African Pentecostalism is that we live in a world that is more than physical and that those forces that impede human progress could be of a negative cosmic nature. In fact, for the human being to come to a full realization of potential and destiny in life, it is expected that people would use all the powers at their disposal to resist the forces of evil that work against their interest and their endeavors. Although other religions may not necessarily use the expression "spiritual warfare," they typically do hold that there are negative unseen forces at work against human life and progress. Thus, for example, in African traditional religions the principal role of the diviner is to work to invoke the powers of beneficence to support human endeavors. Among the Yoruba of Nigeria, the word of diviner is *Babalawo*, meaning "father of secrets," because he has the power to discern the spiritual sources of human affliction and prescribe solutions to them. In virtually all religious traditions, there exist functionaries whose responsibility is to provide those supernatural resources needed to ward off supernatural evil and protect those that ward it off. Thus, for African Christians, it makes religious sense to claim that not only are their everyday problems the results of demonic affliction, but also that by the power of the Spirit, God equips his children to engage in warfare against these powers.

Finally, maturity is an important objective in spiritual formation. To that end, there are obvious difficulties with some of the spiritual warfare ministries that have unfolded in Africa. Its biggest fallout is its inability to get people to be personally responsible for their actions by blaming every misfortune on external spiritual agents. That does not take away from the fact that spiritual warfare is an important Christian ministry. Indeed, one of the reasons for the phenomenal growth of Pentecostalism, especially in Africa, is that they take the spiritual warfare ministry seriously. There is rarely a calamitous situation or misfortune, whether social or economic, political or religious, that is not attributed to the work of the devil working through different principalities and powers. This coheres with both biblical and African traditional perceptions of supernatural evil. For example, one day when the disciples had been unable to cast out an evil spirit tormenting a boy through an epileptic fit, Jesus appeared to deal with the situation. When the disciples wanted to know why they had not been able to deal with the situation, Jesus responded that that type of spirit would only be cast out by prayer and fasting (Mk 9:29). In Pentecostal thought, this is what spiritual warfare is about. It involves "waiting on the Lord" for the power to cast out demons and heal the sick through engaging in warfare that the kingdom of God may come upon people and communities. Jesus was very clear that the Holy Spirit was God's own empowering presence upon the disciples. Without that presence coming upon them, it was impossible to function effectively as disciples bearing a message of salvation. The Spirit is the Spirit of Jesus and, as Keener notes, "the more we know about Jesus from the Bible, the more prepared we are to recognize the voice of his Spirit when he speaks to us."[17]

---

[17]Craig S. Keener, *Gift and Giver: The Holy Spirit for Today* (Grand Rapids, MI: Baker Academic, 2001), 42.

CONCLUSION

An important reason that people give for opting for Pentecostal communities rather than the historic mission or mainline churches, especially in
Africa, is what we have referred to as the peripheral or marginal role that the
Spirit occupies in the theology of the older churches. And yet, in the biblical
material, the Spirit plays a critical role in Christian spiritual formation. In
writing to the Ephesians, Paul talks about the fact that the reason for granting
spiritual gifts is so that the church of Christ could be built up into maturity
(Eph 4:11-16). Peter also refers to the Spirit-indwelled people as "being built
into a spiritual house" (1 Pet 2:5). In other words, as Pentecostal theologian
Frank Macchia would have it, "the Spirit-baptized church is still under
construction" or still being formed. He continues: "We are still becoming
the church as the temple of God's dwelling. We are constantly in the process
of being the Spirit-baptized people, constantly renewed as we drink continu-
ously from the Spirit. We are constantly under renewal and expansion as we
move toward eschatological fulfillment in the new creation of God."[18] In
other words, spiritual formation is a process and not an event. The question
is this: How does this process unfold?

First, the Holy Spirit brings transformation that can only be explained in
terms of the power of God in action. It is power that uproots carnality from
our lives and drives us toward the things of God. You love Jesus because you
know with definite assurance that he died for you: "Those who live according
to the flesh have their minds set on what the flesh desires; but those who live
in accordance with the Spirit have their minds set on what the Spirit desires"
(Rom 8:5). Second, he imparts empowerment that makes it possible for people
to function in the graces of the Spirit. The Holy Spirit begins to manifest in
various ways among his people: "There are different kinds of gifts, but the
same Spirit distributes them. There are different kinds of service, but the same
Lord. There are different kinds of working, but in all of them and in everyone
it is the same God at work. Now to each one the manifestation of the Spirit is
given for the common good" (1 Cor 12:4-7). Third, he grants power for
Christian witness. The Christian and the community begin to reflect the
message of truth: we proclaim the Lord's death and resurrection until he comes.

---

[18]Macchia, *Baptized in the Spirit*, 205-6.

The Spirit comes to guide God's people to evangelize and to encourage one another. He comes to reveal the heart of God to his people and God's heart, Keener explains, is defined by love (Jn 13:34-35; 15:9-14, 17). To demonstrate "unselfish love," he notes, is to know God's heart (1 Jn 4:7-8).[19] For as Paul reminds us, "My message and my preaching were not with wise and persuasive words, but with a demonstration of the Spirit's power, so that your faith might not rest on human wisdom, but on God's power" (1 Cor 2:4-5).

STUDY QUESTIONS

1. Many contemporary Christians in the West have set aside spiritual warfare, demythologizing the reality of demonic spirits in Scripture, replacing them with psychological and medical explanations. How does reading Ephesians, for example, from an African Pentecostal perspective challenge some of those demythologizing assumptions?

2. In this chapter, I introduced the category of "demonic doorways," arguing that according to African Pentecostal theology and praxis, when people lead morally sinful lives, these behaviors are thought to create doorways that give the enemy access into their lives. In applying this concept to your own spiritual life, what might be some demonic doorways that are leaving you vulnerable to spiritual attack? How might identifying these areas of sin, repenting of them, and prayerfully pursuing holy living contribute to your own spiritual health, freedom, and formation?

3. In your own church context, how might incorporating a robust biblical theology of supernatural interventionism—including healing and deliverance ministries—contribute to evangelism and mission? What are some of the key areas of sin and spiritual oppression that are the most pressing issues in need of supernatural intervention? How might the church practically engage with the powers in order to bring the promises and experience of the gospel to bear in these instances?

4. Do you view Christian discipleship as involving spiritual warfare? Why or why not? Do you believe that, as a Christian, one of the ways

---

[19]Keener, *Gift and Giver*, 42.

we exercise our authority in Christ is to proactively battle evil spirits and other powers that are inimical to our well-being? If so, what can the church do to increase congregational and individual awareness of this aspect of our discipleship and mission?

5. In your own theological understanding, how do personal malev-olent spiritual beings relate to the phenomenon of systemic and structural evil? How does your understanding of spiritual powers relate to the cosmological understandings of the New Testament and African Christians?

6. Though the charismatic renewal has made a significant impact on the historic evangelical and mainline churches of the West, these denomi-nations would not, by and large, be labeled by most as "charismatic." What work needs to be done to allow the experience of the Holy Spirit to become more central in the theology and practice of evangelical and mainline denominations? How can this theology make an impact on evangelical networks that minimize the work and experience of the Spirit in favor of an intellectualized version of the faith? How might the Pentecostal hermeneutical triad of *promise, fulfillment,* and *expe-rience,* as discussed in this chapter, help you connect the work of the Holy Spirit at Pentecost with today?

CHAPTER TWELVE

SPIRITUAL FORMATION THROUGH FAILURE AND FAITHFUL PERSEVERANCE

HAYOUNG SON

I AM HONORED TO BE A CONTRIBUTOR TO THIS BOOK, and I hope to supply a viewpoint of spiritual formation from my perspective as a Korean female Christian.[1] In this chapter, I will deal with two stories of Peter's failure. Through these episodes, I want to focus on the relationship between failure and spiritual formation. Cultural understandings about failure and endurance are often held unconsciously. To acknowledge failures and to endure hardships properly, we need to correct our cultural understandings of endurance, failure, and hardship and realign them with the biblical understanding. As an example, I will critically analyze a Korean cultural understanding of endurance that is derived from a particularly Korean environment. I will demonstrate that from this cultural perspective, people often struggle to acknowledge their failures. I will then invite readers to investigate their own cultural assumptions and determine where their own cultural proclivities might need to be corrected by biblical truth.

---

[1]I am an ordained pastor, an evangelical scholar, and an adjunct professor teaching New Testament classes in South Korea. My denomination is Presbyterian, but my denominational engagement is much wider than that. I have studied at interdenominational schools in Korea and in the United States during my MDiv and ThM programs with students and professors from diverse denominations. Furthermore, I studied at one of six Southern Baptist seminaries in the United States for my PhD. Even now, as an adjunct professor at a Korean seminary, I meet students and professors who represent diverse nationalities, denominations, and cultural backgrounds every semester.

Failure is an inevitable component of spiritual formation. Although we hope to grow up smoothly and quickly, we actually grow up while falling down and getting up continually. Therefore, perseverance is an essential element for our spiritual formation. As God promised, we will grow up into the "unity of the faith and of the knowledge of the Son of God, to maturity, to the measure of the full stature of Christ" (Eph 4:13). This promise will be achieved and is even guaranteed (cf. Eph 1:11-14), but we cannot persevere to the last moment solely by means of our own enduring efforts. Only perseverance based on our trust in the faithfulness of God can bring us to full completion in Christ. The faithfulness of God on our behalf empowers us to faithfully persevere so that even our failures become providential instruments of our spiritual formation.

Spiritual Growth Through Failures

The two stories of Peter's failure dealt with in this chapter are Peter's falling into the water on the stormy sea (Mt 14:22-33; cf. Mk 6:45-52; Jn 6:16-21) and Peter's denial of Jesus three times (Mt 26:31-35, 67-75; Mk 14:27-31, 66-72; Lk 22:24-34, 56-62; Jn 13:36-38; 18:15-27). Through these two stories that are familiar to many Christians, I want to think about the question, Why did God allow Peter to experience these kinds of failures? The second failure in particular could have destroyed Peter (like Judas Iscariot) and could have been a fatal flaw for Peter as a leader of the early church. Jesus had even predicted that the denial would occur that very night, but he did not prevent this tragic event. Jesus allowed the bitterest failure of Peter's life to happen. Why?

The first story of Peter. We cannot avoid winds, storms, and waves in our lives. Therefore, we may prefer to empathize with the story of Peter who faltered while attempting to walk on the stormy water. We hope to walk on the stormy water in a dignified manner, full of faith as Peter did (for a while). However, just as Peter sank into the water due to his fear and fragile faith, we also become terrified in our own daunting situations. Overwhelmed by fear, our faith can so often cave in when worries prevail and problems persist. Thankfully, however, the salvation that Jesus brought was not absent or late in bringing rescue and redemption to Peter. Indeed, the mighty arm of the Lord is not absent or late when he sovereignly intervenes in our lives, even if we sometimes feel like his saving actions are too slow or too late in arriving.

The story of Jesus' walking on the water is mentioned in the Gospels (Matthew, Mark, and John, but not Luke) right after the story of Jesus's feeding of the five thousand (Mt 14:13-21; Mk 6:30-44; Jn 6:1-15; cf. Lk 9:10-17). Sometimes a story written in the Gospels can cause the reader to become perplexed due to differences in the elements of the story (e.g., wording, ordering, the number of characters) compared to the parallel accounts in the other Gospels. Concerning Jesus' walking on the water, however, the three different expressions recorded in the Gospels do not cause confusion but increase clarity. Yet, one significant difference is noteworthy: only the Gospel of Matthew deals with Peter's trial and failure to walk on the water.

After the miracle of the feeding the five thousand, Jesus made the disciples get into a boat and go on ahead of him to the other side (Bethsaida). After dismissing the crowd, he then went up on a mountainside to pray by himself. The Gospel of John adds further detail: "When the people saw the sign that he had done, they began to say, 'This is indeed the prophet who is to come into the world.' When Jesus realized that they were about to come and take him by force to make him king, he withdrew again to the mountain by himself" (Jn 6:14-15).

"When evening came" (Mt 14:23; Mk 6:47; Jn 6:16; cf. "it was now dark," Jn 6:17), Jesus was alone on land, and his disciples were in a boat on water. A strong wind was blowing, and the waters grew rough (Jn 6:18). The boat was buffeted by the waves (Mt 14:24), and the disciples strained at the oars (Mk 6:48) because the wind was against them (Mt 14:24; Mk 6:48). Though diverse in expression, these varied details do not result in any theological disharmony. They expand the narrative rather than obscure it. In addition, the boat's location and the precise time at which Jesus approached them are likewise illustrated diversely in the various Gospel expressions.[2]

---

[2]Matthew 14:24: *to de ploion ēdē stadious pollous apo tēs gēs apeichen* (BGT, "many stadia away from the land") is variously rendered with the boat being "a considerable distance from land" (NIV), "a long way from the land" (ESV), "a few miles offshore" (NAB), "many/some furlongs distant from the land" (RSV, NJB), "far from the land" (NRSV, NET), and "many stadia away from the land" (NAS), or for *to de ploion ēdē meson tēs thalassēs ēn* (BYZ, "in the middle of the sea") the boat was "in the midst/middle of the sea" (ASV, KJV, NKJV). Likewise, in Mark 6:47 the boat is described as being *ēn to ploion en mesō tēs thalassēs* (BGT/BYZ, "in the middle of the sea"), which is rendered "in the middle/midst of the lake/sea" (NIV, ASV, NAS, KJV, NKJV) and "[far] out on

These three verses in Greek tell us that the boat was approximately twenty-five to thirty stadia (three or four miles) from the land.[3] Considering the size of the lake (eight to nine miles between the east and the west, and thirteen to fourteen miles between the south and the north), if the disciples had rowed three or four miles from the land, it could be said that they were in the middle of the lake. Therefore, these diverse expressions in Greek, which issue forth in even more diverse English translations, are functionally equivalent.

The story provides another tip that assists the reader in understanding the existential situation of the disciples. When the disciples were struck by the wind and waves, and subsequently encounter Jesus on the water, this is said to be "the fourth watch of the night" (Mt 14:25; cf. Mk 6:48).[4] This refers to the time between 3:00 a.m. and 6:00 a.m. We do not know the exact time when Jesus dismissed the crowd and sent the disciples in a boat to cross the sea. However, it would be before "evening came." Even if we suppose that the time would be 9:00 p.m., at the latest, this means that the disciples would have already spent at least *six hours* on the water, making headway painfully. We also need to remember that even before getting on the boat, the disciples had been with the five thousand people in a remote place ministering with Jesus. Thus, after finishing a full day of ministry, and having been on the water for at least six hours, the disciples would have been totally exhausted. It would have been at this point—the point of exhaustion—that they would have seen something or someone approaching them, walking on the water.

---

the sea" (ESV, NAB, NJB, RSV, NRSV). Lastly, John 16:19 has the boat *elēlakotes oun hōs stadious eikosi pente ē triakonta* (BGT/BYZ, "about 25 or 30 stadia") which is rendered "about three or four miles" (NIV, NAB, NAS, NET, NJB, NKJV, RSV, NRSV) and "about five and twenty or thirty furlongs" (ASV, KJV).

[3]A stadion is 185 to 192 meters (607-640 ft.). Thus, twenty-five to thirty stadia are three or four miles. An outdated Korean unit for length, the "li" is used in Korean translations: "many li(s)" for "many stadia" (Mt 14:21) and "10 and some li(s)" for "25 or 30 stadia" (Jn 6:19). Some older Koreans may know how long one "li" is, but most young Koreans do not know the length. One "li" is approximately 393 meters, and so one "li" is equivalent to about two stadia. Thus, twenty-five to thirty stadia correspond roughly to twelve to fifteen li(s). Therefore, "10 and some li(s)" would be a suitable translation.

[4]Most English Bibles take a literal translation of the time in Matthew 14:25 and Mark 6:48 as "the fourth watch of the night" (e.g., ASV, ESV, N/KJV, NAB, NAS, NJB, RSV). However, some English Bibles take a less literal translation of the time in both verses, such as: "the night was ending" (NET), "shortly before dawn" (NIV), and "early in the morning" (NRSV) in accordance with the perceived meaning.

Can you imagine that situation? I am certain that if I were one of them, I would have been terrified and cried out with them: "It's a ghost!"

Through this story, I want to draw three theological principles that are pertinent to our own understanding and approach to faithful perseverance in the midst of momentary failures.

Jesus knew the disciples' struggles. Jesus saw the disciples straining at the oars because the wind was against them, and he went out to them. The disciples might have thought that they were fighting against the wind and waves by themselves. They probably thought that Jesus was not aware of their struggles because he was not there with them. If Jesus had been in the boat, even if he were asleep, they would have been able to wake up him (cf. Mt 8:23-27; Mk 4:35-41; Lk 8:22-25). This time, however, they were on water, and he was on land. Mark's Gospel highlights an interesting expression: "When evening came, the boat was out on the sea, and he was alone on the land. When he *saw* that they were straining at the oars against an adverse wind, he came towards them early in the morning, walking on the sea" (Mk 6:47-48 emphasis added). Jesus *saw* them. He *knew* the disciples' struggles. And *he came to the disciples.*

Sometimes, like the disciples, we too act and think as if no one—including God—is aware of our struggles. Yet the truth is that even if we do not confess our problems to him, God is intimately aware of our struggles, our failures, and our problems to the deepest depth. Even if we fight against a monster that lives only in our mind and do not tell it to anyone, God knows our battle. God knows us—each of us. In any situation and in any circumstance, we should remember and rest assured that God knows this situation, and he is ready to jump into it. God is the Lord of all creation, and thus he is Lord over our every situation.

Jesus approached his disciples amid their struggle. Let us not miss another key point. Jesus saw the disciples straining at the oars due to the wind blowing against them, jumped into the stormy sea, and walked on the rough waves to approach his disciples and save them. He does the same thing for us. Jesus does not merely *know about* our struggles, but he *jumps into* our struggling situations and approaches us to save us. This is very similar to his incarnation. Jesus jumped into our world. He put himself in the midst of our situation.

Hebrews 4:15-16 says, "For we do not have a high priest who is unable to sympathize with our weaknesses, but we have one who in every respect has been tested as we are, yet without sin. Let us therefore approach the throne of grace with boldness, so that we may receive mercy and find grace to help in time of need." His incarnation, his earthly life, and his empathy with our weakness gives us confidence to approach him and to ask for his mercy and help. Jesus did not merely command his terrified and exhausted disciples from a comfortable distance. Rather, by walking on the stormy sea (into the same situation as the disciples), Jesus *approached* his disciples. And standing in front of his disciples, in the middle of stormy sea, still under the rough weather, Jesus said, "Take courage! It is I. Do not be afraid." He says the same words to us in the midst of our struggles.

Jesus did not stop the wind immediately. Of course, Jesus could have made the wind and waves calm even before he walked on the water. If he had done so, Jesus could have more easily approached the disciples. Even for the sake of the weary disciples, who worked hard with Jesus all day long and struggled against the wind on the water for at least six hours, Jesus could have calmed the wind earlier. If so, the disciples could have had more immediate relief from their struggle. However, he did not. For the sake of Peter, who bravely tried to walk on the water (even voluntarily!), Jesus could have calmed the wind. If so, Peter might have succeeded in walking on the water, and that experience would have been one of his proudest memories. It would have been good evidence that Peter was a fit, faithful, and qualified leader for the early church. However, Jesus did not calm the winds at that time.

In fact, he *delayed* the calming of the wind. Peter tried to walk on the water, sank, and was saved by Jesus. The Lord then said to him, "You of little faith, why did you doubt?" (Mt 14:31). And then, "When they got into the boat, the wind ceased" (Mt 14:32). In contrast to Jesus' delay, the story shows other times that Jesus acted immediately: *immediately* Jesus made the disciples get into the boat (Mt 14:22; Mk 6:45); *immediately* Jesus said to the terrified disciples, "Take heart, it is I; do not be afraid" (Mt 14:27; Mk 6:50); *immediately* Jesus reached out Peter's hand and saved him (Mt 14:31). Yet if Jesus had immediately calmed the wind—or even calmed it in the middle of Peter's walking on the water (before he fell into the water)—Peter might have succeeded in walking on the water, but he would not have learned one of the most unforgettable lessons of his life. Jesus did not stop the wind until after Peter had failed and learned from his failure. Peter's failure is a blessing because it took place in the Lord's time and under the Lord's wisdom and providence. And because of this, Peter's failure led to more a resilient, spiritually formed faithfulness.

Peter voluntarily tried to walk on the water: "Lord, if it is you, command me to come to you on the water" (Mt 14:28). He showed faith that exceeded the faith of any of the other disciples. He even succeeded—for a while. He could have been complimented for his effort, yet he heard, "You of little faith, why did you doubt?" (Mt 14:31). This comment might at first glance appear to be harsh. However, this experience and Jesus' comment engraved the power of the providential faithfulness of the Lord in Peter's mind rather than the failure of his own attempts at faithfulness. Later—especially when he became the leader of the early church—this experience would be a tremendous blessing, not only for Peter, but for the entire church. Losing our focus on Jesus brings doubt and fear, but placing our focus on Christ's providential faithfulness leads to our own faithful perseverance. Therefore, as the author of Hebrews writes, "Let us run with perseverance the race that is set before us, looking to Jesus the pioneer and perfecter of our faith" (Heb 12:1-2).

Sometimes we pray that God would stop the wind immediately, solve our problems quickly, and make the waves die down before we become exhausted. However, God seems to have another goal—to allow us to learn through the situation. For us, our immediate success or failure is the most important thing; but for God, our sustained spiritual growth is the measure of true and abiding success. And often God chooses to allow failures so that our fallible faith can learn to rest on his infallible faithfulness.

The second story of Peter. If Peter could erase one night from his life, he would likely choose the night that he denied Jesus three times. For Peter, however, that night is the occasion for another providential lesson in which greater faith is achieved through momentary failure.

During the Last Supper, Jesus predicted Judas Iscariot's betrayal. After the Last Supper, Jesus went out to the Mount of Olives with his disciples. Before praying at Gethsemane, Jesus predicted the disciples' betrayal: "You will all become deserters because of me this night" (Mt 26:31; Mk 14:27). About this prediction, Peter confidently replied, "Though all become deserters because of you, I will never desert you" (Mt 26:33; Mk 14:29). Then Jesus predicted Peter's betrayal: "Truly I tell you, this very night, before the cock crows, you will deny me three times" (Mt 26:34; Mk 14:30; Lk 22:34; Jn 13:38). Then Peter confidently answered again, "Even though I must die with you, I will not deny you" (Mt 26:35; Mk 14:31; cf. Lk 22:33; Jn 13:37).

Luke adds Jesus' talk to Peter before Jesus' prediction of Peter's denial: "Simon, Simon, listen! Satan has demanded to sift all of you like wheat, but I have prayed for you that your own faith may not fail; and you, when once you have turned back, strengthen your brothers" (Lk 22:31-32). Jesus did not prevent Peter's denials from happening, but he did pray that Peter's faith might not fail.

As Jesus predicted, Peter denied Jesus three times, the rooster crowed, and the Lord turned and looked straight at Peter (Lk 22:61). Peter then remembered the word the Lord had spoken to him and went outside, weeping bitterly. This experience could have resulted in a debilitating defect and fatal moral injury for Peter as a leader of the early church. Jesus knew the pain that Peter would experience after denying him. Why, then, did Jesus not refuse Satan's request to sift all of the disciples, thereby preventing Peter's denials in the first place?

Jesus expected that Peter would pick himself up and continue to run. Jesus prayed for Peter that his faith might not fail, and he expected that Peter would pick himself up and continue to run. Jesus' prayer reminds us of Psalm 37:24: "though we stumble, we shall not fall headlong, for the Lord holds us by the hand."

The truth is, according to the Bible, "God trusts you." Or, to put it another way: God places trust in us because he has entrusted himself to us. He trusts that we will continue running because it is by his own divine power and grace that we continually find the energy and spiritual impulse to run. Consider, for example, 1 Corinthians 10:13, in which Paul writes, "No testing has overtaken you that is not common to everyone. God is faithful, and he will not let you be tested beyond your strength, but with the testing he will also provide the way out so that you may be able to endure it." God trusts, expects, *and equips us* to overcome and to endure the situations or obstacles that we face.

Jesus expected that Peter would turn back and strengthen his brothers.
We need to remember Peter's answers before he experienced this kind of
failure: "Though all become deserters because of you, I will never desert
you" (Mt 26:33; cf. Mk 14:29); "even though I must die with you, I will not
deny you" (Mt 26:35; cf. Mk 14:31); "Lord, I am ready to go with you to
prison and to death!" (Lk 22:33); "Lord, why can I not follow you now? I
will lay down my life for you" (Jn 13:37). Peter never fathomed that he could
betray Jesus, or that the fear of suffering and death would lead him to deny
his Lord. Yet if he did not experience this kind of failure, he probably could
not have understood the pressure on other disciples to betray Jesus out of
the ever-present fear of suffering or death. Through his preemptive, providentially shepherded failure, Peter was crafted by God into an unyielding
leader of the early church who was able to shepherd, comfort, and serve
those who—like him—were drawn to save their lives instead of losing
them for the sake of the kingdom and the Lord Jesus Christ. As Jesus predicted and expected, Peter picked himself up again and turned back and
strengthened his brothers.

In the process of standing up and turning back, Peter experienced forgiveness and acceptance from the Lord. Later, Jesus came to Peter fishing in
Galilee, and he asked the despondent disciple three times, "Do you love me?"
(Jn 21:15-17). How could Peter confess his love to the Lord confidently? Out
of shame, remorse, or embarrassment, we can imagine his voice responding
in a defeated whisper. However, humiliation and punishment were not the
intention of Jesus' query to Peter. Jesus already knew about Peter's love for
him, and he likely also knew how much Peter would be embarrassed by his
questions. However, Jesus gave Peter new opportunities to confess his love
again (and again and again). Just as Peter denied Jesus three times, he
confessed his love three times. The point of this is almost penitential—in a
formative, not a punitive sense. Jesus' commands to "feed my lambs" and
"tend my sheep" (Jn 21:15-17) refreshed Peter's soul and restored his mission.
The last command of Jesus, "Follow me" (Jn 21:19), restored Peter's identity
as a disciple of Jesus, the one he was to follow, and the one to whom he be-
longed. Peter, as the disciple who was restored by the Lord and who experienced the Lord's forgiveness, encouragement, and faithfulness, was equipped
to strengthen his brothers who were terrified by the world's threats.

Through failure and weakness Peter learned about the Lord's faithfulness. While Peter was confident about the prospects of his own loyalty and faithfulness toward Jesus, he failed. After his failures, he became humble and recognized that he could trip any time if he merely relied on his own power to persevere. After he was filled with the Holy Spirit, he was completely changed. Then, Peter was able to keep his words that he confidently said to Jesus before his denial (cf. Mt 26:33, 35; Lk 22:33; Jn 13:37). However, like Paul's confession that "we have this treasure in clay jars, so that it may be made clear that this extraordinary power belongs to God and does not come from us" (2 Cor 4:7), Peter (especially after Pentecost) continually learned to rely on the empowerment and energy of the Holy Spirit and not on his own self-generated strength or skill. When Peter was empowered by the Holy Spirit, he was able to endure all things and to follow Jesus sincerely to the last moment of his life.

Likewise, our failures teach us not to rely on ourselves but on the Lord. This is the strange yet sovereign blessing of failure as well as the most important secret of ultimate success: it comes by way of failure transformed into faithfulness. In our lives in general and in our spiritual lives in particular, our own efforts are necessary. However, the Spirit of the Lord and *his faithfulness* must remain the source of energy for any efforts of our own. Even if we are currently doing well in our spiritual lives, we can—and likely will—fall down at some point. While we are growing up, we must move the center of mass in our spiritual lives from ourselves to the Lord. This is how we spiritually grow up. If our failures can make us less reliant on ourselves and more reliant on the Lord, then the ultimate result is blessing. God is training and equipping his people at all times, but especially through the tough times.

THE KOREAN CULTURAL UNDERSTANDING OF ENDURANCE AND THE BENEFITS FOR GLOBAL EVANGELICALS

For many Koreans, a symbol of "endurance" or "perseverance" would be women of the Chosun Dynasty. During the Chosun Dynasty (fourteenth to nineteenth century AD), a husband could have a wife and several concubines. A wife could be divorced for seven valid causes, and one of the seven was jealousy of other concubines. Even if her husband loved a concubine more than her, the wife was forbidden to express her jealousy. If she was treated harshly by her husband or her mother-in-law, she was not allowed to express any anger or complaint. Women were forced to endure unfair and unreasonable situations, and like two sides of the same coin, endurance became one of the virtues to be praised and a sign of maturity. Due to this kind of traditional understanding of endurance, Koreans' conception of endurance includes the hiding or ignoring of their emotions and desires.[5]

The pressure to ignore one's desires or hide one's feelings seems to be reinforced by the Korean community-centered society and the shame-honor culture. Like Japan and China, Korea has a shame-honor culture. In this culture, *Chae-myun* (face-saving) and reputation are important. These make Koreans more conscious (compared to people of other cultures) of the perceptions, thoughts, or evaluations of others rather than their own thoughts or acts. Usually in shame-honor cultures, an individual's shame or honor is not only about their own actions but about the shame or honor of all of the members of the family or society to which the individual belongs. Therefore, members of one's family or society put unseen burdens on each other to avoid shame and to pursue actions that bring honor.[6] That is why countries that operate according to a shame-honor culture are usually community-centered. Because of this inclination, Koreans tend to "endure," to follow social rules by focusing on what they *should do* rather than what they *want to do*. To do their duties first, Koreans train themselves to ignore their own individual desires from a young age. This becomes the basis of the strength for endurance in any situation.

The Korean competitive environment, as well as their contemporary economic situation, contributes to their impulse toward perseverance and endurance.[7] To secure a job or to enter a school, Koreans must

---

[5] Ignoring one's feelings or desires in some degree by oneself would be one of the essential elements of endurance. However, Koreans' understanding of endurance as the ignoring of one's feelings seems to go further in a somewhat negative way (compared to people of other cultures).

[6] Koreans' view of this value is rapidly changing. Younger generations are more individualistic and less community-centered than the previous generations. They are also more Westernized due to cultural exchanges as a result of traveling, reading, and online access.

[7] After the Korean War in 1950, Koreans lost the foundation of industry. Since the 1960s, Koreans have experienced a stunning economic growth that is referred to as "the miracle on the Han River." South Korea transformed from a developing country to a developed country with the eleventh GDP global ranking in 2015 and twelfth in 2019. However, after the IMF period (1997–2001), the national economic environment was changed. These days, young adults cannot find

engage in exceedingly competitive processes. Thus, Koreans typically spend significant time preparing for exams to gain entrance to schools or careers. This excessive competitive environment in Korea exists within the reality of a high population density, and within a cultural framework that values hard work and rigorous study habits in general. This is a good characteristic of a nation, but when the nation cannot supply enough opportunities for study or work, this national inclination can become a kind of tragedy for the people. This may explain the low happiness score and high suicide rate of Korea.[8] Under the excessive competitive environment, Koreans find it difficult to accept their mistakes or failures easily. This may be caused by face-saving too. Furthermore, they find it hard to agree with the biblical teachings that link hardship and endurance to joy.

It is here that the Scriptures can course correct cultural deviations—Korean or otherwise—by means of the Christian understanding of endurance. The Bible presents us with a God who allows us to face hardship and to go through tough times, for through those difficult situations God causes us to persevere faithfully not only in spite of *but precisely through* our failings. This is because our faith rests not on our own fortitude but on the faithfulness of Jesus Christ. Our suffering and endurance is then reframed within the narrative of Jesus' sufferings because we are his followers. As Jesus did, so we should do. Even though he was the divine Son, Jesus "learned obedience" through what he suffered, and he was perfected through obedience to God the Father (see Heb 2:10; 5:8-9). In other words, suffering strengthens endurance and obedience, and faithful perseverance through failure leads to perfection. The power of God, says Paul, is made "perfect in weakness" (2 Cor 12:9). James articulates the same theological point in 1:2-4: "My brothers and sisters, whenever you face trials of any kind, consider it nothing but joy, because you know that the testing of your faith produces endurance; and let endurance have its full effect, so that you may be mature and complete, lacking in nothing."

---

full-time positions as easily as before. Thus, their study and free time are usually spent for preparing to get a better job.

[8] According to the 2019 World Happiness Report from the Sustainable Development Solutions Network for the United Nations, the Korean happiness score is 54th place. Available at https://worldhappiness.report/ed/2019/changing-world-happiness.

The goal of hardship is perfection, and the point of perfection is to make us mature and complete as the people of God. The image of the perfection of God's people is given focus and clarity in Ephesians 4:13. The goal of God's perfecting plan of salvation is that we all might arrive at "the unity of the faith and of the knowledge of the Son of God, to maturity, to the measure of the full stature of Christ." This is also the reason that God inspired the Bible: so that Christians might be complete/perfect and equipped for every good work (see 2 Tim 3:17). God, who called us as his children, his people, and his servants, desires that we grow up and cross the finish line. And, though it may seem paradoxical, it is through God-empowered perseverance that our momentary failures bear fruit by becoming a primary means to our maturity in faithfulness and spiritual formation.

The path of our spiritual growth will necessarily and providentially include tough times and failures. Yet a season of success or a momentary failure is not in itself a cause for either celebration or lament. Regardless of our successes or failures in our current situation, what matters is that we learn through them. God's intended aim is not the momentary realities of success or failure, but the future faithfulness that comes by persevering through failure. It is this path alone that leads to eternal spiritual growth.

CONCLUSION

The apostle Peter—the one who was formed through failure and whose failure lead to faithful perseverance—wrote this to the early church:

> Discipline yourselves, keep alert. Like a roaring lion your adversary the devil prowls around, looking for someone to devour. Resist him, steadfast in your faith, for you know that your brothers and sisters in all the world are undergoing the same kinds of suffering. And after you have suffered for a little while, the God of all grace, who has called you to his eternal glory in Christ, will himself restore, support, strengthen, and establish you. (1 Pet 5:8-10)

These words echo out from the bottom of a heart whose life experiences were ultimately marked not by perfection but by failure. If Peter had successfully walked on the water without incident, and had never denied or betrayed Jesus, we would—from a human perspective—reckon his leadership potential to be strong, perhaps even ideal. However, God chose to demonstrate that through Christ's faithfulness our failures are transformed into instruments of spiritual formation. Moreover, we have seen that it is through Peter's failures—not through his own inherent cultural or personal fortitude—that God formed him to be a key leader in the early church. That was a blessing, promise, and pattern, not only for Peter, but for the early church. And not only for the early church but also for the church across the ages. For all of us. For you.

STUDY QUESTIONS

1. Sometimes we treat our problems as if God does not know our struggles. Can you think of any times that you have felt like that? What caused you to think or act like that?

2. Why did Jesus wait to stop the wind until he was with his disciples? Why do you think that Jesus walked on the stormy water to approach the disciples?

3. Have you ever had an experience in which God's seeming delay taught you a greater lesson that you would not have learned if the response of God had been immediate?

4. What have you learned through your own failures? How have you seen your failures result in spiritual formation?

5. Do the people of your nation have a specific cultural understanding of perseverance or endurance? What makes it challenging—and even difficult—to acknowledge personal failure in your culture?

EPILOGUE

Spiritual Formation, Catholicity,
and the Multicultural Communion of the Saints

JOHN FREDERICK AND RYAN A. BRANDT

AS WE CONCLUDE THIS CONVERSATION IT is crucial that we, the church catholic, recognize that the fellowship that we have through the Spirit by faith is a participation in the life of Christ, and therefore in the very life of God himself. Since we are partakers of the divine nature by means of the unity that we have in the Spirit (cf. 2 Pet 1:3-8), we must rightly understand our participation in the communion of the saints as a reality that exists not only across cultures and continents (which is the premise of this volume) *but also across the ages.* The great Methodist theologian Thomas Oden has identified a tendency toward a form of "modern chauvinism" that is pervasive in the contemporary Christian church.[1] This allergic attitude toward all things ancient considers everything that is premodern to be intrinsically inferior and in need of progressive replacement. As evangelicals, therefore, it is crucial that we model our new forms of collaborative theological engagement within the framework of faithfulness provided by the apostolic rule of faith, which is evidenced through the ancient Creeds, and in the apostolic, infallible, Spirit-inspired witness of Holy Scripture.

The time for intercultural theological engagement that is substantive and collaborative is long overdue. Yet as we speak to and with one another in

---

[1]Thomas C. Oden, *The Rebirth of Orthodoxy: Signs of New Life in Christianity* (New York: Harper-Collins, 2003), 8.

new and exciting ways as the body of Christ today, we must do so within the coherence and catholicity of the consensual orthodoxy of the saints through the ages. This book is an attempt to do just that. Only if, as Oden says, we learn to theologically engage by developing a "hunger and exposure" to the crosscultural "symphony of voices within classical orthodoxy" will our contemporary global conversations be honoring to God and beneficial to the life and mission of the church.[2] By speaking within the coherence of the cloud of witnesses of the communion of the saints, we will be able to "recognize the dissonance" of theological motifs that are not in the "key" of the historic Christian faith or in "harmony with the biblical faith."[3] Given the massive leaps in communication technologies and instant access to the works of the saints across the ages that we enjoy, to neglect to have conversations like the ones attempted in this book would be at best lazy and at worst purposefully parochial. It would also be insufficiently catholic and therefore lead to a deficient and emaciated form of evangelicalism.

However, as we engage in this fashion, taking full advantage of the benefits of technological progress and the global village, we must do so being fully committed to the notion that whatever theological progress we may make here must be *faithful* progress if it is to be progress at all. It is incumbent upon us, therefore, to take seriously the opportunity and the weighty responsibility to do theology and spiritual life together, doing our best to recalibrate global evangelicalism around the marks of the true and faithful one, holy, catholic, and apostolic church. This intercultural and intergenerational reality has implications not only for the church but also (as we have seen in this volume) for theological education.

Theological colleges and seminaries across the globe are awakening to the transformational reality that cultural, theological, and ethnic diversity in an institution of theological education is absolutely essential. This is not just a politically correct issue; it is a *gospel* issue.[4] After all, how can colleges, seminaries, networks, and denominations truly represent the church, the

---

[2]Oden, *The Rebirth of Orthodoxy*, 119.
[3]Oden, *The Rebirth of Orthodoxy*, 119.
[4]See e.g., Galatians 2:11-14 where Paul responds to Peter's hypocritical ethnocentric conduct as behavior that was "not in step with the truth of the gospel" (ESV). Therefore, the universal, multicultural nature of the gospel is not a political talking point but rather a component of the gospel itself.

kingdom—how can they truly represent God's image and mission—when theology is done in an echo chamber? Yet, while faculty rosters are becoming beautifully more diverse, thereby more faithfully representing the nature and kingdom of God, in theological seminaries and ministry training networks we often end up with a diverse cluster of people who work in the same place but rarely work *together*. It can often feel like the contemporary academy and contemporary theological discourse has traded the echo chambers from ages past for shiny new intellectual silos in the same location.

Christian scholars and pastors can easily do their diverse work as diverse people side by side *but not together*, nor with any real sense of cross-disciplinary engagement or crosscultural impact. Therefore, we must be eager to be colleagues and ministry coworkers who not only work side by side with a diverse team of brothers and sisters but *together with one another*, doing theology and spiritual life for the heart of a global evangelical community. We must work together as a global communion of churches and believers, within the coherence of the catholicity of the saints through the ages and across the continents. We must refuse to settle for mere diversification but press on to diversified collaboration.

In all these ways, we pray that this volume helps to encourage the church catholic toward a greater cultural and historical awareness of the diverse gifts of the body of Christ, helping to foster a more intentional and holistic practice of spiritual formation.

CONTRIBUTORS

Sammy Alfaro (PhD, Fuller Theological Seminary) is professor of theology at Grand Canyon Theological Seminary in Phoenix, Arizona, and pastor of Iglesia Nuevo Día / New Day Church in Goodyear, Arizona. He is the author of *Divino Compañero: Toward a Hispanic Pentecostal Christology* and coeditor of *Pentecostal and Charismatic Movements in Latin America and Latino Communities.*

J. Kwabena Asamoah-Gyadu (PhD, University of Birmingham, UK) is currently president, as well as a Baëta-Grau Professor of Contemporary African Christianity and Pentecostal Theology, at the Trinity Theological Seminary, Legon, Ghana. He is the author of *Christianity and Faith in a Pandemic Era: Lockdown Periods from Hosanna to Pentecost* (2020) and coeditor of *Christianity in Sub-Saharan Africa* (2017). He has many other publications in the areas of Pentecostalism and Evangelical Christianity in Africa. Kwabena is a fellow of the Ghana Academy of Arts and Sciences.

Ryan A. Brandt (PhD, Southern Seminary) is associate professor of Christian history and theology at Grand Canyon University. He serves as managing editor of the *Journal of Biblical and Theological Studies*, and his work has appeared in the *Journal of Spiritual Formation and Soul Care* and *Perichoresis.*

S. Min Chun (DPhil, University of Oxford) is president and associate professor of worldview and Old Testament studies at Vancouver Institute for Evangelical Worldview, Langley, Canada. He authored *Ethics and Biblical*

Narrative: How to Read the Book of Judges [Korean], and *Worldview Preaching* [Korean], and translated *Ethics and the Old Testament* (John Barton), *The God I Don't Understand* (Christopher Wright), and *The Dawkins Delusion* (Alister McGrath) into Korean. He manages a YouTube channel called *MinChun Salon.*

John H. Coe (PhD University of California, Irvine), is director and professor of spiritual theology at the Institute for Spiritual Formation, Talbot School of Theology. He was the founding editor of the *Journal of Spiritual Formation and Soul Care* and has copublished several books in the area of spiritual formation and integration including *Embracing Contemplation: Reclaiming a Christian Spiritual Practice, Psychology in the Spirit,* and recently *Where Prayer Becomes Real: How Honesty with God Transforms Your Soul.*

John Frederick (PhD, University of St. Andrews) is lecturer in New Testament and Greek at Trinity College Queensland in Australia. He is the author of *Worship in the Way of Cross: Leading Worship for the Sake of Others* and *The Ethics of the Enactment and Reception of Cruciform Love.* He is a priest in the Anglican Church in North America (ACNA).

Michael J. Gorman (PhD, Princeton Theological Seminary) holds the Raymond E. Brown Chair in Biblical Studies and Theology at St. Mary's Seminary & University in Baltimore, Maryland, USA. He is the author of numerous books and articles in New Testament theology and spirituality, including *Cruciformity: Paul's Narrative Spirituality of the Cross, Inhabiting the Cruciform God,* and *Participating in Christ.* He has a special concern for theology in the Majority World.

Le Chih Hsieh (PhD, Asbury Theological Seminary) is associate professor at China Evangelical Seminary in Taiwan. His work has appeared in *Sino-Christian Studies* and *Holy Light Theological Journal.*

Markus Nikkanen (PhD, University of Aberdeen) is the academic dean of the Finnish School of Theology (Suomen teologinen opisto) where he teaches New Testament exegesis, ethics, and pneumatology. He is an ordained pastor in the Evangelical Free Church of Finland and leads the school's spiritual formation program.

Alfred Olwa (PhD, University of Western Sydney/Moore College, Sydney) was formerly associate professor of practical theology at Bishop Tucker School of Divinity and Theology at Uganda Christian University. He is an Anglican bishop in the Diocese of Lango and is the author of *Missionary of Reconciliation: The Role of the Doctrine of Reconciliation in the Preaching of Bishop Festo Kivengere of Uganda between 1971–1988*. He serves as coeditor of the journal, *Global Anglican* (formerly *The Churchman Journal*). His work has appeared in *Anthology of African Christianity, Global Renewal Christianity: Spirit-Empowered Movements of Past, Present, and Future, vol. 3: Africa and Diaspora*, and *St. Mark's Review, A Journal of Christian Thought & Opinion* 230, (December 2014) among others.

Jonathan K. Sharpe (PhD, University of Pretoria) is assistant professor of theology at Grand Canyon University. He is the coauthor of "Bonhoeffer and the Way of the Crucified: Methodeia, Doctrine, and the 'Powers'" in the JBTS monograph *Ephesians and the Powers* and the author of "Experiential Obstacles to Faith: Why a Good and Powerful God Allows Christians to Suffer" in *The Beginning of Wisdom: An Introduction to Christian Thought and Life*. He is a cowriter and executive producer for the film *The Heart of Man*.

Ha Young Son (PhD, New Orleans Baptist Theological Seminary) is adjunct professor of New Testament at Asia United Theological University in South Korea. She is the author *Praising God beside the Sea: An Intertextual Study of Revelation 15 and Exodus 15*.

Robyn Wrigley-Carr (PhD, University of St. Andrews) is associate professor of theology and spirituality at Alphacrucis College, Australia. She is on the editorial board and book reviews editor for the *Journal for the Study of Spirituality* and on the executive team of the International Network for the Study of Spirituality. Robyn is author of *The Spiritual Formation of Evelyn Underhill*, edited *Evelyn Underhill's Prayer Book*, and has contributed to several journals in spirituality and theology.

GENERAL INDEX

SCRIPTURE INDEX